GIVE ME A CHANCE

A Primer Advocating for People with Disabilities

JANIS GILBERT

ARCHWAY
PUBLISHING

Archway Publishing books may be ordered through booksellers or by contacting:

Archway Publishing
1663 Liberty Drive
Bloomington, IN 47403
www.archwaypublishing.com
844-669-3957

Interior Image Credit: Tom Gilbert, Janis Gilbert

ISBN: 978-1-4808-9593-5 (sc)
ISBN: 978-1-4808-9592-8 (hc)
ISBN: 978-1-4808-9594-2 (e)

Library of Congress Control Number: 2020917498

Print information available on the last page.

Archway Publishing rev. date: 11/13/2020

CONTENTS

ACKNOWLEDGMENTS

I want to thank my two sons, Eric, and Aaron, and my daughter-in-law, Natasha, for allowing me to utilize experiences from their lives as illustrations and for giving me the encouragement to write this book.

Thank you also goes out to my husband, Tom, for his editing and reference expertise on this manuscript and helping with pictures.

Thank you to all of the people with disabilities for your perseverance and in a lot of cases, paving the way for others in your effort toward self-actualization.

INTRODUCTION

"Mom, the other kids are picking on me again," complained our older son, Eric, during elementary and middle school years. This was a repeated refrain from him reflecting typical interactions with his peers, especially since he was one of the smallest boys in his middle school.

Growing up with a disability is tough. It is tough for the child, the parents, his/her siblings, and for the child's teacher and classmates. Every person, disabled or not, wants to be happy, loved, and respected. They want to be accepted. They want to accomplish their dreams. Parents also want these very same things for their child.

In his article entitled *A Theory of Motivation* from which we get *Hierarchy of Needs* (1943)[1], noted psychologist Abraham Maslow wrote that the basic needs of each individual for food, clothing, and shelter must be satisfied first. Only after these basic needs are met, can an individual go on to other hierarchical needs such as safety and security, then love and belonging, self-esteem, and finally self-actualization (achieving one's full personal potential). Once the initial needs are met we can all make strides in maximizing our abilities.

People with disabilities or special needs have hopes and dreams just like everyone else. They need safety, security, love, and belonging. They want to feel good about themselves and accomplish things in life. They might not be able to make all of their dreams come true, but they still have those dreams. They want their life to have meaning. People with disabilities

---

[1] Abraham H. Maslow, "A Theory of Human Motivation," *Psychological Review*, Vol. 50, No. 4 (1943), 370-396, http://psychclassics.yorku.ca/Maslow/motivation.htm.

sometimes need others to give voice to their hopes and desires and to help them achieve some of their goals.

People with disabilities are people first. They are not their disability; it does not define them. They want to be given a chance to accomplish as much as they can. Many of them accomplish a great deal in spite of their challenges.

People with disabilities are frequently considered "outside the norm" and consequently face marginalization, isolation, loneliness, discrimination, and sometimes abuse. They are pitied, ignored, excluded, stereotyped, and scapegoated. People tend to be afraid of what they do not understand and most people do not understand physical and mental disabilities. Some may even fear that they could acquire a disability from someone who is disabled. Wider education and understanding about disabilities could help change public attitudes toward people with disabilities enabling them to feel more included in our society.

My life experiences have given me many opportunities to learn about mental health disabilities. For the first 16 years of my marriage, my husband and I struggled with his undiagnosed clinical depression. During that time, we adopted our first son, Eric, placed with us when he was 10 days old. When he entered school, the structure of that setting immediately surfaced some challenges. He was diagnosed with Attention Deficit-Hyperactivity Disorder (ADHD). However, as he moved into middle and high school, another diagnosis became clear—Asperger's Syndrome, or Autism Spectrum Disorder. This challenge impacts his life in significant ways and ours too.

When Eric was 10, we adopted a 6-year-old boy named Aaron. He carried a diagnosis of ADHD, which we felt confident we could handle. There was some suggestion that he might have been affected by fetal alcohol. As he progressed in school, the increasing challenges of learning and social adjustment revealed how pervasively he is affected by Fetal Alcohol Spectrum Disorder. He has almost no Executive Brain Function and makes very poor decisions. This has resulted in extensive involvement in the criminal justice system.

While we were welcoming Aaron into our family, I decided to return to school full-time (while still working full-time) to earn a Master's Degree in Special Education. Subsequent to completion of my degree, I taught special education in an urban high school.

I have learned a lot about disabilities through these experiences. I continue to learn how amazing people with disabilities are (just like everyone else) and how creatively they face and manage their challenges.

I have written this book to share what I have learned. It begins with an overview of disabilities, defining what they are, how they are acquired, that two or more disabilities frequently occur together, and some statistics about disabilities in the United States. We take a look at well-known people who have various disabilities and how disabilities have been portrayed in popular culture through movies. The book covers the history of treatment of people with disabilities and how this has changed over the years. It examines diagnosis and treatment of disabilities and challenges associated with this work, including shortages of resources. There are sections looking at aspects of life for people with disabilities including family and social relationships, education, employment, transportation, housing, and others. Chapters discuss caregiving, advocacy, community support services through governmental and nonprofit agencies, and planning for the time when parental caregivers are gone.

Throughout the book I have included personal and professional experiences from our family life. This material is followed by a section of personal stories written by people whose families have been touched by disabilities.

My hope is that after reading this book, you will have a better understanding of disabilities and the many complex issues that people with disabilities and their caregivers face every day and how we can all make accommodations to make a person's life better and more fulfilling.

This book is designed for parents and teachers but may be useful to individuals with disabilities and people who want to learn more about disabilities and have a better appreciation of both the challenges and the victories of living with a disability. To profit from this book, you do not have to read it straight through as you would a novel. The chapters are arranged so that you can pick the subject areas most relevant to you at the time.

It is truly amazing that in the third decade of the twenty-first century there is still a stigma associated with having a mental illness, even though approximately 26 percent of the U.S. population over the age of 18 years has a diagnosable mental illness. While federal and state legislation, such as the American's With Disabilities Act, has enshrined in law the rights of people with disabilities, they still seek the honoring of those rights by people in their everyday lives. They want to be given a chance.

People with disabilities may sometimes feel angry, sad, depressed, afraid, frustrated, confused, helpless, inadequate, embarrassed, ashamed, odd, anxious, and numb. They may have painful memories and emotions from experiences that can lead to alienation, loss of friends, and other symptoms. It is important for them to have coping strategies and a circle of supportive people on whom they can call when they are experiencing these feelings.

Studies show that people who are born with disabilities tend to be better adjusted to their situation than people whose disabilities arrive later in life. Like a pebble tossed into a pond sends out ripples, having a disability affects widening circles of family, friends, and colleagues. This is true whether the disability is physical, mental, or behavioral, such as alcoholism, eating disorders, drug abuse, or other addictions.

People with disabilities sometimes act "strangely," sometimes violently. This behavior causes people unfamiliar with how disabilities manifest themselves to become uncomfortable and even fearful. Consequently, if this behavior occurs in the public arena, the police may be called. Many police officers lack understanding about the best way to deal with someone having a mental health crisis, although more departments are beginning to have specially trained mental health officers and crisis intervention training for all officers. Still individuals experiencing a mental health crisis are frequently arrested, charged with a crime, and enter the criminal justice system. I know from personal family experience.

Other times a mental health crisis ends more tragically. In the past couple of years nationally as well as in our community, lethal force has been used against people with known mental health conditions. Sometimes the lethal force has been used simply because the person "did not obey the commands" of the police officers. Mentally ill people have difficulty comprehending and complying with such commands when they are in emotional crises. (If parents killed their children every time the kids did not obey a directive, our population would be decimated!!)

It is also true, however, that in this same period persons who have mental illness have carried out deadly attacks on persons known and unknown to them. Because of a lack of treatment options and resources, earlier intervention did not occur and police are left to be the intervenors at the crisis stage. It is a sad commentary on the priorities of our society that we have not moved to better solutions for these issues. From one perspective, it is a good outcome when police intervention prevents people in mental health crises from causing any harm and only ends up in their incarceration.

Law enforcement professionals admit that our jails and prisons have become de facto mental health institutions. In jail and prison, people with mental illnesses experience more discrimination and ill treatment at the hands of both inmates and facility staff. Medical staffs working in jails and prisons frequently alter the medications from what the people had been prescribed by their own psychiatrist. Partly this is because jails and prisons have difficulty accessing patient medical records on the outside. It is also because jails and prisons have their own drug "formularies" of preferred medications in order to manage their operating costs.

In the Wisconsin prison system, it is standard practice to strip all incoming prisoners of their psychotropic medications "cold turkey" and then observe them to determine if they really need the medication(s). Again, I have firsthand experience with this practice in my own family. I have also heard this directly from other inmates. There are two things wrong with this approach: 1) the medical staff does not know the individual well enough to make a judgment call regarding discontinued medication prescribed by his regular psychiatrist, and 2) psychotropic medication should be tapered, not cut off cold turkey. This action frequently sets the person up to commit some infraction of institution rules or another crime, resulting in sanctions or more charges.

Does this make any sense? Where is the justification for the actions taken against these individuals with disabilities? Where is the justification for this kind of inhumane treatment to any individual? It almost seems like people with disabilities are merely subjects on which to experiment. Unfortunately, such experimentation has happened before. Read on.

CHAPTER 1

WHAT IS A DISABILITY?

What is a disability and why do we tend to become uncomfortable around a person with a disability? Disabilities come in all shapes and sizes. They can be physical or mental. Dictionaries define disabilities as lack of adequate power, strength, or physical or mental ability, or incapacity. They can be conditions that limit movement, senses, or activities, especially things that limit people's basic life skills or prevent them from holding gainful jobs. They are conditions that disable or put people at a disadvantage.

A person with a disability can be anyone having a physical impairment such as hearing or sight loss, limb problems, cognitive impairment, learning impairment, mental health issues, HIV positive status, or hidden impairments and long term health conditions that progressively worsen, such as multiple sclerosis. This includes everyone who identifies as needing the support of an organization in order to remove a barrier that may have excluded them from participating in the economic, social or political life of their communities (see Chapter 8, Changes in Disability Treatment Landscape).

A chronic illness is defined as any ongoing illness from which one does not heal. People with chronic illnesses can experience lots of pain and distress, or have limits and circumstances brought on by the illness, resulting in disability. People who suffer from a great deal of pain can have problems sitting, walking, standing, or lying for example. They may also have a great deal of trouble concentrating due to the pain.

It is not uncommon for people with mental health or other issues to deny that there is any kind of a problem, even though those around them can see that there is a problem, and that professional help should be sought. Denial can be part of a disability or illness, or it can be fear of going to doctors and receiving a diagnosis.

People with disabilities, especially those with mental illness can have challenging behaviors at times. People may shy away from someone with a disability because they are afraid of what they do not understand. Earlier in history, people feared that disabilities were "catching." (Today there is the witticism, "Mental illness is contagious; you get it from your kids!")

My older son sometimes forgets to take his medications. When he does, he can become angry and belligerent. A family member told me about a neighbor with bi-polar disorder who was chasing his mother and wife around the neighborhood with a knife because he had not taken his medication. My relative described how scary that was. Yes, episodes like that can be scary, but to those of us who deal every day with a person with mental health issues such behaviors are usually just annoying. Most of the time we are not scared but rather annoyed that a confrontational situation is happening yet again that we were not able to quickly diffuse by redirecting the person.

CHAPTER 2

DISABILITIES–BORN OR ACQUIRED

A person can be born with a disability or acquire one during life. Cerebral palsy, cystic fibrosis, autism, limb deformities and heart deformities are just a few of the disabilities with which a person can be born. Diseases such as sickle cell anemia or Huntington's disease are genetically-based maladies that can manifest early in life. A person can have a genetic propensity to alcoholism, schizophrenia, breast cancer, or obesity that develops later in life.

Diseases acquired later in life can result in an individual losing the ability to think, walk, see, or hear, which can become disabilities. These diseases include Alzheimer disease or dementia, Parkinson's disease, multiple sclerosis, diabetes, and years ago, measles, mumps, and polio.

Less than 15 percent of people are born with disabilities. Most disabilities come later in life. There are hundreds of different kinds of disabilities. A perfectly healthy individual can be involved in some type of accident—vehicle, skiing, biking, swimming, to name a few and end up with a traumatic brain injury, spinal cord injury, broken bones, and so on. In addition to healing the physical injury, there can be many months of intense rehabilitation to learn how to walk and talk again. Sometimes getting the brain's neurological paths to connect the right word with the correct object or concept can be extremely frustrating, exhausting, and even disheartening.

Armed conflict and violence such as wars produce many disabilities. Many soldiers have come back from war with every conceivable form of physical and mental disability. More and more they are also coming back with post-traumatic stress disorder (PTSD-called "shell shock" in World War I and "battle fatigue" in World War II). War has produced new "illnesses" such as Gulf War syndrome which affects a person's ability to feel well and productive. Workers at Ground Zero in New York City not only experienced respiratory illnesses but also PTSD.

PTSD can stem from traumatic incidents such as muggings, rapes, and torture; kidnappings and being held captive; child abuse; car accidents; train wrecks; plane crashes; bombings; and natural disasters such as floods, hurricanes, tornadoes, earthquakes, and tsunamis. It can also result from discovering or being on the scene of such tragedies. The majority of people exposed to such events experience symptoms of distress such as sleep problems and jumpiness. Suddenly, life is turned upside down.

People with PTSD may become emotionally numb, especially in relation to people with whom they used to be close. They may lose interest in things they used to enjoy. They may have an exaggerated startle response, be irritable, become aggressive, have trouble falling asleep and staying asleep, or have nightmares. They may avoid situations that remind them of the original incident and often find anniversaries of the incident to be very difficult.

PTSD symptoms seem to be worse if they were triggered deliberately by another person, as in a mugging or rape. Most PTSD sufferers repeatedly relive the trauma in their thoughts during the day and in nightmares when they sleep. These are called *flashbacks*. Flashbacks may consist of images, sounds, smells, or feelings. They are often triggered by ordinary occurrences, such as a door slamming, a car backfiring, or being in a place that looks like the setting where the trauma occurred. A person having a flashback is likely to feel the emotions and physical feelings that occurred during the incident despite no longer being in danger.

Post-traumatic stress disorder did not become a formal diagnosis until 1980. Effective treatments weren't widely available until the 1990s.

Illnesses like cancer, heart disease, multiple sclerosis, arthritis, and diabetes cause the majority of long-term disabilities. Back pain and injuries are also significant causes. Most are not work related and therefore, not covered by workers' compensation. Lifestyle choices and personal behavior that lead to obesity are becoming major contributing factors. Musculoskeletal disorders are the number one cause of disabilities. These include arthritis, back pain, spine and joint disorders, and fibromyalgia (chronic inflammation of a muscle with an overgrowth of the connective tissue).

Many other maladies are also being called disabilities such as obesity, alcoholism, drug addiction, gambling, compulsive eating, anorexia, and video-game addiction. Recent gene experiments have revealed that a faulty version of the FTO gene causes energy from food to be stored as fat rather than burned leading to some forms of obesity. The latest research has suggested that addiction affects different parts of the brain and causes a person to have highs and cravings. While the *DSM V (American Psychiatric Association Diagnostic and Statistics Manual–Fifth Version)* does not list some of these as mental health disorders, they are listed as "possible suggestions" for future research and inclusion in future editions of the manual.

As another section of this book highlights, disability is no respecter of people. Disabilities can affect any race, gender, or socio-economic group. In 2011, US Representative Gabrielle Giffords from Arizona was fine one minute and fighting for her life the next, with months and years of rehabilitation ahead. In 2010, an army psychiatrist at Fort Bragg went on a shooting rampage killing several people and injuring countless others. What was Dr. Nidal Malik Hasan's state of mind or mental condition? A psychiatrist mother killed her adolescent son and then herself leaving a note stating "school–can't deal with school system" and "debt is bleeding me; strangled by debt." Anyone can get to a breaking point or be susceptible to outside influences, causing erratic behavior and perhaps violence.

While alcoholism and prescription drug abuse may be disabilities, they can also be accidents waiting to happen. One person's disability can lead to another person's disability when a drug-or alcohol-impaired person drives and crashes into someone. This happened to some friends of mine, as you will read about later.

Because most disabilities occur later in life, they can cause total paradigm shifts. Family dynamics shift, maybe from one adult being the bread winner to another family member now having to assume that as a primary responsibility. That person may or may not have been employed before, but suddenly it is imperative for him or her to be the primary wage or salary earner. If there are children, then the responsibilities change there too. Perhaps responsibility for primary care of the children is given to the person with the disability; maybe the children, depending upon their ages, take on more responsibility in the household; or if children are very young, the family may have to go on disability so someone is around to take care of the children as well as the disabled parent. The same is true in a single-parent household.

There is a paradigm shift at work also, if the person can still work. Perhaps he or she can only do part of a previous job or maybe none of it and needs a different position. This puts more stress on everyone as co-workers take on additional work, at least initially.

Disabilities occurring later in life can also challenge friendships. People may not know how to respond to the person with the disability or perhaps a friendship was based upon mutual participation in a physical activity like golfing or bowling, and the disabled person can no longer participate in that sport.

Canadian writer, J. Bickenback, states that disability is actually a fluid and continuous condition which has no boundaries but which is, in fact, the essence of the human condition. As a condition which is experienced by us all at some stage in our lives, disability is actually normal. If we are not born with a disability, as we go through life we might acquire a disease, have an accident, or develop a disability in the normal aging process, thereby making it a normal part of life. Western society's social mores, however, do not view it as normal.

We can minimize disabling accidents by thinking an activity through and visualizing an event to its logical conclusion. An example would be jumping or diving into water of unknown depth. If we visualize various scenarios of positive (nice dive, swimming up to surface) and injurious outcomes (dive into too shallow water, hit head, and break neck), we can make better decisions, regulate our behavior, and not take unnecessary risks that could end in disaster.

Sometimes we take unwise risks because of *normalcy bias*—a mental state people enter when facing a disaster. It is a coping mechanism that occurs when we are trying to comprehend a traumatic event or impending disaster. It causes people to underestimate both the possibility of disaster occurring and its possible effects, so they inadequately prepare for it. Even the government has fallen victim to this phenomenon. Inadequate government and citizen preparation for Hurricane Katrina and the denial that the levees in New Orleans could fail was an example of normalcy bias, resulting in thousands of people refusing to evacuate. The denial of the severity of the 2020 coronavirus (COVID-19) pandemic by a large segment of our society is another example of normalcy bias, despite the statistics showing millions of infections and hundreds of thousands of deaths. The belief that the pandemic is a hoax, that the numbers have been inflated for political reasons, and the refusal to take simple measures like wearing a mask is evidence of this bias.

A disability will change your life in many ways. Family member's roles and responsibilities may need to change. Raising children might become more challenging. There will be medical decisions and considerations. There may be a need for home accessibility modifications and adaptive equipment. Often this is not covered by insurance, creating financial pressures on the family. Your new reality may seem like a foreign world for which you are totally unprepared.

Whether a person is born with a disability or acquires one later in life, whether that disability requires minor or major adjustments in life, he or she will still desire safety, security, acceptance, and love in their life.

CHAPTER 3

CO-MORBID CONDITIONS

When people have more than one disease or disabling condition, they are said to have co-morbid conditions. Each condition could stand alone for diagnosis and treatment. Examples of co-morbid conditions are respiratory illness and post-traumatic stress disorder suffered by World Trade Center rescue workers, a psychiatric disorder coupled with substance abuse, attention deficit hyperactivity disorder and Tourette's syndrome, autism and anxiety or gastrointestinal issues, blindness and non-circadian rhythm, and depression accompanied by obsessive-compulsive disorder. A person may have a traumatic brain injury and physical mobility issues. Depression and post-traumatic stress disorder frequently go hand in hand. Children and adolescents with bi-polar disorder almost always have another co-morbid condition.

The more co-morbid conditions a person has, the more complicated and challenging life can be. Frequently, when medication works for one of the conditions, it does not work for the other, or it causes unbearable side-effects for the co-morbid condition(s). This proves to be a challenge for the physician trying to find a good combination of medications that will address all issues satisfactorily and not cause unacceptable side-effects.

Most clinicians and researchers agree that a combination of medication and therapy will lead to the best outcomes for people, whether they have a single condition or co-morbid conditions. While medication is working to stabilize a person's mental, emotional, or physical health, an experienced therapist helps the individual learn strategies to live a satisfying life as well as to advocate for themselves.

CHAPTER 4

SOME STATISTICS

People with disabilities make up a surprisingly large portion of our nation's population. There are approximately 49 million people in the U.S. that are disabled. That is over 19 percent of the population. Any of us can become a member of this group at any time. More than 50 percent of disabled Americans are in their working years, ages 18-64.

- Disability directly or indirectly affects nearly one out of every two adult Americans.
- Less than 15 percent of people with disabilities are born with their disability.
- One third of disabled Americans are 65 or older.
- Of the almost 70 million families in the United States, more than 20 million have at least one family member with a disability.
- Cognitive, physical, and mental health disabilities affect approximately 20% of North Americans of all races, ages, and genders.
- Between 1990 and 2000, the number of Americans with disabilities increased 25%.
- Approximately 90 percent of acquired disabilities are caused by illness rather than accidents.
- The link between poverty and disability is strong and goes in both directions. Poverty causes disability through malnutrition, poor health care, poor sanitation, lack of fresh clean water, and dangerous living conditions. Disability can cause poverty by

preventing the full participation of the disabled person in the economic and social life of their communities, especially if the proper supports and accommodations are not available.

- The EEOC (Equal Employment Opportunity Commission) projects productivity gains of $164 million from the ADA and $222 million net benefit from decreased support payments coupled with increased revenue, i.e., decreasing the number of people collecting some type of disability while increasing the number of taxpayers.

- In many third world countries, disability rates in the population are higher among groups with lower educational levels. On average, 19 percent of less educated people have disabilities, compared to 11 percent among the better educated.

- In developing countries, 90 percent of children with disabilities do not attend school.

- Persons with disabilities are more likely to be victims of violence or rape, and less likely to obtain police intervention, legal protection, or preventive care.

- Just over 1 in 4 of today's 20-year-olds will become disabled before they retire.

- Over 65 percent of working-age adults with disabilities are unemployed. Of those who do work, nearly one third earn an income below the poverty level.

- People with disabilities are nearly twice as likely as people without disabilities to have an annual household income of $15,000 or less. In 2009, 26.4 percent of non-institutionalized persons aged 21-64 years with a disability were living below the poverty line.

- People with disabilities represent the single largest minority group seeking employment in today's marketplace.

- When people with disabilities are working, they maintain above average work attendance and productivity.

- Most people with a disability did not need costly modifications to the workplace to be gainfully employed. Employer fears of expensive insurance premiums did not materialize.

- Two-thirds of people with disabilities who are not working would like to work.

- A qualified person with a disability has a 1 out of 100 chance of getting a job when compared to a non-disabled person with similar qualifications.
- The chance of a black woman with a disability being unemployed is over 90 percent.
- People with disabilities become socially isolated: 66 percent had not been to a movie in the last year, 17 percent did not go out to eat at a restaurant, 66-75 percent did not go to a sporting or live music event, and 13 percent never shop in grocery stores.
- Claims for disability benefits are surging in industrialized nations– up to 600 percent in some nations; encouraging governments, private companies, and unions to search for ways to get disabled people back to work.
- Over 20 percent of people with disabilities of working age live below the poverty line. This is more than twice as high a poverty rate as other Americans.
- For every dollar spent to rehabilitate disabled persons for employment, $10 or more is returned to the economy.
- Globally, people with disabilities represent an emerging market on par with the size of China.
- Even though strides have been made in disability rights in the past 25 years, the majority of people with disabilities are poor, under-employed and under-educated due largely to unequal opportunities.
- Women have a higher overall rate of disabilities (23.2 percent) than men (17.7percent), primarily because women outnumber men in the elderly age groups.
- In the United States, 65-75 percent of us will become disabled simply by living to our full life expectancy.
- One in eight workers will be disabled for five years or more during their working careers.
- Working Americans severely underestimate their risk of disability. Thirty percent have the chance of becoming disabled for 3 months or more during their working careers.
- Medical problems contributed to 62 percent of all personal bankruptcies filed in the United States in 2007 or approximately 500,000 cases.

- There are 50,000 head injuries each year. Most are under the age of 30.
- Prior to the Affordable Care Act (Obamacare), Medicare and Medicaid insured only about one-third of people with disabilities. More than 14 percent of people with disabilities had no insurance.
- Some physically-disabled people who formerly lived in institutions now live in nursing homes.
- If you are disabled, you are 25 times more likely to spend some part of your life in a nursing home.
- The overall rate of disability in the United States for white people is 20.2 percent, 24.3 percent for African-American/American Indian/Alaska native people, 19.2 percent for Hispanic people, and 16.6 percent for Asian people.
- Nearly 40 percent of persons reporting a disability live in the South—twice the 20% of each of the other three geographic areas. Among the states, Alaska, Utah, and Minnesota have the lowest rates of disability—about 15 percent. West Virginia had the highest rate of disability at 24.4 percent, followed by Alabama, Arkansas, Kentucky and Mississippi, each over 23 percent.
- The Social Security Administration denied 65 percent of initial SSDI claim applications in 2009.
- The average Social Security Disability Insurance (SSDI) monthly benefit payment was $1,258 (2020). The maximum Supplemental Security Income (SSI) monthly benefit payment is about $751 (January, 2020). This translates to $9,012/year for SSI recipients, $15,096 yearly for those receiving SSDI benefits. This is not very much money to buy food, pay rent, utilities, etc. The 2020 US Department of Health and Human Services poverty guidelines for the 48 contiguous states and Washington D.C. was $12,490 for one person, $16,910 for two people, and $25,750 for a family of four. At this rate, everyone on SSI is about $3,000 below the poverty level every year.
- Of the more than $3 billion spent annually in philanthropic giving, only 2.9 percent of grants made by philanthropic institutions is directed to programs serving people with disabilities.
- Assistive technology is essential to self-care at home for more than one-third of people with disabilities.

- Eighty percent of persons with disabilities live in developing countries.
- For every child death due to war, three are injured and acquire a permanent form of disability.
- At least 20 percent of veterans of the Iraqi war came home with PTSD (Post Traumatic Stress Disorder).
- PTSD occurs more frequently in women. PTSD is often accompanied by depression, substance abuse, and other anxiety disorders.[2]

[2] "Disability Statistics: Information, Charts, Graphs and Tables," Disabled World, https://www.disabled-world.com/disability/statistics.

CHAPTER 5

DISABILITIES–NO RESPECTER OF PERSONS

Having a disability does not necessarily mean that you cannot achieve your goals in life. Many people have achieved fame in spite of or because of having a disease, mental illness, or physical disability. Some individuals believe their condition gives them more creativity. We would live in a much less interesting and creative world if these individuals hadn't persevered in pursuing their talents and dreams.

Below are names of well-known people who have achieved fame together with information about their disability and line of work. These people have written about their challenges or other writers have told their stories. This list is by no means exhaustive, just a sampling. The asterisk (★) denotes that they are in more than one list, hence having co-morbid conditions.

Notable People with Disabilities	
Person	**Line of Work or Profession**

Speech Differences/Stutterers

Bruce Willis	Actor
Tiger Woods	Golfer
Julia Roberts	Actress

15

Person	Line of Work or Profession
Jimmy Stewart	Actor
Stephen Hawking★	Physicist
Winston Churchill★	Prime Minister, England
King Charles I	King, England
King George VI	King, England (Movie: The King's Speech)
Aristotle	Philosopher
Charles Darwin★	Naturalist
Sir Isaac Newton★	Scientist
Theodore Roosevelt★	President, United States
Washington Irving	Author
Thomas Jefferson★	President, United States
George Washington★	President, United States
Moses	Prince of Egypt/Hebrew Prophet

Hearing Impairments

Helen Keller★	Author
Thomas Edison★	Inventor
Ludwig Van Beethoven★	Composer/Musician
Marlee Matlin	Actress

Visual Impairments

Helen Keller★	Author
Stevie Wonder	Musician/Singer
Franklin Delano Roosevelt★	President, United States
Harriet Tubman★	Slave/Underground Railroad
Louis Braille	Inventor/Author
Galileo	Italian Astronomer
James Thurber	Comedian/Cartoonist
Claude Monet	French Painter
Ray Charles	Musician/Singer

Asperger Syndrome/Autism

Albert Einstein★	Mathematician/Scientist
Sir Isaac Newton★	Scientist

Person	Line of Work or Profession
Benjamin Franklin	Inventor/Statesman
Napoleon Bonaparte★	French Statesman and Military Leader
George Washington	President, United States
John Quincy Adams	President, United States
Andrew Jackson	President, United States
Andrew Johnson	President, United States
Abraham Lincoln★	President, United States
James Garfield	President, United States
William Taft	President, United States
Leonardo da Vinci★	Painter
Ludwig Van Beethoven★	Composer/Musician
Bill Gates	Entrepreneur
Robin Williams	Actor
Tom Hanks	Actor
Dan Aykroyd★	Actor
Marilyn Monroe★	Actress
Clark Gable★	Actor
Temple Grandin	Educator

Depression/Bi-Polar Disorder

Patty Duke	Actress
Abraham Lincoln★	President, United States
Catherine Zeta-Jones	Actress
Wolfgang Amadeus Mozart	Composer/Musician
Richard Dreyfuss	Actor
Boris Yeltsin	President, Russia
Buzz Aldrin	Astronaut
Diana (Diana Frances Spencer)	Princess of Wales
Mike Wallace	Journalist
Jimmy Piersall	Baseball Player
Alfred Lord Tennyson	Author

Schizophrenia

Mary Todd Lincoln	First Lady
Lionel Aldridge	Football Player

Person	Line of Work or Profession
James Robert Mosley	Singer/Songwriter
Tom Harrell	Musician
John Nash	Mathematician (Movie: A Beautiful Mind)

Obsessive Compulsive Disorder

Charles Darwin★	Naturalist
Howard Hughes★	Industrialist
Donald Trump	President, United States
Leonardo DiCaprio	Actor
Michael Jackson	Singer
David Beckman★	Soccer Player
Ludwig Van Beethoven★	Composer//Musician
Albert Einstein★	Mathematician/Scientist
Michelangelo	Painter

Spina Bifida

Hank Williams, Sr.	Singer
John Cougar Mellencamp	Singer/Song Writer

Cerebral Palsy

Christy Brown	Irish Author/Painter (Movie: My Left Foot)
Geri Jewell	Comedian/Actress

Amyotrophic Lateral Sclerosis (ALS)

Stephen Hawking★	Physicist
Lou Gehrig	Baseball Player
Jim "Catfish" Hunter	Baseball Player
Stephen Hillenburg	Cartoonist
Dennis Day	Singer/Comedian/Actor
Jacob Javits	US Senator from New York
Mao Zedong	Chinese Statesman
David Niven	Actor
Sam Shepard	Actor/Playwright

Person	Line of Work or Profession
Steve Gleason	Football Player
Kevin Turner	Football Player
Maxwell Taylor	US Army General

Epilepsy

Vincent van Gogh	Artist
Sir Isaac Newton★	Scientist
Napoleon Bonaparte★	French Statesman and Military Leader
Neal Young	Musician
Agatha Christie★	Author
Charles Dickens	Author
Alexander The Great	Greek King and Military Leader
Alfred Nobel	Swedish Chemist/Engineer
Danny Glover★	Actor
Leonardo da Vinci★	Painter
Julius Caesar	Roman Emperor
Aristotle★	Greek Philosopher
Theodore Roosevelt★	President, United States

Tourette Syndrome

Howard Hughes★	Entrepreneur
Dan Aykroyd★	Actor
David Beckman★	Soccer Player
Wolfgang Amadeus Mozart★	Composer

Dyslexia

Agatha Christie★	Author
Albert Einstein★	Mathematician/Scientist
Alexander Graham Bell	Inventor
Danny Glover★	Actor
Hans Christian Anderson	Author
Henry Winkler	Actor
Leonardo da Vinci★	Painter
Magic Johnson	Basketball Player

Person	Line of Work or Profession
Thomas Edison★	Inventor
Walt Disney	Film Producer
Winston Churchill★	Prime Minister, England
Woodrow Wilson	President, United States
George Patton	US Army General
Edward Hollowell	Child and Adult Psychiatrist
Nolan Ryan	Baseball Player

Physical Impairment (Used Wheel Chair)

Franklin Delano Roosevelt★ (Polio)	President, United States
Christopher Reeve (Equestrian accident)	Actor/Director
Itzhak Perlman (Polio)	Violinist/Conductor
Teddy Pendergrass (Auto accident)	Drummer

CHAPTER 6

MOVIES PORTRAYING PEOPLE WITH DISABILITIES

Movies have been made about people with disabilities practically since movies began to be produced. Some of the movies actually showcase more than one type of disability, such as "I Am Sam", whose main character is autistic, but his friend has agoraphobia.

Here is a sampling of them:

Alzheimer's Disease/Dementia:

Iris (2001)
Away From Her (2006)

The Notebook (2004)
Still Alice (2014)

Amnesia: (3 or 4 different types)

I Love You Again (1940)
The Snake Pit (1948)
Anastasia (1956)
RoboCop (1987)
Overboard (1987)
Regarding Henry (1991)
The Addams Family (1991)
Clean Slate (1994)

Copycat (1995)
The English Patient (1996)
The Long Kiss Goodnight (1996)
Wintersleepers (1997)
Naked Fear (1999)
The Bourne Identity (2002)
Finding Nemo (2003)
Public Domain (2003)

Ocean's Twelve (2004)
50 First Dates (2004)

Spider-Man 3 (2007)
Total Recall (2012)

Amputees, Paraplegics, Quadriplegics

An Affair to Remember (1957)
It's Good to be Alive (1974)
The Other Side of the Mountain (1975)

Men of Honor (2000)
Million Dollar Baby (2004)
Robo Cop (2014)

Anxiety Disorders:

Mrs. Dalloway (1997)
Session 9 (2001)

White Oleander (2002)
Punch-Drunk Love (2002)

Autism:

Rain Man (1988)
Little Man Tate (1991)
House of Cards (1993)
What's Eating Gilbert Grape (1993)
Mercury Rising (1998)
Molly (1999)
Bless the Child ((2000)

I Am Sam (2001)
Marathon (2005)
Mozart and the Whale (2005)
Adam (2009)
My Name is Khan (2010)
Temple Grandin (2010)
Fly Away (2011)

Bipolar Disorder:

A Fine Madness (1966)
Mr. Jones (1993)
On the Edge of Innocence (1997)
The Horse Whisperer (1998)
Pollock (2001)
Sylvia (2003)

The Flying Scotsman (2006)
Michael Clayton (2007)
Observe and Report (2009)
The Informant! (2009)
Boy Interrupted (2009)

Clinical Depression:

The Fire Within (1963)
Ordinary People (1980)
The Butcher Boy (1998)
Prozac Nation (2001)

The Hours (2002)
Shrink (2009)
Helen (2009)
It's Kind of a Funny Story (2010)

Dissociative Disorders:

The Three Faces of Eve (1957)
Psycho (1960)

Sybil (1976)
Never Talk to Strangers (1995)

Fight Club (1999)
Me, Myself & Irene (2000)
The Tale of Two Sisters (2003)

Secret Window (2004)
Frankie and Alice (2010)

Eating Disorders:

The Best Little Girl in the World (1981)
Kate's Secret (1986)
The Karen Carpenter Story (1989)

Sharing the Secret (2000)
Black Swan (2010)

Obsessive-Compulsive Disorder:

Cat People (1942)
What About Bob? (1991)

As Good As It Gets (1997)
The Aviator (2005)

Borderline Personality Disorder:

The Fountainhead (1949)
Play Misty for Me (1971)
Fatal Attraction (1987)

The Hand That Rocks the Cradle (1992)
The Cable Guy (1996)
Chloe (2009)

Antisocial Personality Disorder:

Clockwork Orange (1971)
The Silence of the Lambs (1991)

Natural Born Killers (1994)
No Country for Old Men (2007)

Narcissistic Personality Disorder:

Wall Street (1987)
To Die For (1995)

White Oleander (2002)

Schizophrenia:

Through A Glass Darkly (1961)
The Fisher King (1991)
Benny & Joon (1993)
Conspiracy Theory (1997)

A Beautiful Mind (2001)
K-PAX (2001)
The Soloist (2008)
Shutter Island (2010)

Delusional Disorder:

Repulsion (1965)
Misery (1990)

Alien 3 (1992)
Obsessed (2009)

<u>Visual Impairment</u>:

Scent of a Woman (1992)   Ray (2004)

<u>Miscellaneous</u>:

A Page of Madness (1926)   Shine (1996) [MI]
Harvey (1950)   Patch Adams (1998)
Vertigo (1958)   The Other Sister (1999)
Miracle Worker (1962)   Secret Cutting (2000)
One Flew Over the Cuckoo's Nest(1975)   Radio (2003)
Taxi Driver (1976)   Running With Scissors (2007)
The Secret of NIMH (1982)   Observe and Report (2009)
Children of a Lesser God (1986) [HI]   The King's Speech (2010) [S]
My Left Foot (1989) [CP]   Soul Surfer (2011) [PD]
Nell (1994) [S]   The Theory of Everything (2014)
Forest Gump (1994) [CD/MR]   Concussion (2015) [Brain]
Mr. Holland's Opus (1995) [HI]   Breathe (2017) [Polio]

CHAPTER 7

DISABILITIES IN HISTORY

Disabilities have been with us since the beginning of time. Names for different disabilities or mental health issues have changed over the years. Someone with a cognitive disability might have been described as "feebleminded" in the past. "Idiot" has been used to refer to a person having anything from a cognitive disability to schizophrenia.

In the past and even some cultures today, babies born with physical disabilities are killed immediately. In some cultures females are considered to have so little value that female babies are aborted or killed. Even in this century, a woman in Afghanistan was recently killed by her husband because she had borne another female child. He and his mother, who was also implicated in the death, had berated and abused the wife after the births of her first two girls. This is astounding since science has known for years that the male is the one to determine the sex of the child. Tragedies like this shouldn't keep happening.

The philosopher, Aristotle, advised getting rid of a child if it was imperfect. Greek law even dictated that a newborn baby was not really a child until seven days after birth so that an imperfect child could be disposed of with a clear conscience. From these beliefs arose the enduring idea that "good" looked beautiful and the deformed and disabled were "bad."

Classical Roman and Greek paintings depicted ideal beautiful bodies with perfect complexions, even though most people had impairments and many would have been scarred by smallpox.

In feudal and medieval Europe, when there were plagues, pestilence, or social upheaval, people with disabilities were often made scapegoats as sinners or evil people who brought these disasters upon society. During this time, witchcraft was linked with disabled people. There actually was a book that told how to identify witches by their impairments, by "evidence" of them creating impairments in others, or by them giving birth to a disabled child. Between eight and 20 million people, mainly women, were put to death as witches across Europe during this time. Many of these people were disabled.

Folklore is full of ideas linking disabilities with a negative or evil connotation. Grimm's Fairy Tales depicts the witch in Hansel and Gretel as deformed, blind and ugly.

Unfortunately, history offers many examples of societies exploiting people with disabilities. People with physical disabilities and deformities were featured as entertainment in circuses and freak shows. Categories of people, such as pirates, were stereotyped and depicted as blind in one eye or missing a hand or foot. Cartoons often characterized disabled people as weak, powerless, or incapable. People with physical and mental disabilities who were viewed as unproductive and a burden to society were sometimes literally sailed away as "ships of fools" from port to port. At each stop, people were charged admission to view the strange human cargo. The "fools" were then abandoned at the end of the tour and left to fend for themselves.

People once thought that mental illness was caused by supernatural powers. People believed that psychiatric disorders were the result of patients being invaded by evil spirits, making them evil beings. There is even a recent television show based upon this premise. One possible reaction of viewers is to feel better about their normality and have increased curiosity and fear of those who are different. The highly successful horror film genre is founded on this phenomenon and exploits the stereotypes.

In the Western Judeo-Christian society, the perception of body differences was influenced by Biblical references such as crippled, lame, blind, dumb, deaf, mad, feeble, idiot, and fools. Jesus reached out to heal a paralyzed man saying, "Your sins have been forgiven you." From earliest times within Jewish and Christian thinking, the idea of sin and disability has been linked. The implication is that a disability is a punishment for our sins or the sins of our parents and is caused by evil spirits, the devil, witchcraft, or God's displeasure. This phenomenon was frequently called the Religious Model of Disability.

In feudal and medieval Europe, most people with disabilities were accepted as part of the family or group, working on the land or in small workshops. However, in general Western culture has not done a good job of embracing people with disabilities although things are getting better.

In the late nineteenth century, ordinances were adopted in some US cities prohibiting people with disabilities from appearing in public. Today, these are referred to as *ugly laws*. The first ordinance was adopted in San Francisco in 1867. Chicago's ordinance, adopted in 1881, read: "Any person who is diseased, maimed, mutilated, or in any way deformed, so as to be an unsightly or disgusting object, or an improper person to be allowed in or on the streets, highways, thoroughfares, or public places in the city, shall not therein or thereon expose himself or herself to public view, under the penalty of a fine of $1 for each offense."[3] All of these ordinances were eventually repealed. Chicago was the last city to repeal its ugly law in 1974.

A FIRST LOOK AT PUNISHMENT VERSUS TREATMENT

In the 1840s, people with severe mental illness were kept in jails. A lady named Dorothea Dix was instrumental in lobbying the Massachusetts legislature to provide better treatment for mentally ill inmates. She made it her personal mission. She visited every jail in Massachusetts and documented the mistreatment of mentally ill inmates. After gaining hospitalization for the mentally ill in Massachusetts, she visited many other states advocating for hospitalization versus incarceration. Her movement led to the building of state mental hospitals and the belief that mentally ill persons deserved to be treated, not punished.

THE INFLUENCE OF INDUSTRIALIZATION

When our country was largely an agricultural society, a child or adult with a disability was accepted and accommodated within the family structure unless the disability was very severe. Everyone did their part in making the farm run and caring for family members. Family members with a disability usually took part in activities to the best of their ability. Those whose

---

[3] Wikipedia contributors, "Ugly Law," in *Wikipedia, The Free Encyclopedia*, https://en.wikipedia.org/w/index.php?title=Ugly_law&oldid=962321015.

disability was too difficult to accommodate within the family setting were placed in an institution and often forgotten.

As nations industrialized, people moved off the farms and began to work in factories, changing the dynamics. Machinery in factories was designed to be run by able-bodied people, those without disabilities. Work and production became linked with human worth, value, and profitability. (Ironically, the unsafe nature of early industrialization machinery injured and maimed many workers, generating more people with disabilities.)

Whole families moved off farms and away from their extended families. With only the nuclear family responsible for a person with a disability, care of this person was more challenging. People with disabilities were viewed as unproductive or incapable because they could not work the machines. More and more people with disabilities were put into institutions so that more family members could work and become skilled, productive members of society.

With the advent of institutions and increasing emphasis on social Darwinism (the application of his theory of survival of the fittest to human society) roles of special institutions shifted from places of reform to places of custody for social control. This became known as the Medical Model of Disability. This created new professions such as social work and expanded job opportunities with specialties in nursing. This also led to eugenics in the United States, believing that the quality of the human race could be improved by selective breeding. Social Darwinism even went to the point that, in 1881, an international congress in Milan, Italy, outlawed sign language, fearing that deaf people would outbreed hearing people!

If a child was born with a disability, the parents were encouraged to immediately place the child into an institution to live out their life in that environment. If a person developed a mental health issue sometime during their life, they were placed in an asylum or institution. My grandmother told of having a nervous breakdown and going into an institution until she got better. She said it was run like the military, patients having to make their beds with such tightness of sheets that a quarter could be bounced off of the bed. And this was in the twentieth century.

Early in the twentieth century, language regarding cognitive disabilities was demeaning. Terms such as idiot, imbecile, moron, feeble-minded, and morally defective were used to indicate levels of disability or, in other terms, the person's IQ level. The lower a person tested on the IQ scale, the more derogatory the label they would be assigned such as idiot.

THE EFFECTS OF TWO WORLD WARS

The return of soldiers from World War I had a transformative effect on the image of people with disabilities. Before World War I, many viewed the disabled as unfit to live in normal society. Now the medical community and other supportive aid groups hurried to help the injured heroes. The result was improved plastic surgery techniques and prosthetic limbs, new rehabilitation procedures, sheltered workshops for disabled workers, and special subsidized housing for injured veterans.

World War II brought a very dark chapter to the history of how people with disabilities are treated. Actions of the Third Reich in Germany highlighted the stigma and scapegoating of persons with disabilities. Propaganda films were produced portraying people with disabilities as "useless eaters" and a burden on the state. This propaganda advocated the idea that people with disabilities should be sterilized or eliminated altogether. One film called "Erbkrank" (Heredity, 1936), was intended to degrade, criminalize, and dehumanize people with physical and mental disabilities. Its goal was to make the audience sympathetic toward compulsory sterilization and, later, euthanasia. In 1939-1940, 140,000 adults with physical and mental disabilities were murdered at the hands of the doctors of the Third Reich. Killing of children with disabilities continued until 1945, with over 100,000 murdered.

Many of our returning World War II soldiers suffered from what we now call post-traumatic stress disorder. Their behaviors as they would mentally relive the dangers they had experienced and the atrocities they had seen scared the veterans' families. Some veterans were convinced by their families and doctors to undergo a relatively new type of brain surgery called a lobotomy (severing the connections in the brain's prefrontal cortex). Some veterans said they felt duty bound to have the lobotomies so that perhaps their delusions, paranoia, and nightmares would disappear with the surgery. Approximately 2,000 World War II veterans were lobotomized during and after the war. At the time, this was considered a miracle cure for all types of mental illness.

Finally, treatment started becoming a bit more humane with bed rest, good nutrition, and placing the patient in a cheerful environment. The therapeutic community adopted a philosophy that if patients had a say in their treatment and were treated with dignity and respect, they would get better faster. Finally, in the 1950s medications started being used to treat mental illness with a good measure of success.

Thorazine was one of the first drugs approved for treating psychiatric illness (1954). Almost two million people were treated with it for psychosis. Other drugs that were developed were used to reduce anxiety, discomfort, and bizarre behavior. These tranquilizing drugs were used to modify the emotional effects of the psychiatric disorders without impairing intellectual functioning. As a result, patients were able to become participating members of the community.

THE DARK HISTORY OF EXPERIMENTATION

At one time, US government doctors condoned and participated in experimentation on prison inmates and people with disabilities, using them as guinea pigs for medical research. Several factors made this possible. Many people with disabilities were housed together in government-run institutions where they could not refuse treatment, they had no one advocating for their rights, some thought them to be less-than-human, and many families "forgot" about their members in institutions. The US military also used people as guinea pigs.

[Author's Note: Researching the material for this section was emotionally difficult. Some stories made me angry. Some made me cry at the inhumanity of using people with disabilities as research subjects. What ever happened to the "first do no harm" part of the Hippocratic Oath?]

Eugenics is the "science" of selective human breeding. Between 1924 and 1981, most states in our nation had eugenics programs and more than 30 enacted laws mandating surgical sterilization for certain individuals, mostly African-Americans. North Carolina sterilized more than 7,600 individuals during this time in the name of "improving" the state's human stock. Virginia had more than 7,000 involuntarily sterilized. By the time the program was halted, the majority of those neutered were young, poor, black women. In their medical records, many of them were listed as feeble-minded, which was the term used at the time for mental retardation. These women and girls, some as young as 14, were deemed unfit to procreate. As many as 100,000 people, mostly black, in 33 states may have been sterilized in this country before the practice was discredited. Since 2010,

North Carolina, Virginia, and other states have decided to compensate those women still alive who underwent this horrific procedure. However, compensation is projected to only be $50,000 per person in North Carolina and $25,000 per person in Virginia.

The Tuskegee Syphilis Study started in 1932. The study was conducted by the US Public Health Service to study the natural progression of untreated syphilis in poor, rural black men who thought they were receiving free health care from the federal government. At that time there was no cure for syphilis, only treatments and drugs that made it a little better. The men were told that they were being treated for "bad blood," a local term used to describe several illnesses, including anemia, fatigue, and syphilis.

Study director Dr. Taliaferro Clark's original goal was to follow untreated syphilis in a group of 400 black men for 6-9 months and then follow up with a treatment phase. However, others involved with the study wanted to continue to follow the men but not give them any treatment. These doctors prevailed. For their trouble, the men were given free medical care, free hot meals, and free burial insurance.

During the World War II years, as men were being inducted into the military, the Public Health doctors gave the draft board in Tuskegee, Alabama, a list of the men who had syphilis and should **not** be treated during their induction into the service. (Others were treated). By 1943, penicillin had been shown to be a cure for syphilis. These men were never specifically told they had syphilis, were never treated for it, and once there was a cure, were never told about the cure.

When information came out about the atrocities perpetrated on humans at the hands of Nazi doctors, international law changed to protect the rights of research subjects. Many US doctors essentially ignored them, arguing that they applied to Nazi atrocities, not American doctors. The Tuskegee study went on until a "whistleblower" leaked information about the study to the media in 1972, and there was a public outcry. The study had lasted 40 years.

Another similar study was conducted by American doctors in Guatemala from 1946 to 1948. With the cooperation of Guatemalan health ministry officials, they deliberately infected prisoners, soldiers, and patients in a mental hospital with syphilis. Both men and women were exposed to the disease(s) and, if they contracted it, were treated with antibiotics, although it is unclear if all of the patients were cured. The information on this experiment did not come to light until October, 2010.

Another federally-funded experiment that utilized men with mental health disabilities, begun in 1942, involved testing flu vaccines on the patients of Ypsilanti State Hospital in Michigan. The men were exposed to the flu virus several months later. Dr. Jonas Salk, who 10 years later developed the first polio vaccine, was a participant in this study.

In the 1940s, Dr. W. Paul Havens Jr. exposed men to hepatitis in a series of experiments including one using patients from mental institutions in Middletown and Norwich, Connecticut. Dr. Havens was an expert on viral diseases and one of the first scientists to differentiate between different types of hepatitis and their causes.

In Staten Island, New York, from 1964-1966, a controversial medical study was conducted at Willowbrook State School for children with mental disabilities. Hepatitis was rampant throughout the institution, but medical researcher Saul Krugman intentionally fed live hepatitis virus to sixty healthy children to observe the development and progress of the disease and to see if they could then be cured with gamma globulin. Did these children understand what was happening and give their consent? Did their parents consent to their children participating in the study? The answer is no.

In the early 1970s, psychologist David Rosenhan conducted an experiment in which healthy people or "pseudo-patients" briefly simulated auditory hallucinations in an attempt to gain admission to 12 different psychiatric hospitals in five different states around the United States. After admission to the hospital, the pseudo-patients acted normally and told staff they were no longer experiencing hallucinations. Hospital staff believed that all of the pseudo-patients exhibited symptoms of ongoing mental illness. They were confined for periods ranging from 7 to 52 days. All were forced to admit to having a mental illness and to agree to take antipsychotic drugs as a condition of their release. In the other part of the study, a well-known psychiatric research and teaching hospital was told by Rosenhan in advance that he would be sending fake patients to the hospitals. In actuality, he sent no patients to the hospital, yet hospital staff falsely identified 41 ordinary patients as impostors.

Even though people in the studies were usually described as volunteers, historians and ethicists have questioned how well these people understood what was to be done to them and why or whether they were coerced.

In congressional hearings in 1973, pharmaceutical industry officials acknowledged they were using prisoners for testing new drugs because they were cheaper than chimpanzees! This caused the government to respond with reforms. When the supply of prisoners and mental patients dried up, researchers turned to other countries. Pharmaceutical companies have tested new medicines on populations in third-world countries without full disclosure of what was being done or what the risks of taking the experimental drug were. This story was dramatized in the 2005 movie *The Constant Gardener.*

What do such experiments say about our humanity? Does the prospect of some "greater good" justify the deceptive mistreatment of the individuals involved? Most studies of this nature were not covered by the news media at the time of the experiments. Even when there was contemporary reporting, the focus was on the promise of new cures while ignoring how the test subjects were treated. These experiments did not give people a chance.

EMBRACING DISABILITIES

In the latter half of the twentieth century, the definitions of impairment and disability were challenged. To medical professionals and to people with disabilities and their families, it was becoming clear that the restricted participation in society of people with disabilities was a socially created barrier, not the result of physical and mental limitations or impairments. Instead of viewing disabilities as a welfare or entitlement issue, society at large began to now see it as a civil rights issue. There was a paradigm shift and prejudice, discrimination, and exclusion began to be derailed by federal and state legislation guaranteeing rights to those with disabilities. (Yet today the pendulum has started swinging back. Some people and politicians believe people with disabilities who are not working are a drain on society. They are taking actions to roll back social "safety nets" such as Supplemental Security Income (SSI) and supplemental food programs because the individuals have not worked to earn these benefits.)

Such progress was not universal worldwide, however, Communist ideology promoted a reverence of the healthy, fully able-bodied worker. In nations under communist rule, individuals who were not perfect—those who displayed any type of disability or defect—were removed from the general population.

In Poland, less than 20 percent of people with disabilities are working, whereas Slovakia employs 43 percent and Great Britain employs over 50 percent. Looking to the future, Poland realizes it needs to step up its game. In a few years, it will exhaust the supply of people in the workforce who are ready to work. They will have to professionally solicit people with disabilities as not only a social obligation, but also as an economic necessity. Poland is recognizing that people with disabilities have many qualities to contribute to society.

In other cultures such as the Maori in Aotearoa (New Zealand), disabilities are considered a normal part of life and people with disabilities are included in economic and social life. The Maori's have a philosophical model of disability activism known as the Social Model of Disability. According to the social model theory, a person may have an impairment but it is the way that society is set up and organized that disables the person. Therefore, disability is something that happens to a person because of the social structures that surround them, not something that the person possesses. They believe that to be competitive and effective, workplaces need to ensure they recruit the best person for the job and then retain and develop them. If people are excluded from the job market for reasons that do not relate to their ability to do the job, workplaces will inevitably miss out on skills, talent and energy. This is an incredibly inclusive and progressive approach.

In the summer of 2015, New York City held the NYC Disability Pride Parade with more than 3,000 participants traveling Broadway using wheelchairs, canes, and guide dogs. The grand marshal was former U.S. Senator Tom Harkin of Iowa who in 1990 sponsored the Americans with Disabilities Act. As one participant said, "When I became paralyzed, I thought my life was over, but I have a purpose in life." Participants felt very good about being able to celebrate themselves, including their challenges, especially since society has marginalized them in so many ways. Senator Harkin is still working for disability rights, stating, "We know that when companies hire people with disabilities, they get the best workers, the most loyal workers, the most productive workers."

CHAPTER 8

CHANGES IN THE DISABILITY TREATMENT LANDSCAPE

In the aftermath of the end of the Great Depression and victories in World War II, Americans looked forward with new optimism and confidence. They dreamed of a better future and new opportunities. Attitudes toward disabilities and people with disabilities benefitted from this sweeping new vision.

In 1946, the US Congress passed legislation called the National Mental Health Act creating the National Institute of Mental Health (NIMH). The Mental Health Study Act of 1955 authorized a thorough study analysis of the human and economic problems of mental illness, published in 1961. This report became the basis of the Community Mental Health Act of 1963.

In the 1950's, three developments contributed to a shift in psychiatric care: 1) the use of psychotropic drugs, 2) the development of the philosophy of the therapeutic community, and 3) geographic decentralization in large state mental hospitals. In 1954 when Thorazine was put on the market nearly two million people were treated with this drug for psychosis. By using psychotropic drugs, more people were able to participate in their own treatment in a democratic way. They were able to participate in decision making, working together with staff in therapeutic communities for more effective management of their own mental illness. By organizing patients by geographic location rather than by illness, this allowed more equitable treatment and less people in hospitals. However, this ultimately contributed to the perception that all psychiatric hospitalizations were undesirable.

Starting in 1957, a series of civil rights acts were passed, many dealing with various social welfare programs, but especially the deinstitutionalization of the mentally ill. California led the states in starting to clear the institutions of patients, but without any other safeguards for treatment in place.

President Kennedy signed the Community Mental Health Act of 1963. Nine months before, he had addressed the nation on the subject of mental health. This was the first time a President delivered a message about mental health and advocated for treatment for people with mental illness. The Act provided federal funds for community mental health centers in the United States. The purpose was to provide community-based care rather than institutionalized care in hospitals. This led to a growing wave of deinstitutionalization. States saw this as an invitation to close costly hospitals, but didn't always transfer the monies to communities to open community mental health centers. Many patients who had previously been "warehoused" in institutions were now released to communities, which in most cases, were not prepared to deal with them. Some individuals ended up with family, some in adult homes, and some on the streets, usually without medications.

In 1967, almost half a million people or about 7 percent of all persons with severe disabilities aged 18-64 in the United States were residents of long-term institutions or schools and homes for people with physical and mental handicaps. About 86 percent of the institutionalized adults under the age of 65 were in institutions operated by state or local governments. Eleven percent were in federal institutions and less than 3 percent were in private institutions. Those with mental retardation (the term used at that time) tended to be institutionalized the longest, followed by those with mental health issues.

The stated reasons for people to be in institutions were: the need for permanent care not possible at home, the need to be watched and looked after more carefully than was possible at home, too hard to handle, and need for special training. These people were placed in the institutions and then frequently forgotten. Many of the institutionalized people had not been out of the institutions for a visit with families in the past year or two, especially if their disability was mental retardation.

During the Nixon and Ford administrations, funds for community mental health services were withheld even though approved by Congress. People with severe mental illness were being let out of institutions with nowhere to go and without community services to assist and support them. Patients needed food, counseling, rehabilitation, medication, money, and places to live, yet there was no coordination between hospitals, institutions, and community mental health centers. In fact, the community mental health centers were not even told when a person was being discharged from an institution, so there was no coordination or continuity of care. The patient might suddenly land on the doorstep of the community mental health center or, if the center was informed they had been discharged, they may not know where to find the person.

Community mental health centers were struggling too with how to best provide services to people. Most services provided through the institutional approach had been based on the Medical Model and that was not always conducive to treating people with a mental illness. When they did get it right, they used that model for all mental health patients regardless of race or economic status.

In October 1980, President Carter signed the Mental Health Systems Act (Public Law 96-398) which provided monies to the states to serve minorities, consumers in rural areas, and the poor. It was considered to be landmark legislation. It provided money for services to children, adolescents, and the elderly, especially in the area of emotional disturbance. This Act was a commitment to provide mental health services to anyone who needed them at the state level with minimal interference from the federal government. It provided federal grants for first time projects to prevent mental illness and to promote mental health care. It also provided federal grants to initiate advocacy programs to protect the legal and other rights of the mentally ill.

Unfortunately, President Carter's Mental Health Systems Act ran counter to the financial goals of the Reagan administration which was more interested in providing a business friendly political climate. This meant reducing federal spending, reducing social programs, and transferring responsibility of many, if not most, governmental functions to the individual states. He also promoted *law and order* and *get tough on crime* initiatives. Reagan dismantled the safety net for people using social programs, characterizing people utilizing social programs as lazy and even criminal. Then most of the provisions of the law itself was repealed by Congress and approved by Ronald Reagan on August 13, 1981.

The Reagan Administration's goals of fiscal restraint received support from the general public because he promoted the perception that the federal government was too big, too prone to waste taxpayer dollars, and not addressing other basic concerns such as crime prevention. Increasing numbers of people were being released from institutions. With no one managing their day-to-day life any longer, many former patients became homeless, were unable to work, did not have access to health services and medications, and had lost contact with their families. In such a vulnerable situation, they were more likely to enter the criminal justice system because they frightened the general public and were viewed as threats to the social order. This bears a striking resemblance to many of the situations today.

In one study, replacing inpatient services with residential and outpatient services resulted in a huge cost savings. A 94 percent reduction in state hospital services resulted in cost savings of more than $45 million over a three-year period. These savings were used to fund community mental health services. During the three-year study, the net savings to mental health services was $3.4 million.[4]

Since the mid-1980s, some western countries like Australia have enacted legislation which embraces a rights-based model, rather than a custodial model, that seeks to address issues of social justice and discrimination.

One of the first civil rights laws offering protection for people with disabilities in the US was the Rehabilitation Act of 1973 (PL 93-112). Its reach extended only to federal agency activities and programs and any activity or program receiving federal financial assistance. Within that sphere, however, Section 504 of the Act prohibited exclusion from participation in, or denial of benefits from, such activities and programs solely on the basis of a person's disability.

In the late 1980s, through their own initiative and with the help of others, people with disabilities started advocating for their rights. This included the right to work with reasonable accommodations (additional time to complete tasks, extra training, or modified workspaces); the right to be able to enter a public building, especially if in a wheelchair; the right to accessible public transportation; and the right to go to school and college

---

[4] Edna Kamis-Gould, *et al.*, "The Impact of Closing a State Psychiatric Hospital on the County Mental Health System and Its Clients." *Psychiatric Services*, Vol. 50, No. 10 (October 1999), 1297-1302. https://ps.psychiatryonline.org/doi/pdfplus/10.1176/ps.50.10.1297.

like others. Civil rights legislation such as the Americans with Disabilities Act of 1990 (PL 101-336) or the Disability Discrimination Act (UK 1995) has provided some of these things, but not all, and not universally. People with disabilities do not want to be a burden on society. They want to work if they are able and to participate in public life. They just need to be given a chance—a level playing field. This approach became known as the Rights-Based Model of Disability.

AMERICANS WITH DISABILITIES ACT OF 1990 (ADA)

The ADA is a landmark piece of legislation signed into law by President George H.W. Bush on July 26, 1990. It drastically changed the disability treatment landscape by prohibiting discrimination on the basis of disability in the same way that prior civil rights legislation prohibited discrimination on the basis of race, religion, sex, national origin, and other similar factors.

The changes made by the ADA were monumental. Section 504 of the Rehabilitation Act of 1973 had only prohibited discrimination on the basis of disability in federal and federally-funded programs and operations. The ADA extended the reach of protections on the basis of disability to state and local government programs and operations, to public transportation, to public accommodations and commercial facilities, and to all employers with 15 or more employees. Public accommodations include facilities in outdoor environments such as parks and trails.

The ADA protects individuals who have a disability or have a relationship or association with an individual with a disability (such as your child with a disability). An individual with a disability is defined by the ADA as a person who has a physical or mental impairment that substantially limits one or more major life activities, a person who has a history or record of such an impairment, or a person who is perceived by others as having such an impairment. The condition does not need to be severe or permanent to be a disability. The ADA does not specifically name all of the impairments that are covered. Regulations of the Equal Employment Opportunity Commission provide a fairly comprehensive list of conditions that are recognized as disabilities.

More information on the ADA as it relates to specific subjects discussed in other chapters is provided in those chapters.

THE LANDSCAPE TODAY

Public support remains strong for providing the least-restrictive living arrangements within the community for people with disabilities and for celebrating the diversity that these individuals represent. Nevertheless, there is a dark undercurrent of sentiment that asserts that people with disabilities who are not working and supporting themselves economically are a burden on society. This sentiment is reflected in such actions as rationing of health care services, proposals to reduce spending on programs that support living expenses for people with disabilities, such as Supplemental Security Income, reductions in support services for people who need assistance with daily life activities, and a move toward a one-size-fits-all model of services.

A basic precept of the Judaic, Christian, and Islamic traditions from the earliest times is charity—providing for those who cannot provide for themselves. Charity is normally considered to be a good thing. However, even within religious sectors of American society, this virtue is being discarded and replaced by an attitude of "I should only have to pay for my own, or my family's, needs." People receiving public assistance are viewed as moochers, taking unfair advantage of the rest of society. There will always be those individuals who try to "work the system," who are looking for charity when they are capable of supporting themselves. The growing sentiment is to view everyone receiving public assistance as one of these individuals and not take into account their disabilities or other limiting circumstances.

While writing this book, I received two email messages from friends and relatives forwarding a spam message complaining about lazy people not working and the rest of us having to support them. Having two sons with disabilities who receive public support, I felt a strong need to reply. Both individuals quickly backtracked, saying that they of course didn't mean people with disabilities, but I believe I made my point—that you can't lump everyone receiving public benefits into one category. There are legitimate reasons why some people cannot work or be completely self-supporting and need public support.

These perspectives illustrate the stereotypes and prejudicial attitudes still held by many in our society toward people who find it necessary to depend upon various forms of public assistance, such as people with disabilities. Without knowing any of the details of a person's life, they use a broad brush to paint a picture in their minds of those receiving public assistance. Sometimes it is easy to think this way because they cannot "see" the disability, like the autism and fetal alcohol issues that so affect my adopted sons.

Depression is another one of those disabilities that is largely invisible and is affecting more and more people. It is a serious mental illness that frequently is caused by a chemical imbalance within the brain. Some people are so depressed that they are mentally paralyzed, unable to do anything. A severely depressed person sometimes loses their employment and the family finds it necessary to access public services and support. A depressed person may be unable to do even the smallest daily activities, let alone seeking appropriate treatment. A family member or friend might have to "hold their hand" —make appointments with a doctor, take them to the appointment, take them to the pharmacy, be on the phone with them to help explain the type of assistance they need, etc. People with severe depression invent many excuses for not doing the things that need to be done. The person helping them has to cut through those excuses and help the depressed person do those things, because if not done, the failure to do them feeds the feelings of worthlessness.

In 2015, there were approximately 7.4 billion people in the world, and 350 million people of all ages, or 4.7 percent, were affected by depression. It is the leading cause of disability worldwide and a major contributor to the overall global burden of disease. More women are affected by depression than men. At its worst, depression can lead to suicide. It is not uncommon for someone with an anxiety disorder or many other physical and mental health disabilities to also suffer from depression. Although there are known, effective treatments for depression, fewer than half of those affected in the world receive treatment, in many countries fewer than 10 percent.

Another staggering trend in the landscape of disabilities today is the abuse of prescription opioids and illegal street opioids. In 2018, 46 people died every day in the United States from an overdose of prescription painkillers. Many more become addicted according to the latest data from the Centers for Disease Control and Prevention. The CDC has called on doctors to limit the number of painkiller prescriptions. If people cannot get or afford the painkillers, many have turned to the cheaper and illegal street drugs, heroin and fentanyl. Overdose deaths involving opioids have increased five-fold since 1999. The CDC reports that, on average, 130 Americans die every day from an opioid overdose, or more than forty-seven thousand each year.

One of the most shameful trends in the landscape of disabilities is the lack of access to mental health services. Obtaining treatment for a mental illness in the United States is not easy. By June 2016, the US had only 3.5 percent as many state hospital beds for the mentally ill as it did 60 years ago. We have closed over 500,000 beds without funding and providing sufficient community mental health services and adequate, affordable housing. There are 17 percent fewer beds than there were in 2010. The US now ranks twenty-ninth among Organization for Economic Cooperation and Development (OECD) countries on inpatient mental health beds. Not being able to access a mental health bed can result in a person becoming incarcerated (see Chapter 32 Jails and Prisons). If the U.S. had replaced the lost psychiatric beds with the wrap-around community services that President Carter had set in motion—providing a full range of community services, including case management, supported housing, and work, we would not have the number of people in our jails and prisons that we do. Our jails and prisons have become the largest mental health institutions in our communities. Police, sheriff deputies, and prison guards have become dispensers of psychotropic medications and *de facto* "therapists" (for which they have little to no training). "Treatment" for aberrant behavior is often placement in solitary confinement to punish the behavior. The successful mental health treatment models used by other countries have respected the dignity and freedom of persons with mental illness for "their right to live as citizens in the community, and the great therapeutic value of engaging them in its daily activities."[5] The lack of a coordinated system of services for those with mental health disabilities in the US does little to preserve the dignity and freedom of persons with mental illness.

People with mental illness do very poorly in the criminal justice system that imposes retributive punishment on them, rather than treatment or at least restorative justice. American society has largely abandoned them, especially those who are poor, leaving it to the police to deal with them. Someone with a mental illness is sixteen times more likely to be shot by the police than someone without mental illness. They are the most likely to be put into solitary confinement because they cannot conform their behavior to the rules of an institution that doesn't understand them and is

[5] Allen J. Frances, "U.S. Mental Health Care Goes from the Worst to Even Worse," *Huffington Post*, June 2, 2017. https://www.huffpost.com/entry/us-mental-health-care-goes-from-the-worst-to-even-worse_b_10215720.

ill-prepared to deal with them. They also are raped or beaten much more frequently both in institutions and out.

Numerous studies have demonstrated that it is more cost-effective to provide housing and adequate psychiatric services in the community than placing people with mental illness in jails and prisons, or leaving them homeless. The World Health Organization's Trieste, Italy, model is one example demonstrating this. Since the early 1970s Trieste has substantially reduced the number of persons with mental illness that are institutionalized. It developed a series of community treatment clinics that provide services to patients living in small groups or apartments, or in their own homes. The clinic is open 24-hours a day and even has a handful of beds for emergency use by a person in crisis. Having something like this in the U.S. would contribute to positive outcomes for patients, workers, and communities. Several US cities have successfully pioneered 24-hour mental health urgent care clinics that have provided an alternative to incarceration when police are called to a scene where someone is having a mental health crisis.

CHAPTER 9

OPPORTUNITIES TO MINIMIZE DISABILITIES DURING PREGNANCY

When people think about having a child, they naturally think about the baby growing into a self-sufficient young adult. Their son or daughter will be well on their way to independence by age 18, except perhaps for assistance in paying for college expenses. Spoiler Alert: It doesn't always happen like that.

If your child is born with a disability, your whole world changes in the blink of an eye. Depending on what the disability is, your child may be dependent upon you for the rest of his or her life, or certainly for the rest of your life. If your son or daughter is unable to live independently and self-sufficiently, you will spend huge amounts of time, energy, and likely money trying to make provisions for the special needs of your child during the remainder of his/her life.

Quite logically, pregnancy is where the disabilities a person is born with begin. It is also the time when a prospective mother can make choices that can minimize the chances that her baby will be born with a disability. Women are encouraged to take prenatal vitamins, especially folic acid. In fact, doctors recommend that if you are thinking of getting pregnant, you should make sure that either your diet has an overabundance of folic acid or you start taking supplements with folic acid because it helps reduce the risk of defects in the development of the neural tube during the first six weeks of pregnancy. This is before many women know they are pregnant.

In the 1980's, it was recommended that women take folic acid to reduce the risk of nervous system problems in newborn infants. By 1998, the Food and Drug Administration mandated that folic acid be added to enriched grain products. Somewhere during this time it was discovered that a lack of or diminished amount of folic acid could cause neural tube defects such as spina bifida, or the incomplete closing of the spine and membranes around the spinal cord; anencephaly, which is a severe underdeveloped brain; or encephalocele, when brain tissue protrudes out to the skin from an abnormal opening in the skull.

Unfortunately, even when a mother makes all the best choices during pregnancy, her child can still be born with a disability. Some diseases or disabilities are genetically based and there is little that can be done to change the outcome. A fetus could inherit two recessive genes, one from each parent, for any number of maladies. Some examples of this are Huntington's disease, Tay-Sachs disease, breast cancer, attention deficit hyperactivity disorder, obesity, alcoholism, etc.

My husband received two recessive genes for hemochromatosis (too much iron in the blood). This may have, in part, been the cause of his coronary artery disease. None of his three siblings received these two recessive genes.

Genetic testing can now alert a couple to potential disabilities or problems their offspring may incur because of their genetic make-up. In fact, genetic testing and egg manipulation now makes it possible to prevent passing on a disease to your offspring. I know of a young couple who, instead of spending money on a big wedding, opted to get married at the courthouse and spend their money to "weed out" fertilized eggs that carried the Huntington disease gene. Because her father recently died of the disease, the wife knows she will develop the disease because she carries the gene. Rather than pass the disease on to her children, they used genetic testing to discard any eggs that would carry the disease and to immediately get pregnant through implantation of the "clean" in vitro fertilized eggs.

By doing this they hope the wife will be able to raise her children before the disease takes over her life.

Starting in 1963, it was federally mandated that testing be done on infants shortly after birth to determine if they have any of 29 different disorders. Early detection can prevent brain or organ damage or even death and save on costly medical bills and/or institutionalization by this testing. Pricks are made to the baby's heel and five drops of blood are taken for the testing. The first such tests were for phenylketonuria (PKU) and hypothyroidism. Detected early, these can be treated with a special diet or medication and prevent mental retardation. Many states test for more than the mandated 29 disorders. Wisconsin currently tests for 44 disorders.

Doctors have been telling women for a number of years not to drink alcohol, smoke, take illegal drugs, or take prescription medications known to have harmful effects on unborn children if they are pregnant or thinking about becoming pregnant. Why? Drugs, alcohol, nicotine and the other chemicals in cigarettes can cause a number of illnesses and/or disabilities in their child. The developing fetus' nervous system, brain, and organs can be adversely affected by what the mother ingests. There can be developmental delays in the child. A child could be more prone to certain illnesses, such as respiratory ailments (colds, asthma). Damage to the central nervous system can cause a person (child or adult) to be hypersensitive to noise, lights, and colors. There are so many ways that an unborn child's life can be affected during pregnancy.

Fetal alcohol spectrum disorder (FASD) is a group of mild to severe physical, neurological, and behavioral conditions caused by alcohol consumption by the mother during pregnancy. Studies comparing the brains of normal children versus children who were exposed to alcohol in utero show shocking differences. A normal brain is grayish in color and has two fairly equal halves that are symmetrical and characterized by bumpy ridges. There is a wide corpus callosum between the two halves. The brain of a child with FASD is kind of whitish, not symmetrical, is comparatively smooth (fewer bumps and ridges) with a narrower and irregular separation between the two halves to almost nonexistent corpus callosum. One picture of an FASD brain that I saw reminded me of a hard-cooked egg. These impacts on the brains of individuals with FASD affects their ability to handle emotions, ability to solve problems, utilize cause and effect thinking, and identify, understand, and respond to social cues. As they get older, these deficiencies affect the individual's ability to maintain a job, form and maintain meaningful relationships, and parent children. They can be impulsive, explosive, and irritable. If the level of alcohol abuse during pregnancy was significant, the child may be born with altered facial features.

This disorder does not have to happen. It causes multiple problems for the child and lasting consequences. No child should have to bear the consequences of a mother's use of alcohol or illegal drugs during pregnancy and be condemned to their own lifetime of bad decisions. For insight on what an adoptive father experienced with his son who was severely disabled by FASD, read *The Broken Cord*.

Even if the most conscientious person who tries to eat correctly, exercise, get sufficient sleep, and who has no genetic anomalies in her family history can give birth to a child with a disability. Anomalies of nature happen. Thousands of women in the southern hemisphere have recently given birth to babies with microcephaly. How did this happen? It appears that the Zika virus from being bitten by an Aedes mosquito is to blame. However, there are other causes of microcephaly, such as chromosomal abnormalities, malnutrition, and exposure to drugs or other toxins (lead being one of them). Microcephaly is diagnosed when a baby's head is at least two standard deviations below the average size for age and sex. Some of the heads of babies in Brazil are five to ten standard deviations below the norm.

Another source of diseases and disabilities is the many chemicals in our world. They are in the air, water, food and food containers, carpets, laminate flooring, the wood that frames our houses, detergents, clothing and other fabrics, etc. All of these exposures put us at risk for harm to our bodies and the developing bodies of unborn children. Chemicals like BPA (bisphenol A), which is in many plastics, canned food linings, and used to be in plastic water containers and baby bottles, can have a weak, hormone-like effect on the body. It is one of a whole class of chemicals that have worked their way into our environment that have estrogen-mimicking effects on pregnant women. They can interrupt the network that regulates the signals which control the reproductive development in humans and animals. The result can be miscarriages, birth defects, and behavioral and academic problems.

Many books have been written on the subjects of various disabilities. None are more poignant than those written by parents about their child's struggles, what their family's life is like, struggles getting a diagnosis, challenges getting services for their child, and the worry about what will happen to the child (frequently an adult at this point) once the parents are gone. These stories are not about an 18-year parenting commitment as we usually think about when getting pregnant. It is a life-long commitment because many of these children will need continued support, either minimally or extensively. Medical science is advancing every day and some disability-causing diseases may soon be eradicated, but people who already have a disability will most likely have it for their entire lives. Once it is there, you can't undo it.

CHAPTER 10

THE BRAIN AND THE ROLE IT PLAYS IN DISABILITIES

The brain is one of the largest organs in the human body and the most complex. It is made up of more than 100 billion nerves that communicate in 4 trillions of connections called synapses. It is like a master computer. It tells all organs how and when to function. It tells our limbs when to move and how to move. It tells our heart to beat, our lungs to breathe. It is a music conductor conducting an orchestra. When a musician or section does not play their instrument according to the music/expectations of the conductor, it causes problems.

The brain is made up of many specialized areas that work together. The cortex is the outermost layer of brain cells. Thinking and voluntary movements begin in the cortex. The corpus callosum is a wide, flat bundle of neural fibers beneath the cortex. It connects the left and right cerebral hemispheres and facilitates interhemispheric communication. The brain stem is between the spinal cord and the rest of the brain. Basic functions like breathing and sleep are controlled here. The limbic system is a border around the brain stem. The limbic cortex, hypothalamus, and associated structures are concerned with "non-thinking" activities of internal environment and self-preservation, provocative emotions such as fear, rage, anxiety, agitation, sexual and defensive reactions. (In a sense, emotions go round-and-round in the limbic system and are diffusely projected to other parts of the nervous system. Excessive persistent reverberations of emotions are thought to be factors in neuroses, psychosomatic ailments, and mental illness.) The basal ganglia are a cluster of structures in the center of the brain. They coordinate messages between multiple other brain areas. The cerebellum is at the base and the back of the brain. It is responsible for coordination and balance. The brain is also divided into several lobes. The frontal lobes are responsible for problem solving, judgment and motor function. The parietal lobes manage sensation, handwriting, and body position. The temporal lobes are involved with memory and hearing. The amygdala is two almond shaped groups of nuclei located deep and in the middle of the temporal lobe. They perform a primary role in the processing of memory, decision-making, and emotional reactions. This is part of the limbic system. The occipital lobes contain the brain's visual processing system. The brain is surrounded by a layer of tissue called the meninges. The skull (cranium) helps protect the brain from injury.

It is important to have a healthy brain. For that we need to have a healthy diet, physical exercise (especially young children as body movement develops the brain), mental exercise (such as doing puzzles, word games, math problems), have plenty of social interaction (because actively engaging with others requires using different regions of the brain).

Scientists estimate we lose between 30,000 and 50,000 brain cells (neurons) every single day. This leads not only to common occurrences like the loss of car keys and reading glasses, but difficulty with management of our time and household tasks. As we grow older our brains start to slow down and literally shrink, although at different rates for each person. Most everyone will show about a 15-30 percent drop in brain weight and size over a lifetime.

There are six factors that kill brain cells. They are: traumatic brain injuries, sports concussions, disease processes, lead or mercury exposure, pesticide exposure, and the normal aging process. These killers have ten consequences for us in memory loss, inattentiveness, the inability to focus, fogginess, forgetfulness, difficulty learning, mental fatigue, emotional issues, poor sleep patterns, and low energy.

Brain trauma and exposure to toxins, such as mercury and lead in the environment can contribute to deteriorating brain health. Lead is a neurotoxin that can damage a child's brain development, cause behavioral problems, and sicken adults. Poor brain function results in memory loss, loss of the ability to focus, pay attention or stay on task.

We can be taught to alter the operation of our brains through meditative practices. This is especially helpful for people who have suffered post-traumatic stress disorder. MRI scans taken of the brains of PTSD sufferers both before and after being taught yoga-based breathing exercises or mindfulness martial arts, show a marked improvement in the function of and communication between two brain structures involved in PTSD–the amygdala and the anterior cingulate, believed to have a role in filtering information that is funneled into the amygdala.

MRI's taken of prison inmates have found what could be called "widespread" abnormalities in the brains of inmates diagnosed as psychopathic. There were differences in the size of brain structures, especially those involved in emotion, and big differences in connectivity within the brain parts. This information leads one to question, "Can someone be held responsible for a crime if a physical malfunction of the brain caused the illegal behavior?"

EXECUTIVE BRAIN FUNCTIONING

Executive brain function describes a set of cognitive abilities that control and regulate other abilities and behaviors. Executive functions are necessary for goal-directed behavior. They include the ability to initiate and stop actions, to monitor and change behavior as needed, to modulate emotions, and to plan future behavior when faced with novel tasks and situations. The ability to form concepts and think abstractly is often considered components of executive brain function. Executive functions are high-level abilities that influence more basic abilities like attention, memory, and motor skills. Executive functions also influence memory abilities by allowing people to employ strategies that can help them remember information. Without instructions, executive function allows most people to figure out the task demanded through trial and error and change strategies as needed.

Executive function allows people to change plans quickly when something arises. It contributes to success in work and school and allows people to manage the stresses of daily life. Executive function also enables people to inhibit inappropriate behaviors. People with poor executive functions often have problems interacting with other people since they may say or do things that are bizarre or offensive to others. When executive functions are impaired, urges to make negative comments to another person or mouth off are not suppressed so there is a problem fitting in socially. There is great difficulty self-reflecting and self-monitoring.

Executive function deficits are associated with a number of psychiatric and developmental disorders, including obsessive-compulsive disorder, Tourette's syndrome, depression, schizophrenia, attention deficit/ hyperactivity disorder, and autism.

A person may not being able to start a task because they have no idea of how to start the task or steps needed to perform the task. There can be perseveration on a topic or the inability to stop a behavior once it is started. There may be an inhibition of behavior according to social norms and the person may appear selfish, rude, or uncaring. They may not be able to plan or problem solve. They may be creative, but in limited areas, i.e., can draw and design cars, but cannot draw in perspective or design houses or other objects. There may be no concept of time. While a person with executive brain functioning problems may be able to solve numerical arithmetic problems, they may have difficulty solving that same problem if it is in story-problem format.

The frontal lobes of the brain play a major role in executive function. The cortex is the site in the brain where lower level processes like sensation and perception are processed and integrated into thoughts, memories, abilities, and where actions are planned and initiated. People with frontal lobe injuries have difficulty with the higher level processing that underlies executive brain functions. Because of its complexity, the frontal cortex develops more slowly than other parts of the brain so many executive functions do not fully develop until late adolescence or even the early twenties. The frontal cortex, where the brain's reasoning side connects to emotion related areas, helps put the brakes on unhealthy behaviors. It is among the last neural regions to mature, which is one reason it is harder for teens to withstand peer pressure, especially pressure to experiment with drugs. Some executive functions also appear to decline in old age, and some executive function deficits may be useful in early detection of mild dementia.

Adolescence is a time of great brain development, especially late adolescence or the early twenties. It is during this time that the brain matures in the area of adult-level cognitive control of behavior by synaptic pruning and myelination allowing the brain to become more efficient while getting rid of neurons that it hasn't used. This period is characterized by improvements in performance of existing abilities such as speed and capacity of information processing and an ability to have more consistent cognitive behavioral control. When this happens, a person can maintain information in active form and use it to control various processes.

Because this brain development takes place so relatively late, there have been many court cases where lawyers have engaged the expertise of specialists in the area of brain functioning to argue that their client could not be responsible because their brain was not yet developed in those areas where they could make a reasonable judgment. This reality of brain development has factored into the debates regarding whether 17-year-olds (or anyone younger) should be tried as adults rather than as juveniles for serious crimes, or whether they should be given sentences as long as older adults for the same crime.

A person with normal brain function usually remembers their life experiences. When a child touches a hot stove, he/she learns not to touch the stove again. A person who has problems with executive brain functioning can have an experience over and over again but each time is like the first time they have had it. My sons can frequently watch a movie numerous times and laugh at funny scenes like it was the first time they saw it. Consequences resulting from some activities are not remembered and a current situation is processed as brand new, without recollection of an identical or similar situation in the past. Therefore, people lacking executive functioning cannot generalize behaviors and situations. The movie *50 First Dates* portrays a woman with a traumatic brain injury from a car accident whose executive brain function has been seriously damaged. Every day is brand new for her even though she does the same tasks every day.

After examining my mother and asking her some questions, her physician said that she had lost the "governor" on her mouth. What she was thinking popped out her mouth regardless of whether or not it hurt peoples' feelings. She was losing her executive brain function.

A friend of ours who had multiple surgeries explained that she had trouble understanding what she reads if it is of a more technical nature because during four of her surgeries her heart stopped and she was brought back to life using "the paddles." The oxygen deprivation and sudden electrical jolts damaged her executive brain functioning.

TRAUMATIC BRAIN INJURY

Brain injuries can be either closed or open injuries. Examples of a closed injury are a baby who is shaken, a person in a car crash, or being tackled on the football field and the brain rattles back and forth in the skull. Many times this produces swelling of the brain and a great deal of pressure that can impair its function if not relieved.

Studies and research has proven that one of the most dangerous ways to obtain a brain injury is through contact sports. American football presents the greatest risk of concussion—more than twice that of the next closest sport. Football is literally beating some players' brains into incoherence, and they won't realize it until it's too late to prevent an early and excruciating death. Years of continual pounding of the brain is found to cause a condition called chronic traumatic encephalopathy (CTE). Participants in boxing, hockey, basketball, soccer, mixed martial arts, wrestling, rugby, lacrosse, and other sports involving varying degrees of intentional or unintended contact are also liable to develop CTE. CTE is caused by relatively minor head injuries—concussions and subconcussive hits (but mostly subconcussive hits) to the head—that appear to pass with little or no short-term effect, leaving victims unaware of the difficulties to come. While they may not notice any symptoms for years, they actually have an organic brain disease called neuro-degeneration. It results in structural changes in their brains. Once a person suffers a concussion, he/she is more susceptible to having another one; the cumulative effect of repeated concussions does the long-term damage to an athlete's brain.

Unfortunately, as we have seen in the news in the last couple of years, CTE has taken its toll on many former athletes. There have been several that died young, as early as age 45. There are others that committed suicide because they could no longer stand their diminished and chaotic life. CTE affects your judgment, the control of your emotions, and affects your suicidal tendencies. Recently, some younger players have quit the sport, citing not wanting to put their brains in any more jeopardy. The movie *Concussion* poignantly depicts the progression of CTE in football players with sub-concussive and concussive injuries.

Some teams have now started using the ImPACT test (Immediate Post-concussion Assessment and Cognitive Testing). These test results can act as a baseline for coaches at the start of the sport season. Doctors can use this assessment in conjunction with other factors to determine if an athlete has fully recovered from a concussion when they retake the test following injury and recuperation.

Any jarring of your brain can lead to CTE. Military personnel and civilians in combat zone experience this from explosions. A child with behavioral issues who repeatedly bangs his/her head can develop CTE. It is the repetitiveness of the trauma to the brain that triggers CTE. While the name CTE is relatively new, the condition has been known for about a century. Professional fighters were described as being "punch drunk" or having boxer's dementia.

The changes made to the brain show up as behavioral and personality changes in mid-life for those who played sports as kids, teens, and young adults. The problems caused by this disease usually result in a person being put on pain medications and many times this leads to addiction to or abuse of these medications. Others have had success with Eastern medicine such as acupuncture.

A person with CTE can suffer from not only severe headaches, but also bouts of amnesia, depression, and dementia. It has been linked to memory loss, dizziness, vertigo, impaired judgment and impulse control, aggression, increased risk of suicide, and Parkinson's. The disease first manifests as a loss of attention and concentration, memory deficits, confusion, dizziness, and headaches. It can also lead to slurred speech, difficulty swallowing, drooping eyelids, deafness, slowed movement, and staggering gait.

An open brain injury (also called a penetrating injury) could be caused by a fall, a car accident, a military accident, or a gunshot—any trauma to the head which fractures the skull. This could include damage to the grey matter of the brain or fluid discharge. Open injuries must always be treated in a hospital to minimize the risk of complications and infection. Antibiotics will probably be prescribed. Depending upon the type and severity of injury, control centers of your brain may have been damaged. This will determine whether the person will have a disability and how severe it will be.

If the fracture is severe, surgery will probably be necessary. A piece of the skull is removed, if need be, to stop any bleeding in the brain or to remove either foreign debris or pieces of bone. Any pieces of bone will be removed from the wound and returned to their correct position. If necessary, metal wire or mesh may be used to reconnect the pieces of skull. In many cases, the piece of skull is reattached using small metal screws.

The speed at which a person recovers from an open head injury will depend upon the severity and nature of the injury as well as his/her general health and individual needs. It may take several months or sometimes years before full recovery. The care of a physiotherapist may be needed if the injury results in weakness, stiffness, or poor coordination and balance. Everyday tasks and activities, at home or at work, may be a challenge. Sometimes a head injury can affect speech and the person may struggle to communicate the same way as before the injury. If the pituitary gland which is in the center of the head is damaged, it may lead to a reduction in the production of hormones. The sense of taste or smell may be lost or affected. The injury might create blind spots in a person's vision. It may even affect the body's ability to control its temperature as well as before, leaving the person feeling too hot or too cold.

There may be some cognitive effects from the injury. The ability to think, process information, and solve problems may be affected. The person may experience memory problems, particularly with short-term memory. There may be changes to emotions and behavior such as feelings of irritation, anger, or selfishness. There can be less sensitivity to other people's feelings. Inhibitions to behaviors that other people may consider inappropriate may be diminished. A person with a traumatic brain injury may also laugh or cry more.

Having a serious head injury may affect the ability to drive. There is a legal responsibility to inform the state driver and vehicle licensing agency and insurance company of such an injury. A person with such an injury will not be able to drive until a doctor has confirmed the person has made a full recovery and the state licensing agency has given its approval.

CHRONIC ORGANIC BRAIN SYNDROME

Chronic organic brain syndrome refers to impaired mental functioning that has a physiological cause such as a stroke (bleeding into the brain or the space around the brain or blood clots cutting off blood flow to a part of the brain), low oxygen or high carbon dioxide levels in the body, or other conditions including abnormal heart rhythms and heart infections. It does not include psychiatric disorders. Chronic organic brain syndrome is long-term. For example, some forms of chronic drug or alcohol dependence can cause organic brain syndrome due to their long-lasting or permanent toxic effects on brain function. Other common causes of chronic organic brain syndrome are the various types of dementia, which result from permanent brain damage due to strokes, Alzheimer's disease, or other damaging causes which are not reversible. Other disorders that are related to injury to the brain and contribute to organic brain syndrome include attention deficit/hyperactivity disorder, autism, concussion, epilepsy, fetal alcohol spectrum disorder, and Parkinson's disease to name a few.

Symptoms of chronic organic brain syndrome vary with the disease that is responsible. However, the more common symptoms are: confusion; impairment of memory, judgment, and intellectual function; and agitation. Chronic organic brain syndrome is not a primary diagnosis but secondary to one of the ailments listed above, so the cause needs to be sought out and treated.

NEW RESEARCH

As the most complex organ in our body, the brain holds many mysteries that science is trying to understand. It took years of study and research to finally understand and explain the syndrome we now call CTE, and to convince the doubters of its reality. Decades of research has still not revealed complete understanding of such diseases as Alzheimer's, Parkinson's, ALS (amyotrophic lateral sclerosis—also known as Lou Gehrig's disease), and many others, let alone identifying cures. Nevertheless, research to date has enabled us to identify safer and healthier practices to minimize harm to the brain and resulting disabilities. It enabled sports to become safer by educating athletes and coaches about cumulative impacts of repeated head injuries, informing them of the signs and symptoms of concussion and warning them of the consequences of ignoring signs of traumatic brain injuries, continuing to play with a concussion, or returning to play before fully healed.

CHAPTER 11

DIAGNOSING CHILDREN

Diagnosing children, especially with mental health issues can be a real challenge because their behavior often does not "present" (display) the typical or classical symptoms that doctors may be more familiar with in adults. Symptoms can change at different ages and maturation levels and present much differently. This is similar to the symptomatic differences between men and women having heart attacks. Most of the popularly known "familiar signs" of a heart attack are those that are typically experienced by a male. Females may present with much different symptoms. It has taken doctors a while to realize this. Medicine is an inexact science and diagnosing behavioral disorders in children is even more inexact because symptoms present so differently than in late teens and adulthood. The symptoms may change dramatically during a child's growing years due to hormonal changes and the child's cumulative efforts to cope with the world around him/her. There are many more psychiatrists and psychologists than there are child psychiatrists and child psychologists because of the extra schooling involved and the difficulty in correctly diagnosing and treating the child's issues.

Our son, Eric, is a young adult now, but starting at age five, he was diagnosed with a lot of different maladies. The first was attention deficit hyperactivity disorder (ADHD). Eric was started on trials of medications. It took about six months to come up with a good match of meds. We also started counseling with our son. My husband and I educated ourselves about ADHD, joined the national support organization known as CHADD (Children and Adults with Attention Deficit Disorder), and attended its conferences. This assisted us in helping Eric in school, at home, and in the community. It also helped us be able to advocate for him in all of these arenas. Forming a circle of family support around a member who has a disability is extremely important. Using more than one mode of treatment provides a greater success rate (medicine plus counseling). This is called multi-modal treatment.

As Eric grew older, his issues changed. The medications no longer seemed to work as well. There were outbursts at home, in school, in the community. By the time he was in sixth grade, things were not going well at all. A tentative diagnosis of bipolar disorder (manic-depression) was offered and Eric started taking medications for that. The first medication tried gave him extreme stomach aches and made him vomit. There were several outbursts at school and consequences which eliminated him from class. He was suspended from school. Finally he was hospitalized. Eric was eventually stabilized and returned to school. The diagnosis of bipolar disorder lasted approximately three-and-a-half years. During this time, the medication Eric was on stunted his growth so as a freshman in high school, he was still almost the same size he had been in 6th grade. This led to a lot of teasing, harassment, and bullying. Now we added trips to an endocrinologist to our routine to see how to remedy his failure to grow. Shots of testosterone solved this problem, and the bipolar disorder diagnosis was discarded.

Finally at age sixteen-and-a-half Eric was diagnosed as having Asperger syndrome (high-functioning autism), as well as the ADHD, a mood disorder, and high anxiety. Autism is usually diagnosed much earlier in life. There are many programs that start working with children before kindergarten, such as the birth to age 3 programs.

As with many developmental disabilities, however, autism is a spectrum disorder. This means that a person can be very disabled to mildly-disabled with the disorder. They can also "slide" along the scale depending on their age and other issues in their life. With remediation (therapies), the person may move along the spectrum from more disabled to less disabled. Eric did not exhibit the more classical symptoms: trouble with language, quiet and withdrawn, and rhythmic rocking. He was just the opposite. When he was age 2, he had the vocabulary of a four year old, according to his pediatrician. He was very outgoing, easily meeting people, even complete strangers. But his social skills were lacking. He did not pick up on social cues from others.

This diagnosis really hit Eric hard. He thought it meant that he was mentally retarded. It was only with a lot of talking, using logic, that I was able to convince Eric that his thinking was flawed. However, this demonstrates the popular perceptions that people have, whether right or wrong, about what a certain disability is. I was able to convince Eric that he was no different today than he was yesterday, that he hadn't suddenly lost any intelligence. Probably the most famous person with autism is Temple Grandin. I explained to Eric who she is and what her credentials and accomplishments are. I asked him if someone who is mentally retarded could get a Ph.D. Only by walking him through this thought process, step by step, was I able to convince him that he hadn't changed but that his diagnosis had.

Sometimes it takes multiple trips to the doctor or even multiple doctors and numerous tests to rule things in or out to settle upon a correct diagnosis. This is extremely frustrating for everyone, especially the individual who is undergoing the tests.

My other son, Aaron, had fourteen different diagnoses during the course of his childhood and adolescence. Most of them were eventually ruled out. The doctor would put forward a diagnosis for Aaron and then start treating him with medications that had been approved for that malady. Only when trials of those medications didn't work did the diagnosis get discarded and changed to something else. All of this trial and error was complicated by Aaron's early life in various foster homes.

As was the case with Eric, it wasn't until Aaron was in his late teens that the doctors had confidence that a particular diagnosis was correct and the others could be ruled out. But we all got through it. Aaron now has yet another diagnosis *caused* by the prison system. (Read more about that in Chapter 32, Jails and Prisons as Institutions for the Disabled.)

In seeking a diagnosis, doctors may have a child go through many tests that fail to indicate why the child is having some problem. They are probably looking for typical or classical symptoms or causes for a problem, and in some cases those typical indicators just may not present themselves. Sometimes this goes on for years with everyone becoming frustrated while the child may be getting worse medically or behaviorally.

Even when the correct diagnosis has been determined, medical management can be a problem in and of itself. With a diagnosis such as epilepsy, a seizure disorder, doctors can still have trouble lessening or controlling the seizures. The medications they have tried might have had no effect on the seizures or actually make the child worse, either through more seizures or through side-effects of the medication. There is nothing worse than watching your child go through painful episodes and be powerless to alleviate it. Again, because of the age of the child or how the malady is presenting, it may be very difficult to definitively diagnose exactly what is wrong.

Treatment of seizure disorders has had a high public profile since some parents have found that certain types of cannabidiol (CBD oil) has had an effect of lessening the number or intensity of seizures for their child. However, because CBD oil was originally derived from marijuana plants, it was deemed illegal in many states. While the ingredient in marijuana that is psychoactive and makes a person "high" is THC (tetrahydrocannabinol), CBD oil with no or very small amounts of THC has medicinal properties.

Prior to 2018, families who were desperate to help their child when nothing else seemed to work made the difficult choice to move all or part of the family to a state that had approved medical use of marijuana products. Of course shipping it across state lines was out of the question since marijuana is still considered an illegal drug federally.

Thankfully, CBD oil is also present in high levels in another variety of cannabis known commonly as *industrial hemp*. This plant has very low levels of THC. The 2018 federal farm bill (Agriculture Improvement Act of 2018, PL 115-334) legalized CBD oil derived from low-THC hemp nationwide and it has become a growing industry for supplying CBD oil. There are still some restrictions on how such oil is marketed and some states have enacted legislation placing restrictions and controls on it, but at the federal levels it is no longer illegal.

Still, wider research into the potential medical uses of marijuana cannabis (with THC) is stifled by its listing at the federal level as a Schedule 1 Controlled Substance. Many believe there are other potential health benefits of this drug, but the medical community is divided in its support for such research.

My friends who were eagerly awaiting their state to legalize CBD to possibly mitigate their son's seizures, found that the CBD actually made his seizures worse.

There are happy stories and sad stories from the history of trying to tap the medical benefits of cannabis and hemp. A parent in my state advocated for legalizing CBD, hoping to move legislators as her daughter's health deteriorated from uncontrolled seizures. She spoke out any chance she got, worked tirelessly. She eventually won, sort of. Legislators passed a bill making use of CBD legal in our state. However, there were numerous caveats attached to the legislation, which made the bill basically useless. All of this came too late for her daughter, who had already died from the effects of the unrelenting seizures.

CHAPTER 12

DIAGNOSING DISABILITIES

Getting a correct diagnosis of a physical and/or behavioral disability is essential to getting proper treatment and setting a course that will make life better. Getting to a correct diagnosis, especially in the case of a behavioral disability, is going to take some time and will require answering a lot of questions to give the professional the best picture of what the problems are and what the person's life is like.

In the case of a child, input may be sought from many people such as the parents, teachers, and pediatricians. Professionals may schedule periods of observation of a child as well as various kinds of testing, including blood tests, before a diagnosis is forthcoming. This diagnosis may be temporary because children's bodies are still growing and problems manifest themselves differently at different ages and maturation stages. Both of my sons have been treated for and carried diagnoses that were later discarded as they grew and matured and it became clear to the professionals that these diagnoses were no longer correct.

If you have a loved one whose behavior concerns you and seems abnormal, it is very important to not ignore it. Mental illnesses such as schizophrenia and post-traumatic stress disorder manifest themselves in the late teens or early twenties and occur suddenly or occur months later in the case of PTSD. Any change in a person's behavior or performance in school or at work is cause for an evaluation.

Please, please, please DO NOT ignore signs that something is wrong. When signs and symptoms are ignored, tragic things can happen. The young man who shot U.S. Arizona Rep. Gabrielle Giffords and several other people in Arizona, killing six, showed signs of trouble that were ignored. So did the young man who opened fire in a crowded movie theater in Aurora, Colorado, and the young man who opened fire at Sandy Hook Elementary School killing 26. All of these individuals showed signs of being troubled, were acting strangely, and people close to them ignored the signs. Clearly, ignoring behavioral changes in loved ones or acquaintances can have disastrous results.

We truly need to stop treating mental illness as a shameful or embarrassing secret, trying to pretend it doesn't exist. It does exist and we need to embrace the changes that come with a mental health diagnosis, educate ourselves concerning it, and adjust our lives to live as best we can. After all, one in five people in the US suffer from some form of mental illness, even if it is something like depression or anxiety.

Some people have a mental health issue from the very early years of their life and to them that is their normal frame of reference in life. They grow up never knowing any different way of feeling or thinking. Such was the case with my husband's depression that was not diagnosed until his early 40s. Even if a mental health condition is suspected, perhaps the issue just didn't seem to be serious enough to warrant going to the doctor and enduring a variety of tests and possibly being put on medication and/or referred for counseling.

If you suspect such circumstances in your life or in the life of a loved one or friend, I strongly urge you or your family member or friend to see a professional to be evaluated. Identifying a mental health issue and receiving proper treatment can change your life for the better. Ask my husband. He will tell you how much better his life has been since being treated for his depression. (And it has been much better for me too!)

CHAPTER 13

MEDICATION VS. NO MEDICATION AND/OR SELF-MEDICATION

MEDICATION AS A PART OF TREATMENT

Whether medication is a part of your or your child's treatment for a disability is a decision that you need to make with the physician. It will depend on what the health diagnosis is, how efficacious the medication is for that malady, and what might be the side effects. The best thing you can do is to educate yourself about the choices of medications and the benefits and risks of each so as to have an informed discussion with your physician.

If you are contemplating medication for your child, the child's self-esteem and classroom socialization needs to be taken into consideration. If the child's behavior without medication is repeatedly getting him/her into trouble with school authorities, for example, or drawing ridicule from his/her peers such that they do not want to be around your child, it could severely stigmatize your child leading to other inappropriate behaviors. The same can be true if the child's challenge is a physical disability that could be somewhat mitigated if medication is included in treatment.

When my son, Eric, was officially diagnosed with attention deficit hyperactivity disorder he was six years old and in first grade. As we were working through this process of diagnosing, educating ourselves, and weighing the pros and cons of putting Eric on medication, he shared his decision with us. One evening in the kitchen Eric was on his knees banging his head on the floor, saying, "Mom, I can't live like this anymore." This from a six-year-old! I have no recollection as to what factors precipitated this cry for help, but when I related the incident to my husband, we decided that we needed to take his feelings into account and had stimulant medicine prescribed for him. It continues to be a very important medication for his mood/behavior to this day.

Medication is not the only treatment option. Some people try alternative things such as vitamins and herbal remedies, bio-feedback, yoga, therapy animals, or psychological counseling (without any medication). This is a personal choice. The one thing that is crucial for you or your child is that once you have educated yourself about the options and your or your child's special needs, you need to make your decision and be comfortable with it. There will be well-meaning people who try to change your mind, citing all kinds of resources. You need to stick to your guns about your decision, advocating for yourself and/or your child.

SELF-MEDICATION

Self-medication is using drugs or alcohol or engaging in behavior that is self-soothing in an attempt to treat poorly-treated or untreated and often undiagnosed mental distress, stress, and anxiety. The person chooses to use drugs or alcohol to deal with some of the symptoms of the disease or disability, or the side effects of medications being taken. The drug of choice to provide relief is usually specific to the user. The individual may have tried different options before finding the substance that makes them feel better or more emotionally stable. Issues in the mental health arena are the most common causes leading people to self-medicate. While not a drug, food can be included in this category as the self-soothing item. Self-medicating frequently starts with mild remedies and graduates to stronger and sometimes even illegal substances.

People who suffer from PTSD as well as other illnesses and disabilities have been known to self-medicate whether or not they have been formally diagnosed, and whether or not they are taking medications for their malady. If a person is self-medicating, then all is not right in their world and more action is required. This action could be additional counseling, medication changes, support groups, and stress relievers such as exercise.

Depression is another malady for which people commonly self-medicate rather than seeking treatment. Alcohol is frequently the substance of choice even though few people understand that alcohol itself is a depressant, so drinking only exacerbates the depression. Tobacco, cannabis, and benzodiazepines (Xanax, Valium, and Ativan) are other common choices. These are all central nervous system depressants and produce feelings of relaxation, but they also lower inhibitions, leading to other potential complications. These substances may provide some immediate short-term relief of some symptoms such as anxiety, but they may also exacerbate other symptoms of a mental illness. They are ineffective compared to true antidepressants that would be prescribed by a physician. Self-medicating this way could lead to addiction or drug dependence and certainly does nothing to improve a person's overall mental health.

Another class of drugs used by some to self-medicate depression or other issues is known as psychostimulants. This includes such drugs as cocaine and amphetamines, which are illegal or controlled substances, but it also includes caffeine and nicotine which are not controlled. They produce improvements in mental and physical functioning, including increased energy and feelings of euphoria. Hence, the popularity of energy drinks and energy shots. Some people who are depressed may use them to increase their sense of self-esteem.

Heroin and morphine are powerful drugs used to reduce pain and increase pain tolerance. They are also effective as mood-stabilizers and anti-depressants. People may use these to self-medicate to bring these benefits or to reduce aggression and rage.

Cannabis is a psychoactive drug and can have both stimulating and sedating effects depending on the individual and their circumstances. Occasional users like the depressant or relaxing effects and chronic users like the stimulating effects. However, if the individual is already depressed, using marijuana may increase the odds of suffering from even more serious mental health problems. These can include schizophrenia, other forms of psychosis, and suicidal ideation. Also, as discussed earlier, cannabidiol (CBD) derived from cannabis has proven helpful in treating some seizure disorders as well as other health issues.

A person with drug dependence and another mental illness often exhibits symptoms that are more persistent, severe, and resistant to treatment compared with persons who have either disorder alone. Reasons for self-medication can be numerous. Some people are just resistant to seeking professional help, such as counseling, and are trying to feel better by self-medicating. Others who are getting treatment might feel that the medication they are receiving is not a good match to treat their condition. Finally, a person may simply have a substance abuse issue as a co-morbid condition. People who self-medicate will continue even when the underlying condition is eased because they may have become psychologically dependent on the "medication" or they are afraid that the condition will become worse unless they continue.

Many people with bipolar disorder say that the medications they take stifle their creativity. They like being in a manic phase as they are tremendously creative and productive and don't want to lose this feeling, ignoring the reality that they cannot sustain it forever. The things they do are often self-destructive, but they are unable to realize this while manic. Some individuals don't want medication at all or stop taking it because they don't like how it makes them feel physically or they feel they will lose that creativity. Then they self-medicate with alcohol or drugs trying to find a balance between feeling bad and feeling like they haven't lost themselves. Actress Patty Duke wrote a wonderful expose on her experiences with bipolar disorder in her book, *Brilliant Madness*.

Whatever the circumstances or reasons, a person who is self-medicating needs to see a trained professional. Together they can explore the reasons for self-medication and determine a better way forward including appropriate and safe medications.

CHAPTER 14

ACCEPTANCE OF THE DISABILITY

Accepting a disability that you have, or a family member like a child has, follows the same stages of grieving as bereavement over the death of someone close to you. Grief is the emotional suffering we feel after a loss of some kind. Grief is part of the healing process.

The five stages of grief, as they were first introduced by Elisabeth Kubler-Ross in her 1969 book, *On Death and Dying*, are denial and isolation, anger, bargaining, depression, and acceptance. These stages can last minutes, hours, days, weeks, months, or years. You do not need to go through the stages one after another, in order, nor do you need to feel or go through all of the stages. A person can flip back and forth between/ amongst them. It is an individual process.

These grief stages may also be revisited during developmental milestones, such as when your child graduates from high school. Although you may have known it from early on, the current reality that your child is not moving on to college or moving on to "being an adult" and having an adult relationship with them is like a new, fresh loss.

Denial and isolation: This stage helps us to cope. We are in the state of shock and our feelings go numb. We wonder how we can go on. We just try to get through the day. This helps to make survival possible and helps us to pace our feelings of grief. This is the beginning of the healing process.

Anger: This is a necessary stage of the healing process. We must acknowledge and feel our anger in order for it to dissipate. We ask ourselves, "Why me?" or "Why my child?" We may be mad at everyone: friends, family, neighbors, God. Under the anger is our pain. Anger can help to define the loss we are feeling.

Bargaining: We may try to bargain with God, like "Please let there be something that can be done to make my child normal." We want our life to go back to the way it was before. We suddenly feel guilty. We wonder if there was something we did or didn't do or could have done to prevent this. *If only* and *what if* plague our thinking. We try to negotiate our way out of the hurt and loss. We want the situation made "all better" while we promise God all kinds of things.

Depression: The reality that our loss is not going to go away sets in and our empty feelings overwhelm us. The grief becomes deeper and feels as if it will last forever. We are intensely sad, withdraw from life, and wonder if there is any point in going on. This particular depression is not a sign of mental illness unless it persists for a very long time and we don't move on to acceptance.

Acceptance: Acceptance is the mental perspective that we are okay, able to go on, accepting the reality of the disability in ourselves or a person close to us, including the life limitations that go with it. We accept that the disability will not go away, but commit to learning to live with it. We resolve to learn all we can about the disability and how to care for our loved one. We resolve to go on the best we can and to make the best of the new situation. Acceptance may be discovering we can have more good days than bad. This is especially true if we get involved with a support group and take comfort from the fact that others have the same or similar struggles. They know how we feel; they understand us.[6]

Acknowledging disabilities requires education, training, and acceptance at all levels of services, including policymaking, administration, and practice. To value diversity is to respect human worth. A system is strengthened when it recognizes and appreciates the varied backgrounds of those it serves, as well as those working in the field. Awareness and acceptance of differences in communication, life view, definition of health, and family are crucial elements of a well-functioning system. Commitment to the provision of quality services regardless of background is the most

---

[6] David Kessler, "The Five Stages of Grief," http://grief.com/the-five-stages-of-grief.

important characteristic of a system. Providing individualized quality services to all people bridges gaps in service delivery, eliminates barriers, and builds communities. We all contribute and benefit from the broad spectrum of unique human qualities. Diversity is the energy that makes our world colorful. Acceptance is the key to success; you have to be accepted in order to grow.

If you are the parent of a newborn with a disability, you suddenly realize that your child will continue to look to you for more continuing support in life compared to other children who are able to independently assume their place as part of the adult world. The needs of your child become the driving force behind major decisions in your family. Sometimes you will wish that life was different. I recall the poem by Emily Perl Kingsley, entitled "Welcome to Holland", who compares raising a child with a disability to thinking and preparing to go to Italy but ending up in Holland.

Loneliness will probably become a new reality for you. While you will still have friends and family, there are certain aspects of your life in which you will feel very, very lonely, because your life is now very different and other people are simply unable to relate to your experiences. You will feel isolated because people will either be uncomfortable around you or your child or believe that coming to participate in whatever they have planned will make it uncomfortable for you or be too taxing on the family.

Taking care of yourself and your spouse are very important. The grief and the stress resolve more quickly if you get enough sleep, eat a balanced diet, refrain from excessive drinking of alcohol, and get some exercise.

Unfortunately, there are people who cannot handle being close to a person with a disability or parenting a child with a disability. It is as if the individual is stuck between the denial and anger stages and can't get passed them. These strong feelings are very stressful. Not infrequently, marriages have ended because a parent found having a child with a disability was too challenging. The mother usually then has sole custody of the child and all or almost all responsibility for the care of that child. Living in Holland when you wanted Italy is very difficult and sometimes an insurmountable disappointment for some couples.

CHAPTER 15

SERVICES AVAILABLE

The number and kinds of services available to support you or a family member with a disability will vary depending on where you live. More will be available in urban areas and less in rural areas, necessitating longer travel to access these services. The services that support people with disabilities can include:

- Medical services, especially specialty physicians
- Counseling services
- Physical therapy
- Occupational therapy
- Speech therapy
- Sensory integration therapy
- Tutoring or other educational services, such as American Sign Language
- Hyperbaric pressure chambers
- Community support programs
- Community psychosocial and rehabilitative services

You might need classes to gain instruction in how to administer some therapy that you can do in the home such as the lung clearing for cystic fibrosis, administering nebulizer treatments for asthma, or special movements for manipulating limbs. Hopefully many if not all of these services will be reasonably available in your locality.

The internet and the yellow pages of a phone book are the places to look when searching for services. Look up anything you can think of and start making a list of possible contacts. Some phone books list community services in the beginning of the book. One place we lived had an agency that was the "first call" source for helping you identify and get connected to agencies and services that you needed (by dialing 211 on the phone. More and more communities have this "first call"). If you live in an area that has a big teaching hospital, that may provide you with more resources. They will have a social worker on staff that can assist you in getting connected to the specific services that you are looking for at the time.

There are many different types of therapies available to help a person cope with and manage their disability, whether it be some underlying problems or becoming comfortable and dealing with a newly acquired condition. My uncle had Type A (juvenile) diabetes. As he got older he started having major problems with his eyesight. One day he woke up and was completely blind. He had been warned by his physician that this might happen. Since he lived in the Chicago area, he was able to access services from The Chicago Lighthouse for the Blind (today, called simply The Chicago Lighthouse). He started attending classes there and learned to read braille, how to travel out in public, count money, and other skills. He was most fortunate in that the company he worked for continued his employment. They allowed him to take vacation and sick leave while he attended the Lighthouse classes and then gave him a job within the company that he was able to do with his new challenges and skills.

The services a person needs will vary according to their age or stage of life. There will be developmental needs during the growing years. There may be financial services that are needed (see Chapter 29, SSI/SSDI). There will be school issues (see Chapter 23 on Education). There may be needs for assistance with housing for the family of a person with a disability or for that person individually as they move into adulthood. In our area, there is an agency whose mission is to help people with disabilities and their families purchase permanent housing by loaning them money for the down payment. It draws together funds that are available for this purpose from federal, state, and local government sources and works with banks willing to give a mortgage to a person with a disability who has very limited income (see Chapter 26, Housing). There are also agencies that can be a person's "representative payee" for SSI/SSDI, or track monies made at a job so other services are not lost because a person is working.

There can be challenges with accessing these kinds of services. There may be waiting lists to get services from a particular agency, either because of staffing or funding limitations, or both. There may be waiting lists to see a particular specialist or therapist. Sometimes the limitation or waiting list for a licensed professional in your area is due to the health insurance coverage you have.

SUPPORT BROKERS

People with developmental disabilities can get "support brokers." The support broker is a person who:

- Helps identify the individual's goals
- Develops an individualized support plan which includes how the individual wants to live, and what things are not negotiable
- Identifies formal and generic supports as well as traditional human service agencies that can assist
- Helps to choose supports that fulfill the goals of the individualized plan
- Uses the allocated budget creatively
- Negotiates rates and contracts for services with the chosen providers
- Monitors the supports for quality on an ongoing basis
- Acts as a case manager

DIVISION OF VOCATIONAL REHABILITATION (DVR)

Title I of the Rehabilitation Act of 1973 authorizes federal support to provide assessment and coordination of vocational rehabilitation services for individuals with disabilities so that such individuals may prepare for and engage in gainful employment. Funding that is available can pay for education, training, workplace modifications, or even a job coach to enable an individual to continue working or do their job efficiently.

CHAPTER 16

SHORTAGES OF MENTAL HEALTH PROVIDERS, COMMUNITY SERVICES, AND FUNDING

There are many challenges in obtaining services and supports for people with disabilities. It is disappointing that public and private institutions have not responded to the existing and growing needs for such services.

PSYCHIATRIST SHORTAGE

To serve those with mental health disabilities, there is a nation-wide shortage of psychiatrists. Currently 59 percent of psychiatrists are 55 or older, the fourth oldest of 41 medical specialties, signaling that many may be retiring soon or reducing their workload.

According to the American Medical Association, the total number of physicians in the US increased by 45 percent from 1995 to 2013. However, the number of adult and child psychiatrists rose by only 12 percent, from 43,640 to 49,079. During that time span, the US population increased by about 37 percent. Also since 2010 millions more Americans have become eligible for mental health coverage under the Affordable Care

Act.[7] Mental illness is a leading cause of disability in America, yet medical students' interest in psychiatry is so low that nearly 14 percent of the 1,360 psychiatric residencies up for grabs in 2013 went to non-US citizens who graduated from foreign medical schools—a higher percentage of foreign participation than in many specialties' residency programs.

There appears to be a perception amongst medical students that the field of psychiatry isn't as well respected or compensated as other specialties, so medical students are not choosing psychiatry. The latest federal data show a mean annual salary of $182,700 for psychiatrists, slightly below the mean for general practitioners and 28 percent below that for surgeons.[8] While medical students are excited about scientific developments in psychiatry and brain studies, there remains concern about the profession's stature and pay levels.

Some psychiatrists are switching to a cash-only practice out of frustration with what they view as inadequate reimbursement from government (Medicare and Medicaid) and private insurance plans. All physicians seem to be complaining about the amount of paperwork and time consumed to get reimbursed for their services which erodes the amount of time they have to actually serve and interact with their patients—what they trained to do. Psychiatrists have mostly ceded psychotherapy or talk therapy to other mental health professionals and focus on the medical management component (prescribing and monitoring medications).

Some states are promoting wider use of long-distance telepsychiatry to fill gaps in care. Some legislatures have voted to pay student loans of psychiatrists willing to work in underserved areas. There have been bills in Congress to forgive student loans for child psychiatrists. Another strategy is to ensure that primary-care physicians have solid training in mental health so they can handle some straightforward cases themselves and make proper referrals for more complex cases. Grants have been given to universities to graduate more psychiatric nurse practitioners, who are trained to provide therapy and prescribe medications. Some psychologists with doctorates, but

---

[7] Associated Press, "Across Much of the United States There is Serious Shortage of Psychiatrists," News-Review (Petosky, MI), September 15, 2015, https://www.petoskeynews.com/featured-pnr/across-much-of-the-united-states-there-is-serious-shortage-of-psychiatrists/article_59c96bbe-4e37-5d51-aa4b-c34747d97a22.html.
[8] Ibid.

not medical degrees, have been granted medication-prescribing privileges after receiving additional training.

Also in demand are "culturally-literate" psychiatrists for racial and ethnic minorities, those willing to work for the US Department of Veterans Affairs, and those willing to work with people with substance abuse problems, people in jails and prisons, and people on probation and parole with severe personality disorders or histories of sexual deviance. It is hard to have a meaningful chance when there is insufficient funding, inadequate numbers of professionals to serve you, and no political will in society to change the situation.

SHORTAGES IN OTHER SERVICES AND SUPPORTS

Some people and families dealing with disabilities are challenged by the geography of where they live compared to the location of services and providers. You may live in a rural area and have to drive some distance to find services or your state or locality may have little to offer.

A friend told me that one state she lived in had few services to help her children with disabilities. When her husband's job moved them to another state, that state had a multitude of services for their children. People from all over the country have moved to the area in which I live because we have very good services for early autism intervention. Since my older son was not diagnosed with Asperger syndrome (high-functioning autism) until he as 16, there was little that the Wisconsin Early Autism Project could do for him.

We live in a time when the budgets of governmental and social service agencies are severely strained or being reduced. Social services is one of the favorite areas to reduce expenditures when budgets need to be trimmed. People who utilize social services are often not good self-advocates or are too overwhelmed to add budget advocacy to their activities. They rightly depend on other organized people and agencies to advocate for the money for these services. In the county in which I live, the county executive takes calls and emails from people regarding proposed budget cuts before they are put into place. This is a great opportunity to advocate for people with disabilities, their needs, and what loss of funds will do to their lives and independence. More weight is usually given to input from organized groups and agencies than from individuals. This may be because they represent multiple clients and users of the services.

The area in which I live also has a great deal of services for people with schizophrenia or cognitive/developmental disabilities. However, if you do not have one of these diagnoses, you may not be able to access the services. For example, there is an adult day-treatment facility that my son applied to attend. The facility helps with socialization, job finding, job coaching, and other life skills. It took one and a half years for his name to come up on the waiting list. We took the tour and he was interviewed. He was very excited about being able to come to this center. The facility staff had requested his medical records, but did not know a lot about Asperger syndrome. Coincidentally, they had a number of people with Asperger syndrome applying for their services. The medical director did a presentation on Asperger syndrome and together with the staff decided they did not want to serve this population. So after waiting one and a half years, our son was turned down! He was very disappointed.

Case management is an important service that has been a point of great frustration for me. Case managers arrange, coordinate, and monitor services for people with disabilities or other special needs so that they can live as independently as possible and have a satisfying life and contribute to their community. Case management services exist in our town, but not in sufficient quantity to meet needs. Eric is now 35-years-old and has been on the waiting list for case management since he graduated high school. At one point several years ago county social services staff were completely blunt with us, telling my husband and I that since we were doing such a wonderful job of managing things for Eric, he would not be a high priority for limited case management services!!

We who have children or younger family members with disabilities all worry about what will happen to our loved one when we die. If they have not been accepted by a social service agency for case management and other services, we have reason to worry. Once accepted, most of these programs will continue serving their clients until the clients move or die. However, this is also a reason for the long waiting lists. We need more agencies providing case management and other services.

Both Eric and his long-time girlfriend, Natasha, have both been evaluated and found to qualify for developmental disability services. They started receiving some services this past fall, and their workers are checking in with them monthly. Although not true case management, it will suffice until we can get that piece and perhaps more services, such as a support broker.

Perhaps the services you or a loved one need are available, but you do not have the money or insurance coverage to pay for them. Some agencies charge fees according to a sliding scale depending on your income, but others do not. Sometimes if you do not have the money to pay for services, you may be able to access them through an agency that pays for them, but that agency may have a waiting list as explained in my examples above. Most agencies will do their best to work with you to find some way to cover the costs.

A service for which there is a perennial shortage is respite care for both children and adults. Without this service, it is difficult for caregivers to take care of themselves and avoid burnout from their unrelenting responsibility of caring for someone with a disability (see Chapter 21, Respite, and Chapter 22, Taking Care of the Caregiver).

CHAPTER 17

NON-MEDICAL THERAPIES

There are non-medical therapies or activities that people with disabilities can engage in that may help them have a chance at a more normal, fulfilling life. Some of these services are performed at the person's home, but sometimes you may need to go to the therapy location to participate in the activity or service.

ANIMAL THERAPY

The benefits of having a pet are well documented. For people with disabilities or those over 60, owning and caring for an animal can contribute to a healthier outlook on life, promote a feeling of safety, and improve health, including lowering stress and blood pressure. The decision to get an animal should not be taken lightly. In return for affection, companionship, and assistance, you will need to provide them food, shelter, exercise, and medical care.

If you are not in a position to own and care for an animal, there are programs that provide opportunities to interact with trained therapy animals. These animals can assist a person with disabilities emotionally, mentally, and physically. These organizations can provide services for a young person with a disability or a returning veteran, especially one who has been wounded in action. Therapy can be with animals such as horses, but the animals we are probably most familiar with seeing are service dogs.

Horse therapy programs can stretch and strengthen a person's muscles, give them control of movement, help the person overcome fears, build self-confidence and self-esteem, and improve balance and coordination. Horseback riding is a commonly recommended activity for people with multiple sclerosis. Because the natural walking gait of the horse is similar to a human's, riding helps restore balance, coordination and posture, all of which can be affected by MS's assault on the spine and central nervous system.

Horseback riding is a huge benefit to people with mental health issues. There is a horse therapy program in our area with trained horses that are gentle and safe. The rider wears a helmet and at first is led around a track while another person walks alongside the rider. When the rider develops enough skill in handling the horse and has enough strength and coordination to be able to be on their own, then the handlers can give them more freedom. The effects of a horse's large, gentle, warm body and soft breath and accepting presence are soothing. The horse and rider usually develop a friendship that could last a lifetime. Participation in caring for the horse is usually part of the therapy program. This can be therapeutic for the horse too.

As of March 2011, miniature horses are recognized as service animals under the Americans with Disabilities Act. A young horse in Alaska has assisted a kindergartner in his classroom. The boy moves around a lot better and has more energy because he can hold on to the horse. The horse is providing balance and mobility and learning tasks such as how to pick things up and eventually hand them to the boy.

In terms of human interaction, dogs can fit into one of three categories. There are assistance or service dogs, trained therapy dogs, and companion dogs. An assistance or service dog is trained to do specific tasks to assist a person with a disability, such as guiding, picking something up dropped on the floor, opening doors, turning lights on and off, alerting the person or another person to sounds, dangers, or something about to happen such as a seizure. These dogs have full public access under ADA law. Despite this authority, they are sometimes denied entrance to places, and therefore, so is the person with a disability. This usually indicates the people running the establishment are uniformed about the legal requirements.

A therapy dog has had obedience and other special training and provides companionship to a person or groups of people. A therapy dog may be brought to a hospital, rehabilitation center, assisted living facility, or nursing home for interaction with patients or residents. These dogs provide temporary diversion from the challenge of disabilities and an alternative interaction with another living being besides humans. The therapy dog is not specifically trained in tasks like the service dog. Therapy dogs **do not** have public access under ADA law.

Assistance dogs and therapy dogs can be very helpful during various medical procedures, especially when physical or speech therapy is required. These dogs can provide great comfort and distraction from unpleasant medical procedures, and are allowed into facilities in many instances. For speech therapy, reading to a dog has been repeatedly proven to provide great benefit. The child sits next to a dog, petting the fur while reading aloud to it. This literally lowers blood pressure and other stress factors as well as making the reading experience much more pleasant for the child. Time spent practicing reading leads to improved performance.

A companion dog is just that, a companion. The dog has no specific training or certification and is merely a family pet. They do not have public access rights.

While dogs may be a big help, they also require time and effort for their care. If the person with a disability is a child, then the dog's care usually becomes mom's or dad's job. However, there is a benefit to having the child do as much as possible in terms of dog care to develop and maintain the all-important bond between the dog and child. This means feeding, grooming, and other care tasks can take much, much longer. The pros and cons need to be carefully weighed before including a dog in the family.

Children with disabilities are often viewed negatively by peers. A child with a canine partner is frequently seen as "different" in a good and appealing way. All three categories of dogs will provide the most important service of all, bringing comfort, security, and benefits of a loyal best friend. They will provide love, affection, acceptance, and companionship to children too often disenfranchised and lonely.

ART THERAPY

Art therapy is a form of expressive therapy that uses the creative process of making art to improve a person's physical, mental and emotional well-being. It can be beneficial for people who experience illness, emotional or physical trauma, domestic abuse, anxiety, depression, and by people who want to develop personally. Through creating art and reflecting on the art products and processes, people can:

- increase awareness of self and others
- cope with symptoms, stress, and traumatic experiences
- manage behavior and addictions
- enhance cognitive abilities
- develop social skills
- improve reality orientation
- increase self-esteem
- heal
- enjoy the life-affirming pleasures of making art

It can be used with people who have suffered a traumatic brain injury.

Art therapists are healthcare professionals who are trained in both art and therapy. They have a minimum of a master's degree in art therapy or a related field. They are knowledgeable about human development, psychological theories, clinical practice, spiritual, multicultural, and artistic traditions, and the healing potential of art. They use art in treatment, assessment, and research, and provide consultations to allied professionals. Art therapists work with people of all ages, in all settings. They work in mental health, rehabilitation, medical, and forensic institutions; community outreach programs, wellness centers, schools, nursing homes, corporate settings, open studios, and independent practices. Licensure in some form is available to art therapists in most states. Depending upon the state, a person can be licensed specifically as an art therapist or more generally as a mental health counselor. A person can also get a license in a related mental health field such as counseling, social work, and marriage and family therapy after completing requirements for those professions.

Art therapy may be used in conjunction with other psychotherapy techniques such as cognitive-behavioral therapy or group therapy. It may be used with children suffering from behavioral or social problems at school or at home, children with learning disabilities, adults experiencing severe stress, people experiencing mental health problems, individuals suffering from a traumatic brain injury, and with children or adults experiencing traumatic events. Usually the person is asked to focus on feelings, perceptions, and imagination while creating their product, expressing images that come from inside the person rather than something outside that anyone can see.

A variety of art methods may be used with clients, including drawing, painting, sculpture, photography, and collages. The therapist usually guides the session in some way, such as giving the client a specific topic. Art therapists choose materials and interventions appropriate to their clients' needs and design sessions to achieve therapeutic goals and objectives. A person in therapy learning to express their feelings through art can use some simple techniques at home to reduce anxiety and get their mind "back on track" such as coloring preprinted pages and then reflecting on why they chose that picture and those colors.

The British artist Adrian Hill coined the term "art therapy" in 1942. While recovering from tuberculosis in a sanatorium, he discovered the therapeutic benefits of drawing and painting. Another artist, Edward Adamson, extended Hill's work to patients residing in long-term mental hospitals in Britain.[9]

Margaret Naumburg and Edith Kramer, US art therapy pioneers, began practicing around the same time as Hill. Naumburg was an educator who thought that art therapy was psychoanalytically oriented and became a form of symbolic speech, which could then be translated into verbal speech in psychotherapy or counseling. Kramer was an artist who pointed out the importance of the creative process, psychological defenses, and artistic quality because these bring out anger, anxiety, or pain.[10]

Doctors during the mid-twentieth century noted that individuals suffering from mental illness often expressed themselves in drawings and other artworks, which led many to explore the use of art as a healing strategy. Since then, art has become an important part of the therapeutic field and is used in some assessment and treatment techniques. It has become a valuable technique used with soldiers suffering from PTSD. The Wisconsin Veterans Museum, near where I live, has featured art of all forms (paintings, sculptures using various media, pen and ink, chalk/pastels, etc.) that have been done by veterans suffering from PTSD.

A 2009 study of people in prison by David Gussak showed that art therapy aided in the improvement of their mood. Because so much of a prisoner's life is outside of his/her control, there is a tendency toward depression and poor mood among the prisoners. Using art therapy, there

---

[9] Wikipedia contributors, "Art Therapy," *Wikipedia, The Free Encyclopedia.* https://en.wikipedia.org/w/index.php?title=Art_therapy&oldid=972345983.

[10] Ibid.

was a shift in the mental perspectives of prisoners to feel that they had some control while creating with art materials, thereby changing their mood to be more positive.

The first use of drawing as an assessment tool for psychological purposes was by German psychologist Fritz Mohr in1906. In 1926, researcher Florence Goodenough created a drawing test, called Draw-A-Man, to measure intelligence as well as personality in children. Other psychiatric art assessments created in the 1940s were found to be successful and have been used ever since.[11]

Art and the creative process can aid in recovery in many illnesses. Hospitals have found that patients participating in art programs had better vital statistics and less trouble sleeping. Even having a picture of a landscape in a patient's room improved recovery time and lessened the need for pain medications. Pre-teens and teens with autism were found to increase their social skills when participating in art therapy. Retired people had better health when participating in art therapy. Cancer patients were able to reduce their emotional distress when utilizing the creative process. It becomes a coping mechanism and a tool to create not only an art object, but causes a paradigm shift in the person and people around them showing they are not only cancer patients but also artists. Art can be painting, drawing, pottery, and crafty things such as scrapbooking or card making.

My father used art as pain management when he was fighting cancer. He created stained glass objects such as lamps and boxes, as well as several dozen window hangings. When he was focused on the intricacies of cutting and fitting the glass, his mind was diverted from the pain he was having. He was able to go several months with minimal pain medication before he had to start relying on the heavier sedating medications.

MUSIC THERAPY

Music therapy is an interpersonal process in which the trained music therapist uses music and all its facets—physical, emotional, mental, social, aesthetic, and spiritual to help clients improve or maintain their health. They help clients improve their communication, cognitive functioning, motor skills, attention, emotional and affective development, behavior and social skills, and quality of life by using music experiences such as singing,

---

[11] Ibid.

songwriting, listening to and discussing music, and moving to music. In some cases, the client's needs are addressed directly through music; in other cases, they are addressed through the relationships that develop between the client and the therapist. Sessions can be one-on-one or in a group, both working equally well.

Music therapy can be used to enhance communication and motor skills with individuals with special needs. It can help promote wellness such as lower blood pressure and relaxed muscle tension; anxiety and stress reduction; alleviation of pain; expressing feelings appropriately with control, confidence, and empowerment; and enhanced memory. It is used in songwriting and listening in reminiscence or orientation work with the elderly, and in processing and relaxation work and rhythmic retraining for physical rehabilitation in stroke victims.

While music therapy will not cure or solve problems brought on by crisis, music therapy can help children and adults in crisis learn and use positive coping skills and express difficult feelings and emotions. The directed use of music and music therapy is highly effective in developing coping strategies, including understanding and expressing feelings of anxiety and helplessness, supporting feelings of self-confidence and security, and providing a safe or neutral environment for relaxation.

Brains and behavior can be functionally changed by engaging in music therapy. Neurological music therapy studies how the brain is without music, how the brain is with music, measures the differences, and uses these differences to cause changes in the brain through music that will eventually affect the client non-musically.

With adolescents, music can provide a sense of identity, independence, and individuality. It can serve as a creative outlet to release or control emotions and find ways of coping with difficult emotions. When someone is singing about what you are feeling, this becomes a relatable message giving the adolescent the feeling of being understood by others, i.e., the singer. Music can break down barriers bringing people of different backgrounds, age groups, and social groups together. While adolescents may listen to music for its therapeutic qualities, it does not mean that they all need music therapy. School music programs provide adolescents a safe place to express themselves and learn life skills such as self-discipline, diligence, and patience, as well as instilling confidence and improving self-esteem.

In special education, music therapy is considered a related service under the Individuals with Disabilities Education ACT, or IDEA (see

Chapter 23, Disabilities in the Educational Realm). When music therapy is deemed necessary to assist a child in benefiting from his/her special education, goals are documented on the Individualized Education Program (IEP) as a related service intervention. Music therapy can be an integral component in helping the child with special needs attain educational goals identified by his/her IEP team. Music therapy interventions can address development in cognitive, behavioral, physical, emotional, and social skills. It can also facilitate development in communication and sensory-motor skills. Music therapists can support special education classroom teachers by providing effective ways to incorporate music into their academic curriculum. Music therapy involvement can stimulate attention and increase motivation to participate more fully in other aspects of the educational program. Interventions apply the inherent order of music to set behavioral expectations, provide reassurance, and maintain structure for children with special needs. Music therapy can adapt strategies to encourage a child's participation in the least restrictive environment.[12]

Individuals with diagnoses on the autism spectrum may display "qualitative impairments in social interaction and communication" and often manifest "restricted repetitive and stereotyped patterns of behavior, interests and activities." Delays and/or abnormal functioning usually occur before age 3 and may be marked by a lack of symbolic or imaginative play.[13] Music therapy provides bridges in a non-threatening setting between people and/or between individuals and their environment, facilitating relationships, learning, self-expression, and communication.

Music captures and helps maintain attention. It is highly motivating and engaging and may be used as a natural "reinforcer" for desired responses. It can stimulate clients to reduce negative and or self-stimulatory responses and increase participation in more appropriate and socially acceptable ways.

Music therapy can enable those without language to communicate, participate, and express themselves non-verbally. Music therapy also assists in the development of verbal communication, speech, and language skills. Music therapy allows individuals with diagnoses on the autism spectrum the opportunity to develop identification and appropriate expression of emotions. Because music is processed in both hemispheres of the brain, music can stimulate cognitive functioning and may be used

[12] American Music Therapy Association website, https://www.musictherapy.org.
[13] Ibid.

for remediation of some speech and language skills. Many people with diagnoses on the autism spectrum have innate musical talents; thus, music therapy provides an opportunity for successful experiences. Emphasis is placed on strengths, which in turn may be utilized to address each individual's areas of need.[14]

The Nordoff-Robbins approach to music therapy developed from the work of Paul Nordoff and Clive Robbins in the 1950/60s. It is grounded in the belief that everyone can respond to music no matter how ill or disabled. The unique qualities of music as therapy can enhance communication, support change, and enable people to live more resourcefully and creatively. They now have programs throughout the UK, US, South Africa, Australia, and Germany.[15]

Music therapy helps stroke victims recover faster and with more success by increasing the patient's positive emotions and motivation, allowing them to be more successful and eager to participate in traditional therapies. When music therapy is used in conjunction with traditional therapy, it improves rates of recovery and emotional and social deficits resulting from the stroke. Families reported that the patient responded more easily to social interactions and more positively. There was a decrease in anxiety, fatigue, and hostile moods. There were physical and emotional reactions to music, such as when one man smiled and lifted his posture in response to a performance of a certain piece of music. The people seemed to be more actively involved and more cooperative when music therapy was used. Although sometimes stroke victims reported that they had the same amount of pain with music as without, it was interesting to view a video tape of therapy sessions. There was more positive affect displayed and more verbal responses while performing upper extremity exercises with both music and karaoke accompaniment. Music therapy improved both mood and social interaction.[16]

It is not just the medical or educational community that recognizes the benefits of music on clients as evidenced by special music during happy

---

[14] Ibid.

[15] Wikipedia contributors, "Music Therapy," *Wikipedia, The Free Encyclopedia*, https://en.wikipedia.org/w/index.php?title=Music_therapy&oldid=970533561

[16] B. L. Wheeler, *et al.*, "Effects of Number of Sessions and Group or Individual Music Therapy on the Mood and Behavior of People Who Have Had Strokes or Traumatic Brain Injuries," *Nordic Journal of Music Therapy*, Vol. 12, No. 2 (2003), 139-151.

hours at assisted living & nursing homes. Children's hospitals, family resource centers, facilities for people with developmental disabilities also use special music, including instrument playing to take a person's mind of their issues for a little while. The residents are happier when participating in this group activity. In addition to listening to the performer(s), they can participate with small percussive instruments such as shakers or hand bells they can ring. Alzheimer's patients have shown to be calmer when listening to music. Effects of music therapy can be observed in the person's demeanor, body language, and changes in awareness of mood and emotion. The work is gratifying for the musicians as well because of the connections they make with their audience members.

With heart patients, some music reduced the heart rate, respiratory rate, and blood pressure in patients with coronary artery disease. There is some research to suggest that listening to Mozart's piano sonata K448 can reduce the number of seizures in people with epilepsy.[17]

Music therapy in the United States has been around since 1944. A degree in music therapy requires proficiency in guitar, piano, voice, music theory, music history, reading music, improvisation, as well as varying levels of skill in assessment, documentation, and other counseling and health care skills depending on the focus of the particular university program. Music therapists work in psychiatric treatment centers, outpatient clinics, community mental health centers, substance abuse programs, group homes, rehabilitation facilities, medical hospitals, senior centers, schools, hospice, and other facilities. Some therapists are self-employed and may be hired on a contractual basis to provide assessment, consultation, and treatment services for children and adults.

Music therapy has been used in various countries in Africa during male and female circumcision, bone setting, or traditional surgery to therapeutically reduce anticipated pain. In the United Kingdom, music was used in hospitals after both of the World Wars, as part of the regime for some recovering soldiers.[18]

Some theater arts are functionally a combination of art and music (therapy). A local group that was started in our community several years ago is Encore Studio for the Performing Arts. It is the only professional theater company for people with disabilities in our state and one of only a

---

[17] Ibid.
[18] Wikipedia, "Music Therapy."

few in the country. Performers have various physical, cognitive, and speech disabilities. Their productions are written by the producer who also has a disability.

MINDFULNESS MEDITATION

Mindfulness is the practice of bringing one's attention to the internal and external experiences occurring in the present moment, which can be developed through the practice of meditation.[19] The practice of mindfulness is strongly correlated with well-being and perceived health because rumination and worry contribute to mental illnesses such as depression and anxiety. Mindfulness-based interventions are effective in reducing both rumination and worry.[20] It is said that mindfulness is the key to overcoming suffering and recognizing natural wisdom, both our own and others'.[21]

Mindfulness meditation has its origins in Buddhism. Buddha taught that the source of suffering is our attempt to escape from our direct experience. We cause ourselves suffering by trying to get away from pain and attempt to hang on to pleasure. Sometimes this causes us to only partially participate in our lives, or spend time wishing things were different. Instead of lessening our suffering or bolstering our happiness, this strategy has the opposite effect. Instead of struggling to get away from experiences we find difficult, mindfulness teaches a person to accept them and integrate them into our lives.

Instead of struggling to get away from experiences we find difficult, mindfulness helps us practice being able to go through them. A good example of this is when my daughter-in-law was in a great deal of pain from a condition she has. The pain woke her up very early in the morning

[19] Ruth A. Baer, "Mindfulness Training as a Clinical Intervention: A Conceptual and Empirical Review," *Clinical Psychology: Science and Practice*, Vol. 10, No, 2 (Summer 2003), 126-143. http://www.wisebrain.org/papers/MindfulnessPsyTx.pdf.

[20] Wikipedia contributors, "Mindfulness," *Wikipedia, The Free Encyclopedia*, https://en.wikipedia.org/w/index.php?title=Music_therapy&oldid=970533561.

[21] Karen Kissel Wegela, "How to Practice Mindfulness Meditation," *Psychology Today* (blog), January 19, 2010, https://www.psychologytoday.com/blog/the-courage-be-present/201001/how-practice-mindfulness-meditation.

and she had not been able to get any relief from it. The longer the pain went on the more anxious and distressed she became. My son called and said she was in so much pain that she was crying and wanted to hurt herself. I asked to speak with her. I described mindfulness meditation and asked her to do it for 10 minutes. She agreed. When I talked to my son about an hour later, he said that she was asleep. When she awoke, she felt somewhat better—on two accounts—she had gotten some additional sleep and she wasn't in as much pain as she had been before.

Mindfulness practice is being employed in psychology to alleviate a variety of mental and physical conditions, such as reducing depression, stress, and anxiety, and in the treatment of drug addiction. It is also being employed in schools, especially elementary schools, to help children refocus their minds to be able to learn better.

Mindfulness meditation is practiced sitting either with eyes closed or open and focused on an object four to six feet in the distance. You can sit cross-legged on a cushion or in a straight-backed chair. Hands rest on the thighs, facing down. Attention is put on the movement of the abdomen when breathing in and out or on the awareness of the breath as it goes in and out of the nostrils. Distractions such as TV, radio, or computer need to be turned off. At first, mind-wandering is common. Just refocus on the breathing in and out. Feel the breath as it comes into your body and as it goes out. Do not try to control your breath. Just pay attention to it.

The last part is working with thoughts. As you sit breathing, thoughts arise. Sometimes there a many thoughts, maybe even one overlapping the next: memories, plans for the future, snatches of something seen on TV. When you notice that you have gotten so caught up in thoughts that you have forgotten to pay attention to your breathing, just gently remind yourself to refocus on your breathing. If you are new to mindfulness meditation, try to sit for 10-15 minutes and gradually increase to 20-30 minutes. Eventually you could extend it to 45 minutes or an hour. If you want to do the meditation for longer, learn how to do walking meditation as an alternative.

Mindfulness meditation is about practicing being mindful—acutely aware, thoughtful, and accepting—of whatever happens in life. It is not about getting ourselves to stop thinking. It can make a person more aware of their body, more aware of how they regulate their attention and their emotions. Mindfulness meditation can enhance quality of life, enhance empathy levels, manage stress better, and decrease stress symptoms such as anxiety or depression. It has been shown to have a positive effect on individuals suffering numerous diseases such as cancer.

YOGA

Yoga is a mind-body exercise that combines breath control, meditation, and movements to stretch and strengthen muscles. It places as great an emphasis on mental fitness as on physical fitness. There are several types of yoga. The most popular form practiced in the United States is Hatha yoga. Breathing deeply through the nose is a vital component of yoga.

Yoga is very helpful to children. Through the practice of yoga, children learn to concentrate better, reduce their hyperactivity, enhance their creativity, and improve motor coordination, strength, endurance, balance, and aerobic capacity. Yoga can improve focus, memory, self-esteem, academic performance, and classroom behavior. It can even reduce anxiety and stress in children. Yoga poses are designed to stimulate and strengthen children, bringing physiological and mental processes into balance. At a basic level physically, yoga creates organization and integration. It increases lung capacity and energizes the central nervous system, especially improving executive brain function which is especially important for people with Down syndrome because they typically have low nervous system tone. If the individual is able, they can be taught breathing techniques and internal self-examination.

Yoga can help with anger issues through various breathing techniques and relaxation poses. It appears to modestly lower blood pressure, though not to a greater degree than other forms of exercise. There is a lot of emotional and mental work associated with yoga.

Yoga can help children with attention deficit hyperactivity disorder (ADHD). It may do so by improving the core characteristics of ADHD: inattentiveness, hyperactivity and impulsivity. It can also boost school performance in children with ADHD.

Research finds that yoga may help relieve pain in people with a variety of chronic pain conditions, including arthritis, fibromyalgia, migraine headaches, and low back pain. Researchers targeting low back pain found that a weekly yoga class increased mobility more than standard medical care for the condition.[22] They also found that people with carpal tunnel

---

[22] A.L. Komaroff, "Yoga Can Help Ease Chronic Pain," *Wisconsin State Journal* (Madison, WI), August 20, 2015.

syndrome had significantly reduced pain when practicing yoga. Yoga appears to calm inflammation in the body and boost the immune system.

A growing number of schools are integrating yoga and mindfulness meditation into physical education classes or into the classrooms.

The big difference between non-medical therapies is that some may be covered by health insurance, whereas you have to pay out-of-pocket for the others. However, the cost of some of these services may be covered by funds allocated to you or your loved one through support brokers or programs like Family Care and IRIS (Include, Respect, I Self-direct).

CHAPTER 18

PLAYERS, PROCEDURES, AND PROTOCOLS THAT WILL DRIVE YOU CRAZY

Living daily life with a disability, or with a family member with a disability, is challenging enough. It is all the more challenging when there is a lack of access to, or obstacles to accessing, services and resources needed to make daily life workable. Obstacles could include not having a disability recognized as severe enough to qualify for services, lack of case management for you or your loved one, providers who won't speak with you if your family member is of adult age, complications with health insurance coverage, or any number of other problems. It is a little hard to have a chance when so many obstacles keep popping up.

MEDICATION MANAGEMENT
(OR THE MEDICATION REFILL FROM HELL)

Just when you think everything is humming along just fine, life serves you lemons. One of the problems that I encounter every couple of years revolves around medication that my son has been taking for years. He has tried other medications in the same class but they do not work as well as this particular one. This medication is a Class II drug that is closely regulated by the federal government. This means that you have to have a written prescription for every 30 days (cannot be called into the pharmacy), it has to be turned into the pharmacy within seven days of when the doctor wrote it, is only good for 60 days from the date he wrote it, and cannot be partially filled like other medications (and get the rest later when the pharmacy gets their shipment). There are now electronic ways to get around the paper prescription, but it also has its drawbacks.

I was filling my son's pill strip for a particular upcoming week and knew that I needed to get the Class II medication refilled. The written prescription was on file at the pharmacy. When I called to ask that it be filled, the pharmacy staff found that they did not have enough of the pills to complete the order. They were having difficulty getting their orders for the medication filled. They did not know when or if they would be getting any more in and said they had heard a rumor that this medication was being discontinued by the pharmaceutical company.

I explained that my son needed that medication or we would face dire consequences such as behaviors that might result in a police contact, because this medication is essential to stabilizing his mood. The pharmacy volunteered to call around to other stores in the same chain to see if they had enough to fill the entire script as written. Of course it was a weekend! They did this and found one store in another community about 20 miles away. That store told me they were reluctant to fill my son's prescription because there was a boy in their community that was on the same medication and strength, and they would not be able to service him when he needed a refill.

The other option was to drive to a community about 70 miles away. They had the medication in one-half the strength but could give me double the amount so that it would equal the same strength that my son was taking. However, before we could complete this transaction, they would need permission from the doctor for the half-strength medication. That meant I would have to wait until Monday when the doctor would be back in the clinic and I needed the medication for tomorrow, Sunday. On top of that, there was a snow storm going on outside!

I called other non-related pharmacies in the area and got the same story, that their orders for this Class II medication had gone unfilled for weeks. No one else had enough of the tablets left to fill the entire prescription order.

I picked up the written prescription from our pharmacy and drove the 20 miles in the snow storm to the closest pharmacy that had what I needed, praying that with script in hand, they would have to fill it for me. I was fortunate to get the prescription filled and to get back home in one piece. Monday I called my son's psychiatrist. He called my regular pharmacy, talked to the pharmacist, found out just how wide-spread this problem was, and with the pharmacist figured out another medication that met my son's need.

Eric was switched to the new medication when his prescription ran out because his medication was no longer on the formulary. It does not work as well. However, the pharmacy does not have it as readily available as the previous Class II drug. Fast forward about two years. We picked up the January prescription and there was a note attached that said the health insurance company was filling the prescription as a courtesy because the formulary (list of approved drugs) just changed and this Class II drug was no longer in the insurance company's formulary. Really? I had to write a letter to the insurance company, give my letter and the other information to the prescribing psychiatrist, and have them handle it per the insurance company's protocol to have an exception approved.

Less than a month later, the same scenario repeated with the new medication. The pharmaceutical company discontinued making it. Again, multiple phone calls, finally finding enough of the medication at the twelfth pharmacy I called, then driving a distance to pick up the prescription so there was no break in medication for my son. I just wanted to scream, "GIVE ME A BREAK, STOP MESSING WITH PEOPLE'S LIVES." I put his psychiatrist on notice in case this was not resolved by the following month. It wasn't, but I managed to find the amount of medication I needed at the same pharmacy (#12) at which I had gotten it the previous month. For several months, I continued to drive the approximately 20 miles round-trip to this other pharmacy to get Eric's class II medication.

The federal Food and Drug Administration decides the quantities of controlled class drugs each pharmacy can have. If they believe your pharmacy is serving too many clients on classified drugs, they may curtail the amount of these drugs the pharmacy can get. It can seem like "luck of the draw" as to whether your local pharmacy is able to serve your needs or not. I know of another woman who is also driving to another community in order to get her medications.

As a side note on this story: With his autism spectrum disorder, anxieties, and low frustration tolerances, Eric could not navigate these challenges and obstacles if he had to handle refilling his medications on his own. He also does not have transportation to drive to another community to fill his prescription. My husband and I have great fears about how things will go for Eric after we are gone. He could very likely give up trying to overcome these kinds of obstacles and without his medications would decompensate, manifest behaviors that are dangerous to him or others, and end up in trouble with law enforcement authorities. For just the complications of filling a prescription, he could end up in our largest mental health institutions of today—our jails and prisons.

Every parent of a son or daughter with disabilities shares these fears about how their child will manage and survive once they are gone. Who will care about giving them a chance for a safe and meaningful life?

Yearly, health insurance companies review and make changes to their formulary, especially as patents run out on name-brand medications. If a generic version of the medication has become available, you should be able to get the same medication in that form for cost or copay. If the medication you are taking is no longer on the insurance company formulary, it will either no longer cover that particular medication or you will have to pay a higher price for it. So for most of us who want to keep our prescription costs as low as possible, we go back to the doctor to get a new prescription for a similar medication that will be covered by the insurance company.

Even when your medication is on the insurance company's formulary, some medications require a prior-authorization from the insurance company before they will cover it for you. This requires the doctor to fill out more online forms or paperwork justifying why he believes you must be on that particular medication. Once approved, the prior-authorization is usually good for a year. Several times I have had to pay full price ($600) out-of-pocket for a prescription until the paperwork was completed to the insurance company's satisfaction and the prior-authorization was granted. The monetary difference that I had paid for the prescription was then returned to me by the pharmacy. But how many people are in a financial position to do this.

These are the players, procedures, and protocols that can make you crazy and cause your blood pressure to rise. But there are more. Read on.

PRIVACY AND PERMISSION NIGHTMARES

While the authorities vary across the US, many states allow minors over the age of 12 or 13 to decide whether or not they want to be hospitalized in a mental health facility or take medications. This can be very problematic when dealing with someone who is mentally ill and experiencing hormonal changes. Many patients are not able to make informed decisions about their own medical needs or their need for medication.

After our sons turned 14, each time we needed to put one of them into the hospital, we had to get them to agree to go in there. Sometimes it was telling them that it was either the hospital or we believed their behavior would spiral out of control to the point where law enforcement authorities might become involved. They could take their pick, but we believed life would be much better for all concerned if they picked the hospital. Fortunately, they were able to agree with us. However, in many states people as young as 13 or 14 can make the choice to check themselves out of a hospital or not take the medication that help them function.

It is not uncommon for people to feel better on medication and conclude that they don't need it anymore. Or they decide they don't like the side-effects or they don't *feel like themselves*. I have heard of numerous stories of people with bipolar disorder who discontinued medications that were keeping them stable because the drugs interfered with their creativity and the accompanying adrenalin *rush*.

Another common and very frustrating problem is not being able to communicate with service providers after your loved one has turned 18 unless you have legal guardianship or he/she has signed a waiver authorizing the release of information about their care to you. In the strictest sense, without a waiver a provider cannot talk with you about anything to do with their care. Without this authorization, you lose most of your power to advocate for your now-adult son/daughter in numerous decisions that may come up. You can find yourself unable to do something as simple as canceling an appointment! I have.

This restriction was put in place at the federal level by the Health Insurance Portability and Accountability Act (HIPAA) of 1996. The HIPAA Privacy Rule is a set of regulations governing the use and disclosure of *protected health information* about an individual's healthcare treatment, including billing and payment for services. It went into effect on April 14, 2003.

While it was designed to protect a person's private information, it can lead to many frustrating situations. Once, when one of our sons agreed to be hospitalized in an adolescent mental health facility, he initially refused to sign a release of information, so the hospital staff could not talk with us. Without a release of information, we cannot even speak to the billing department of a provider concerning charges for their care.

In 2013, the coverage of the Privacy Rule was expanded beyond direct healthcare providers to include associated businesses. We have learned that this includes prisons in which our younger son has been incarcerated. When we go to visit him, we always call the prison before we leave to make sure he is eligible for a visit. On one occasion when we were told that he was eligible, we made the 45-minute drive only to learn upon arrival that he was not eligible. He was in solitary confinement. When we explained that an hour ago we were told he was eligible, the staff said that he must have done something after we called to get him thrown into solitary as a consequence. When we asked what he had done, they said they couldn't tell us because of the HIPAA Privacy Rule. American prisons consider solitary confinement to be *treatment*. As previously stated, our jails and prisons are the largest mental health institutions in our society

OTHER FRUSTRATING ISSUES

Sometimes in addition to one diagnosis, a behavior or physical condition resulting from the stress of the disability will pop up. While the new issue could be a co-morbid condition, it is usually of shorter duration. So, while it could have a diagnosis of its own, it is often not the primary or even secondary diagnosis. Such a behavior or condition might be something like *cutting*, a self-injurious behavior. Cutting is a painful addiction in which a person cuts themselves to deal with emotional pain. It is an impulse-control disorder—the inability to resist acting on impulsive thoughts and often characterized by the intentional harming of oneself. It is usually associated with trauma. Cutting usually manifests itself when a person becomes overwhelmed with situations and resorts to cutting as a relief; calming them down. It is a behavior that, once a person has engaged in it, he/she will be drawn to it again for the rest of his/her life. It may help express feelings that cannot be put into words by the individual, distracts from current stresses, or releases the emotional pain. A person may be trying to cope with feelings like sadness, self-loathing, emptiness, guilt, and rage.

Cutting is calming because it causes the body to release endorphins, which are the body's narcotic. They minimize pain by providing a sense of well-being. When our bodies experience pain, our brains release endorphins to soothe and energize us so we can take action to get out of harm's way. Cutting switches the pain from being emotional to physical. Physical pain eventually goes away while emotional pain feels as though it won't.

Self-harm can also include less obvious ways of hurting oneself or putting oneself in danger, such as driving recklessly, binge drinking, taking too many drugs, and having unsafe sex. Unfortunately, self-harm keeps a person from learning more effective strategies for feeling better. Understanding the reason for the self-harming behavior is necessary for a person to recover and stop that behavior. The self-injury serves a need. Other wholesome ways to meet those needs must be learned.

Another kind of challenge comes from people closest to you. When someone you love has a disability, there are many well-meaning people who will give you solicited or unsolicited advice. When Eric was diagnosed with ADHD, people sent us newspaper clippings on ADHD, medications, harm that medications do, and other related matters. These people mean well, but many times they just don't get it. They haven't taken the time to ask about the situation or understand it fully. Nor did they ask how we are feeling about these decisions.

Sometimes family members have made comments on our children's behavior when their own behavior in the past has not been much different. These comments have stirred up my anger. Sometimes I say something and sometimes I just keep silent. However, keeping silent is not advocating for my kids.

Not understanding a situation and then making comments can be very hurtful and upsetting. Then the person doesn't understand why you are now upset. They have just added to your stress, probably without meaning to, but I am tempted to avoid them in the future, but this becomes isolating. Once I left a vacation with extended family and took a bus home because I could no longer stand their judgmental attitude and comments. I had made a lot of accommodations to include them in our vacation and they were making negative comments about our parenting and what my children needed.

Isolation from family and other social circles is a frequent experience of those with disabilities or a loved one with a disability—an experience we had not anticipated and for which we were unprepared. We were asked by some to not visit again if our kids were with us, and consequently we also felt hesitant to invite these people to our home. We were asked by a church-sponsored summer camp to no longer sign up our younger son to attend the camp. These were emotional wounds that truly hurt and took time to heal.

CHAPTER 19

ADVOCACY

Advocacy is defined as pleading the cause for or defending someone. People with disabilities often need someone to advocate for them. Advocacy could be for a child, a sibling, a spouse, a parent, a friend, or someone you see on the street. There are lawyers that specialize in disability law. They are advocating for someone with a disability in the courts or advising parents or other caregivers on legal matters, such as establishing long-term financial support for a person with a disability.

Advocating often includes educating others about the person's disability. There are national and local agencies that are involved in advocating and educating. They might also provide services to disabled individuals and their families. The National Alliance on Mental Illness (NAMI), Children and Adults With Attention-Deficit/Hyperactivity Disorder (CHADD), and United Cerebral Palsy (UCP) are such agencies, just to name a few. There is easy access to information about these and other service organizations via the internet.

If you are the parent of a son or daughter with a disability, the most important advocate your child has is you. At some point, your child may be able to start advocating for him/herself, but they need your modeling of how to do it. You will have to advocate with friends, neighbors, the public, the school system, professionals in your child's life, and with governmental agencies. You may have to advocate with the legal system. You may need to advocate even after they die. The best way to advocate is to learn all that you can about your loved one's issues and be able to state them clearly and concisely. Ask questions of the professionals, prioritize your concerns, and share tips that work at home. Make files and save copies of all paperwork. Ask caregivers to articulate to you what the needs and protocols are for the person with a disability to make sure they understand them.

There was a recent news story of a mother suing a group home after her 49-year-old daughter choked on a bagel and later died. The daughter was living in an assisted living center because she had sustained brain damage during birth. The lawsuit contends that staff knew the daughter was on a special diet. However, she would steal food from the kitchen even though she knew she wasn't allowed to eat without staff supervision because she ate her food quickly and required reminders from staff to slow down and chew her food. She was a known choking risk to the staff. The lawsuit contended the daughter was left unsupervised for an unspecified amount of time, during which she found bagels and peanut butter, ate them quickly, and began to choke. She then ran to her bedroom where she collapsed on the floor. Her death was due to lack of oxygen to her brain.

Advocacy can be finding services for yourself or your loved one, talking to people, joining or starting support groups, and other *soft* actions. It can also mean repeatedly calling, writing, and emailing officials and agencies to get services, or even suing them to get services. This is the *hard* or *in your face* advocacy that is sometimes necessary.

This *hard* advocacy reality is illustrated by the story of a man whose son had autism. The school system provided a learning environment and daily structure for his son until he graduated from high school at age 22. While in many ways the young man still had the abilities of a one year old, in the news report video he seemed to be able to follow simple directions and could feed himself. The father applied for services through an agency that would take care of his son during the day while he worked. The agency denied the services. The father found it necessary to sue the agency because providing such services was this agency's mission and responsibility. He won his case and the agency will begin providing this service to his son. However, while pursuing this outcome for his son, the father had to quit his job to take care of his son and was out of work for two years. These are the seemingly unnecessary burdens that some parents experience in advocating for their loved ones.

A mother sued a YMCA in Ohio because they excluded her six-year-old son from a summer camp and other programs because of his Down syndrome. She felt this was hypocritical after the YMCA used a photo of him in its promotions extolling opportunities for everyone! Yet they were guilty of not making reasonable accommodations and discriminating against her son based on his disability.

Advocating for a child with a disability is a constant and ongoing effort. Sometime after our son, Aaron, turned 18, he got in trouble by confronting a friend who was supposed to allow him to sleep over that night. He ended up being arrested and charged with disorderly conduct. The judge gave him six months in jail, 30 days of which had to be served but the other five months were stayed if he successfully completed an AODA (alcohol and other drug abuse) program. We were given the name of the individual who would be contacting Aaron to talk with him about the program.

After a couple of weeks, Aaron told us the jail staff started giving him messages saying that he was not eligible to go on electronic monitoring (ankle bracelet). We were all confused, including his attorney, since Aaron had not applied for the electronic monitoring program. Aaron had been interviewed by a man from the AODA program. but then we heard nothing. I obtained the contact's phone number and called him. He said Aaron would benefit from the program and had given Aaron's name to the jail staff.

In the course of speaking with him, I learned that Aaron would need to be on electronic monitoring to participate in the AODA programs. Suddenly, I got the picture! I asked him if he was telling me that he approves people for AODA treatment, but the jail staff can veto his recommendation by denying electronic monitoring. He said he "did not get involved in the *politics*" of the matter. I thanked him and went to the computer to write a letter to the judge. By this time I was steaming angry. The sheriff department was effectively countermanding a judge's order! My husband had to tone down my letter a bit, but then we faxed the letter to the judge and received a quick reply. She stated the sheriff's department did not have the authority to override her decision and she would make sure Aaron was released by Friday on electronic monitoring. If he was not released by then, we were to let her know.

The sheriff department seemed none too happy that we had worked through the judge to overrule their attempt to sabotage her order of AODA treatment. They told us we would need to have another phone line installed to which they would hook up the bracelet monitoring station. When the phone company said it would take three days to install a new line, they had to look for an alternative. Finally, Aaron was brought home Thursday night on a GPS monitoring bracelet. He was able to attend the program and successfully completed it. Without my advocacy, Aaron would have simply spent six months in jail and received no treatment.

One of my duties as a special education teacher was to find out whether each student on my caseload wanted to take exams in the Resource Room or in their regular classroom. If they wanted to take their exam in the Resource Room, I had to get the exam from their instructor, put it in a file in the room, and then return it to the instructor after the exam period.

One of my students had a writing disability which required him to use a laptop. When I went to his math teacher to get the exam, the instructor refused to give it to me stating that the student might have math information on his computer and could cheat. We agreed that he would take the exam in the regular classroom so the teacher could monitor and make sure he was not cheating. The teacher also wanted the computer wiped clean first to make sure there was nothing on it that the student could use to help him on the test.

I thought this was unreasonable and so did the student. I went to the department chair and was told that it was up to the instructor. My next stop was the school principal. After explaining the situation and what concessions we had made, I asked for her help. She told the teacher to stop creating obstacles and let the student take the exam in the classroom with his laptop intact.

I recently spent about one hundred dollars making photocopies, five or six trips to the Social Security Administration (SSA), about ten to fifteen hours of my time, and lots of frustrating hours advocating for my older son after he got a job with the help of a job developer/coach. Apparently getting a job, even if it was only four hours per week, was enough to significantly reduce his disability benefits. The fact that he was making only $116 a month gross didn't seem to make a difference, nor that he was paying a job coach almost double that amount per month to be there with him. At one point when the job coach was filling out some paperwork for me to send to the SSA, she looked at me and asked, "What happens to people who don't have someone advocating for them?" She knew, of course, but was just making the point. After six months of advocating for Eric with SSA, his full benefits were restored; but what a hassle!

During one of our younger son's prison stays, my husband and I wrote a couple of letters to the prison psychologist, and copied to our son's attorney, advocating for his health care needs in the prison. He was being given medications that were previously determined didn't work for him, and he was in solitary confinement which was affecting his mental health. Our sharing of information and advocacy was ignored by the prison medical staff.

As a result of the incorrect medications and five months in solitary confinement, Aaron became totally psychotic. He lost 70 pounds of weight. Aaron had to be transferred to a locked medical facility. We again wrote a letter to the medical staff of this facility. This time the response was much different. The staff was receptive to the information we shared and put Aaron on medications that actually worked for him. They also thanked us for writing the letter because it enabled them to avoid trial and error with different medications and allowed Aaron to quickly come out of his psychosis.

These are examples of the constant and ongoing advocacy efforts that are needed for the success and well-being of those with disabilities. This advocacy gives the person a chance at a *normal* life. Advocacy can be frustrating and time consuming, but ultimately very rewarding to know that you have accomplished this for your loved one. However, you also wonder who will be available to do the advocacy once you are gone.

There is a wonderful saying that shows the impact that advocacy can have on a child with a disability. I don't know who said it and I couldn't find the citation but the sentiment is apt. "When you change a child, you change the family. When you change the family, you change the community. When you change the community, you can change the world."

CHAPTER 20

THE REALITIES OF EVERY DAY LIFE

When you have a child with a disability, *you* have to be *very* flexible. Most children with issues do much better if they have a routine schedule. When this schedule is varied for whatever reason, there may be problems such as acting out. If you know that there will be a disruption in the child's normal schedule, it usually works better if you can prepare them for this schedule change ahead of time. Our strategy was to tell our sons that they had a doctor's appointment tomorrow, and then remind them of it in the morning, and after school. It also helps if you bring along some items that the child likes, such as certain toys, foods, etc. Some parents keep a *go* bag that has items that the child likes, but the only time the child sees them is when they are on the go. I had items that I would purchase at the dollar store or at an educational store that my kids could only use when we went to church gatherings. They were allowed to take other items from home as well, such as their newest Lego creation.

If a child with a disability is able, he/she needs to be responsible for things just like any child might be. This helps them feel *just like the other kids.* Putting toys away and straightening their room are two key responsibilities. I am still working on these with Eric who is 35 and Aaron who is 31! They know what they are supposed to do but frequently are "too busy." Such tasks are difficult for them because it isn't fun and their executive brain function deficits make the multiple organization decisions of straightening up a room very challenging and emotionally frustrating. They will complete a task such as cleaning if others direct them and make the organizational decisions, but they have to be prepared for it ahead of time. They have made some incremental progress at doing such tasks.

Life with someone with a disability can be rewarding but also exhausting and frustrating. Sometimes these stresses lead to divorce because one or both spouses could not handle the constant challenges. There is a higher rate of divorce when a spouse becomes disabled or chronically ill. If a child with a disability is born to a couple, there is a slightly higher than average chance that the couple will divorce and the mother usually becomes the primary caregiver and custodial parent. Interestingly, the divorce rate is not higher if the disability is Down syndrome. Also, the studies show that if additional children without a disability are born into the family, the slightly higher divorce rate declines.[23]

Over a period of many years, the experiences of my husband and I brought us closer together and deepened our relationship. This is not always the case however. Parents, whether single or a couple, need other outlets, need adult time away from their kids, but especially if they have a child with a disability. When we were going through the adoption process, the social workers kept stressing how important it was for the adults to keep a good, healthy relationship. Later, when our younger son was having major behavioral problems, social workers were telling us to get respite so we could be by ourselves and *recharge our batteries*. However, we quickly learned that getting any kind of respite care for our children can be extremely challenging. (See Respite Section)

Frequently, even extended family members don't understand why your child behaves the way he/she does, even if you have explained their challenges *ad nauseam*. Grandparents and siblings and their spouses may make comments about your child's behavior, your parenting, and your lifestyle that can be very hurtful and isolating.

I have a friend that experienced the comments from her grandparents and her aunts regarding her son's behavior. This of course was in addition to getting an earful from her son's teacher every day. My friend was doing

---

[23] Eun Ha Namkung, *et al.*, "The Relative Risk of Divorce in Parents of Children with Developmental Disabilities: Impacts of Lifelong Parenting," *American Journal on Intellectual and Development Disabilities*, Vol. 120, No. 6, 514–526. https://www.ncbi.nlm.nih.gov/pmc/articles/PMC4624231/.

everything humanly possible to find the root cause of her son's problems. She and her husband spent about $10,000 out-of-pocket taking him to different doctors, psychologists, and having different tests performed on him to see if he was in pain or allergic to something that he couldn't articulate. She worked a full time job but spent her weekends buying and preparing organic foods, all while being criticized by her family. She certainly couldn't ask them to assist and give her respite. This only isolated her and her husband even more and continued to make them question their parenting skills. (They have an older child who seemed to be doing just fine under their tutelage). Their son was eventually diagnosed with Asperger's Syndrome and is getting therapy and doing well.

My husband's parents told us we just weren't showing our younger son the love he needed. They had little understanding about what our life was like until I bailed in the middle of one vacation with them. Then they got a little taste of what love and discipline couldn't do as far as our son's behavior was concerned. This judgmentalism on the part of friends, relatives, teachers, and others serves to isolate the family all the more and adds needless stress to their lives.

Life with a child with a disability is very stressful, more so if you are a single parent. There have been news reports of a parent killing their disabled child, either because they were overwhelmed and saw no pathway to reducing the stress in their life or because there were additional stressors such as financial problems with which the parent could no longer cope. This can happen to anyone, even professionals. In the summer of 2011, a psychiatrist shot and killed her son and then herself leaving a note that said she could not deal with the school and school system for her son with special needs and that debt was strangling her. This woman should have known the warning signs of too much stress and to ask for help, but sometimes that is difficult to do for any of us.

There have also been news reports of individuals with autism (both young children and adults) who have been locked in the basement of homes or in cages. They were denied adequate food, clothing, toilet facilities, warm sleeping quarters, and stimulation with other people. The antidote to such horrible treatment is for our society to provide more and better services to support those with disabilities and their caregivers. The ease of accessing these services needs to be streamlined and widely published. These services must include meaningful respite services so that the stress on caregivers will not drive them to desperate actions like locking loved ones in basements or killing them.

Some parents, who have a child with *profound* developmental disabilities, after much soul-searching, have made the very hard choice to stop the child's growth. The procedure or treatment is called *growth attenuation* or *Ashley treatment,* named for the girl whose case brought public attention to this procedure. It is a hormone treatment that stops the physical growth of the child. Ashley is unable to move or talk or do anything for herself. Her parents feared they would no longer be able to move or lift her as she grew without the assistance of mechanical lifts (which I know from experience with my aged mother are cumbersome for the operator and uncomfortable for the person being lifted). Ashley's parents felt that by the child remaining small, they could continue to provide her care much longer in their lives without placing her in an institution, and they could continue to take Ashley with them to various places and have her participate in family activities.

While still a controversial procedure, parents of both boys and girls with severe developmental disabilities have chosen this for their child. Parents of females have also had the womb removed to prevent any menstruation, which would be painful and totally not understood by the young person. This "treatment" first showed up in medical journals in 2006; however, it was tried in the 1950s and 1960s. Without this choice, the child might have to be placed in an institution rather than remaining in the family.

A very interesting side effect of the hormone treatment can be a lessening or remediation of some of the co-morbid conditions affecting the person, such as cessation of seizures and stiff joints becoming more pliable.

Jobs and disabilities can be a challenging combination—your job and your kid's disability. Life is easier if you work for an employer that is family friendly. My husband worked in a supervisory position for the federal government, which is family friendly. I was a special education teacher in a high school two and a half miles from home. Both of our jobs gave us degrees of flexibility and availability to minister to the needs of our children and their challenges when there was a crisis. For many people, however, caring for their children and holding onto a job doesn't work. Their job or employer does not permit the flexibility for them to be able to leave whenever there is a family crisis. I have known women who have lost their jobs because the kids called the office too much and, therefore, mom was on the phone with them rather than doing her job.

If you are working outside the home, you probably need some sort of day care. It is crucial that the provider understand your child's challenges and strategies that work well for that child. There were days when we would get calls that one of our sons needed to be picked up immediately because he would not settle down or was in a major confrontation with another child. There were other times when the infractions or problems could wait until we picked them up at the normal time.

Recently we received the newsletter from the Adoption Resource Center that explained that there are times and events that trigger adoption issues, such as birthdays, Mother's Day and Father's Day, first days of school, or other milestones. I could have used this information about 30 years ago!! There was about a ten-year period when every Mother's Day or my birthday (or brother's birthday) was "ruined" by the misbehavior of one son or the other.

I remember one time when we had reservations to celebrate my birthday (birthdays were always a family affair) at a restaurant about ten miles away. The youngest started having a tantrum just before we left, and continued it during the car ride. When we got to the restaurant, he was still not settled down, so my husband went in and cancelled our reservation, explaining our dilemma. It took about 1½ hours back at home to get our son settled down before we could go out to dinner—at the same restaurant.

Another time we were on our way to a restaurant to celebrate our older son's birthday when the younger son again became out of control. We said we were going to turn around and go home. This so incensed our older son that he threw a Matchbox car, hitting and breaking the rear-view mirror on my car. Then we definitely went home! Both boys understood their part in the cancelled evening event. We later made arrangements to go celebrate the older son's birthday a couple of weeks later, telling the younger son that he had lost the privilege of going with us. The day arrived for us to go to dinner. Because he could not go with us as a consequence, the younger son again began to tantrum. It necessitated getting the police involved before he would settle down, eat the macaroni and cheese (his favorite) we made for him, and stay by himself until we got back (without doing any damage to the house or his brother's belongings).

It is difficult to carry on conversations with other adults when your child is throwing a tantrum. If they are parents too, it may be a little easier, but if your child has special challenges, even those people can steer clear of you after a while.

Your child's challenges may make it difficult to reason with them. With a disability, their reasoning and problem-solving skills are frequently below average. All of this can be isolating for the parent(s). You find that your family has not been included in something because of your child's behavior.

In our case, it was both our kids' behaviors. One time we were invited to the wedding of a relative. It listed only my husband and I on the invitation. We could not get a baby sitter, so we *bribed* our kids with good behavior rewards if they stayed home by themselves (ages 10 and 14). We went to the wedding which was about two hours away. We were in frequent phone contact with the boys at home. When we got to the wedding, there were other kids that had been invited, but not ours (we assumed because of their behaviors). We were hurt, felt like failures, and felt set apart from others.

Another time, we were going to go on a trip to China, just the two of us. The boys' Special Education para-educator volunteered to stay with our sons. Our sons' behaviors began to deteriorate to the point that we decided we could not leave them in the care of someone else, even though this person knew the boys and was highly qualified. Having bought trip insurance, we thought we would get our deposit back. However, needing to care for a family member with a *mental* health condition was not covered by the policy, so we lost the $5,000 deposit.

Some of the closest relationships I have today are with people who *have walked a mile in my shoes* and understand what having a child with a disability is like. For those who don't understand, my relationship with them is not so close. Overall, relationships are slightly easier now that my sons are adults and, to a limited degree, on their own.

To those heroic parents who are raising a child with a behavioral disability, I can say that I know from experience how much it hurts to overhear people talking about your child and making the comment, "Stay away from those two; they are bad news." The person didn't know my sons at all, probably didn't care why they were acting the way they were, but just didn't want their behavior influencing their own child.

My sister-in-law tells us that we compartmentalize our lives very well, and I guess when I think about it, we have. Otherwise we would never get anything done or be able to move on following some crisis. We certainly wouldn't have been able to do our jobs, function in our volunteer activities, or do much of anything else if we hadn't learned how to *stuff* our sons' behaviors and our family's challenges into a little box, and then move on. You learn to *roll with the punches.*

CHAPTER 21

RESPITE—SO IMPORTANT BUT OFTEN ILLUSORY

Respite is defined as an interval of rest or relief. Having some rest or relief from parenting or caring for a person with disabilities is essential to a caregiver's physical and mental health. Caregivers will need different amounts of respite based on their individual needs. When they get respite, they will be able to sustain caregiving for longer periods than if they do not get any respite.

Respite care, as distinguished from respite, is the alternative care arrangement made for the person needing the care. Without respite care options, there is no meaningful opportunity for caregivers to enjoy a period of respite. Respite care can be for a couple of hours, a day, a weekend, or longer. It can be in your own home or somewhere else. You may be able to hire someone to be in the home while you are still there, but they are tending to the person with a disability while you accomplish whatever it is you need to accomplish. This can include taking a nap for much needed rest.

My mother's first 24/7 caregiver did not take any time for herself even though it was built into her contract. After only a few months, I got a call from my step-sister saying that things had rapidly deteriorated and that the caregiver was not taking care of mom, the apartment was a mess, and the caregiver was drunk! I was on vacation over 1,000 miles away! I had checked on things before I left on vacation and was told that everything was fine.

When the kids were younger, my husband and I usually spelled one another. However, there were times when we wanted to go *on a date* or to a conference. Because of our sons' behaviors, we had trouble getting babysitters. One time when our son was admitted to the adolescent psychiatric hospital, the social worker reminded us that we needed to be taking care of ourselves by getting some respite. We explained that we had looked into it but we could not access the service, and besides it was only for a few hours at best if we could access it. She told us unequivocally that respite care was available. We checked again, found it was not available to us, and told her at the next meeting we had. She was shocked. She said she had never heard any feedback like that before.

Another time we argued with a social worker regarding access to respite care. We told her that since we couldn't access the respite care, she needed to find some place to put our younger son (Eric was older by that time and could stay alone) while we attended a conference on Reactive Attachment Disorder for which we had already paid. At the very last minute, she was able to get Aaron into the Respite Center, but the condition was we had to be back to pick him up immediately after the conference. So, while services may be available, if you can't access them for one reason or another, it is as if they don't exist. In our case, we were a two-parent family with a moderate income. These factors worked against us because most of the parents who were able to access respite services were single parents who were poor and engaged with numerous community support services.

So, our family's experience taught us that respite services often proved to be more *on paper*—touted in some agency's brochure—than real, or we found that they did not serve children with our sons' challenges. We didn't experience much respite.

A news anchor in our area could not get respite for her son with severe disabilities. She became so frustrated at not being able to find anything or being on never-ending waiting lists that she started her own respite center for infants and children to age 6 who had severe disabilities. Ironically, by that time her own son was 6, going on 7, and would not be able to use the center (see Chapter 30, Grassroots Groups and Support Organizations).

One of the special education teachers I worked with was able to get respite care for her wheelchair-bound daughter by advertising in the university job listings. She actually was able to secure someone that got along well with her daughter and eventually was interested in more hours.

This turned into regular periods of respite care, which was a big help to the family. We tried advertising for someone on that site and got no takers. Back to square one.

I remember a friend telling me that once, when her husband was out of town and her daughter was about two and a half years old, she set up some toys for her daughter to play with and ran to take a shower. She said she was only in the bathroom for about 7 minutes. However, her daughter had apparently decided that the toys mom had laid out were not interesting. She managed to get the top off a container of Vaseline and smeared it all over some vinyl records. It was in all the grooves of the records, on the record jackets, and on the carpet. I don't remember where she said she put her daughter, but she then called the "parental abuse hotline" because she was so mad and frustrated that she was afraid she would hurt her daughter. After talking to someone for about 10 minutes, she was settled down and could now tackle the task of cleaning up the mess. Something as simple as a shower or a phone call can be a respite, as long as you are able to totally release yourself from worrying about where your child is and what he/she is doing.

Several years ago, our neighbors were taking care of her mother in their home. When they needed some respite, they were able to drive the mother to a hospital in a community about 30 miles away that provided adult respite services, and then retrieve her when they came back from a trip.

CHAPTER 22

TAKING CARE OF THE CAREGIVER

A survey from 2013 reported that more than 65 million people—29 percent of the US population—provide care for a chronically ill, disabled, or elderly family member or friend in any given year. They give an average of 20 hours of care per week. Much of that care is for an adult sibling.

It is extremely important for caregivers of a person with a disability to take care of themselves. If they cannot or do not take care of themselves, they will become ineffectual in caring for the person with the disability. Caregiving is not only time consuming, but also very stressful. I have known caregivers that have ended up in the hospital or died before the person with the malady or disability because caregiving was so stressful. Caregivers need to find ways to reduce the stress so that they can continue their very important job of caregiving. Stress can rob us of sleep, increase our anxiety levels, lower our immune system, and make us more vulnerable to various illnesses, heart disease, increased blood pressure, and depression, just to name a few.

Caregivers may need some classes or instruction on assisting the person with a disability. They need to have the skills to deal with both the physical and emotional aspects of the disability. Without the necessary knowledge and skills, a frustrated and overwhelmed caregiver could do as one Michigan woman did—lock her sister in a closet with little food, water, or clothing, and only a bucket for toileting.

People find many ways to relieve stress. It could be some form of exercise, i.e., yoga, playing a team sport, running, or taking a walk or a hike. It could be *retail therapy* (although this can get very expensive), going to see a movie, or reading a good novel. Drinking alcohol is not a good idea; it will only add to the stress. The point of whatever approach one takes is the time away from care giving to refocus the brain. Usually some form of physical exercise is the best, because physical activity increases the production of the brain's feel-good neurotransmitters, called endorphins. Even five minutes can improve one's mood. The key is to do this regularly to achieve the maximum benefit.

Mindfulness meditation can be helpful. "It is about being in the moment and noticing what is going on with your breathing, your body, your thoughts, your feelings, without analyzing or judging or reacting to it. Studies have shown that mindfulness significantly reduces stress, anxiety, and depression, improves sleep, and lowers blood pressure." [24]

I wasn't sure my mother was eating properly and she refused to have "Meals on Wheels" coming in so I bought a bunch of plastic containers and every night when I would cook for my family, I would make enough for my mom. I would then put a meal in the plastic container, label it, and put it into the refrigerator. Once a week, I would drive from Madison, Wisconsin, to the northern Chicago suburbs with a cooler to check on my mom and deliver the meals to her. Later she had a live-in care-giver, but I still drove to the Chicago area every week to pay bills & grocery shop for the two of them. I made the trip every week for almost 4 years. That was about $60,000 worth of gas, tolls, and extra oil changes to say nothing of the wear and tear on both me and my car. Another winter was coming up and I dreaded continuing this so I told my mom that I was burning out and could no longer make these weekly trips; that she would have to move to Wisconsin to be closer to me. This was when we moved her into an assisted living facility 6 miles from me. My husband and I visited her 3 times a week for about 1 hour each time. Still time consuming but not nearly as wearing as a 5-8 hour trip there and back to Chicago depending on weather. This provided me with much needed respite on an ongoing basis so I could take care of myself and better assist my mom.

---

[24] "Mindfulness Exercises," Mayo Clinic, https://www.mayoclinic.org/healthy-lifestyle/consumer-health/in-depth/mindfulness-exercises/art-20046356.

So, who is going to take care of your family member with a disability after you are no longer able? Who will be the new caregiver? And will they take care of themselves so they can take care of the loved one? Frequently, the responsibility falls to one of their siblings, if they have one. Sometimes siblings live far away from other family members and taking on responsibility for a family member with a disability can be extremely disruptive. If the family member is well-connected with supportive services in their community, moving them to where the sibling lives is not a good option. Sometimes siblings have made the difficult decision to quit a good job to move back to where the family member lives. (This is also sometimes true in order to care for an aging parent.) Many people with disabilities need help with activities of daily living, vocational support, and behavioral support. They may need a payee for financial considerations (see SSI). They may need to be taken to appointments.

One family we know makes frequent visits to another state so their son with a disability can spend time with his older sister who lives independently. Mom and dad then leave for a getaway on their own, giving the sister an opportunity to experience the care she will one day need to provide for her brother when mom and dad are gone. Another family we know had their son with a disability move to another state shortly after his sister moved there, ahead of the parents, so everyone could find out what life would be like without the parents around.

I remember one person telling me that she felt she was an adult at 8 years-old because her mom left her in charge of her older brother who had a developmental disability. This young woman (and her husband) keeps a watchful eye over her brother, who lives nearby, while mom lives in another state. The sister makes decisions and advocates for her brother with agencies when necessary and keeps track of how things are going for her brother. While still supportive, the parents have only occasional personal contact with their son, although mom calls her son every day.

When a sibling has a disability, it changes the dynamics in their sibling relationships. Some siblings are able to show a caring attitude toward their brother or sister with a disability. Others are struggling just to manage their own lives, let alone that of a sibling with a disability. Caring for someone is a huge commitment of time, resources, and energy. It can, however, be extremely rewarding, bringing people closer together, enhancing the quality of life for both individuals. About 80 percent of siblings say that they have a close relationship with their sibling with a disability and that this relationship enhances their life, having an impact on the quality of life, helping them develop patience, understanding, compassion, and providing important perspectives about life.[25]

Most siblings of adults with disabilities understand that they need a long-term plan in place. However, most have not completed the planning necessary to ensure their loved one's care. Some have done no planning and don't know if any planning has been done by their parents. Having and knowing about a long-term plan will lessen anxiety, and lessening anxiety will go a long way in preserving the caregiver's mental health. (See Special Needs Trust and Life Care/Life Style Plan sections.) Having a Life Care Plan in place for future care of a sibling with a disability, and updating it as the siblings' life circumstances change, can ensure the best possible outcome for families.

Some things to think about when deciding to take on the care of a sibling with a disability:

- Is this something you really want to do? The responsibility is best taken on freely and with love—not as an obligation. You have to do what is right for you.
- Decide how much effort you want to put into your sibling's care. It can range from calling him/her on a regular schedule to taking him/her into your home. You need to do whatever is appropriate for you (and your family).
- Are you willing to take on managing your sibling's finances? Or would you name a trustee to oversee them?
- Educate yourself about care of your sibling. You will then be able to make an informed choice about whether you are truly capable of caring for him/her.
- Organizations abound for everything from mental illness to specific maladies such as cystic fibrosis. They can provide education, support, networks, local affiliations, referrals to doctors, therapists, and other information to help you in making a decision.
- Is the person already on SSI and Medicaid? Are they already involved in community services? If so, what are these services? How does the person access these services (transportation)?

---

[25] "Caring for a Sibling with a Disability: Easter Seals Siblings Study" (Springfield, MA: MassMutual Financial Group, 2013). https://www.massmutual.com/mmfg/pdf/Sibling%20Study%20Key%20Findings_SC8200.pdf.

- Find out what kind of financial resources are available. Is there a special needs trust for the person with a disability? If not, will there be money available from insurance or an estate to put toward their care? Financial concern is the area most worrisome for people. There is the fear that there will not be enough money for the care of the loved one throughout their life.

CHAPTER 23

DISABILITIES IN THE EDUCATIONAL REALM

FEDERAL LEGISLATION OVERVIEW

In the K-12 educational realm, there are two laws that govern services for students with disabilities or suspected disabilities. One of these is a civil rights law called the Rehabilitation Act of 1973 (PL 93-112). Section 504 of the Act prohibits exclusion from participation in, or denial of benefits from, federal and federally-funded activities and programs, such as public education, solely on the basis of a person's disability. The protections of Section 504 apply during the K-12 years as well as after a student graduates from high school. It applies to post-secondary education (college) because most colleges and universities accept federal financial assistance.

The other, Public Law 101-476, is called the Individuals with Disabilities Education Act (IDEA). The IDEA is only for the pre-K-12 period of time–while the student is in elementary, middle, and high school. These two laws give students with disabilities a chance to reach their full potential.

Children with disabilities do better in year-round learning situations. Both IDEA and Section 504, along with the regulations that implement them, have provisions for students who need *summer school* if your school district is not on year-round schooling.

The rights of children with disabilities who attend public schools, all of which receive some federal funding, are protected under the IDEA.

If your school district allows the taking of vouchers and you opt to send your child with a disability to a private school, in most states you are waiving your child's rights to the special education services guaranteed under IDEA. Those schools are not <u>required</u> to have therapists or special educators on staff. Vouchers give you a set amount of money that is being taken from the public schools. If the services that your child needs go over this amount, you are the one who needs to pay the difference, if those other services would even be available to your child. In some cases, the public school district where the private school is located may be willing to collaborate in providing some special education services, but this is not guaranteed. If you are considering enrolling your child with a disability in a private school, make sure you know exactly what special services will be provided and by whom.

Mental health services are the largest unmet need of children and families. The schools that are the most successful in dealing with children with mental health issues are those whose staff have been trained in identifying students with such needs and trained in providing for their needs. These schools often collaborate with area agencies to provide training for the staff and/or assistance with therapy/therapeutic activities.

SECTION 504 OF THE REHABILITATION ACT OF 1973

Section 504 is a federal civil rights law designed to protect the rights of individuals with disabilities to participate in federal and federally-assisted programs and activities. This includes educational programs that receive federal financial assistance from the U.S. Department of Education. Recipients of this federal financial assistance include public school districts, institutions of higher education (colleges), and other state and local education agencies. Federal regulations implementing Section 504 require a school district to provide a "free appropriate public education" (FAPE) to each qualified student with a disability who is in the school district's jurisdiction, regardless of the nature or severity of the disability. A FAPE consists of the provision of regular or special education and related aids and services designed to meet the student's individual educational needs as adequately as the needs of non-disabled students are met. A student must be evaluated before any type of services can be provided. Sometimes a student will start out with a *504 plan* while testing and investigation is done to determine what the student's disability is and how best to help the student. After testing, many times a student will then qualify for special education and the provisions of IDEA will kick in with an IEP being written for the student.

A student is qualified under the provisions of Section 504 if he/she is determined to: (1) have a physical or mental impairment that substantially limits one or more major life activities, (2) have a record of such an impairment, or (3) be regarded as having such an impairment. Section 504 regulations define a physical or mental impairment as: (1) any physiological disorder or condition, cosmetic disfigurement, or anatomical loss affecting one or more of the body systems such as neurological, musculoskeletal, special sense organs, respiratory including speech organs, cardiovascular, reproductive, digestive, genitourinary, hemic and lymphatic, skin, and endocrine, or (2) any mental or psychological disorder, such as cognitive disability, organic brain syndrome, emotional or mental illness, and specific learning disabilities. The regulatory provisions do not set forth an exhaustive list of specific diseases and conditions that may constitute physical or mental impairments because of the difficulty of ensuring the comprehensiveness of such a list.

Major life activities, as defined in the Section 504 regulations include functions such as caring for one's self, performing manual tasks, walking, seeing, hearing, speaking, breathing, learning, and working. This list is also not exhaustive. Other functions can be major life activities for purposes of Section 504 such as eating, sleeping, standing, lifting, bending, reading, concentrating, thinking, and communicating. Major bodily functions include such functions as the immune system, normal cell growth, digestive, bowel, bladder, neurological, brain, respiratory, circulatory, endocrine, and reproductive functions.

While IDEA authorizes federal funding and grants to states to support special education services, attaching many specific conditions to the receipt of such funds, Section 504 (and similar laws like the Americans with Disabilities Act) prohibits discrimination against people with disabilities, but does not provide any type of funding.

Section 504 and its implementing regulations require schools to provide students with disabilities appropriate educational services designed to meet the individual needs of such students to the same extent as the needs of students without disabilities are met. An appropriate education for a student with a disability under Section 504 regulations could consist of education in regular classrooms, education in regular classes with supplementary services, and/or special education and related services.

At the elementary and secondary educational level, a "qualified student with a disability" is a student with a disability who is of an age at which students without disabilities are provided elementary and secondary educational services; at an age which is mandatory under state law to provide elementary and secondary educational services to students with disabilities; or a student to whom a state is required to provide a FAPE under the IDEA.

IDEA

In 1975, Congress passed Public Law 94-142; the Education for All Handicapped Children Act which later became PL 101-476 identified as the Individuals with Disabilities Education Act (IDEA). The goal of this federal legislation was to ensure access to a free, appropriate public education, or FAPE, for all children, regardless of disability. In its reauthorization in 1986, provisions were added to extend services to infants and toddlers. In amendments to the law in 1990, the name of the law was changed to the Individuals with Disabilities Education Act (IDEA). It has been reauthorized and/or amended several times since then, in 1997, 2004, and 2010,

A child with a disability refers to children with mental retardation or cognitive disabilities, hearing impairments, speech or language impairments, visual impairments, serious emotional disturbance, orthopedic impairments, autism, traumatic brain injury, other health impairments (this is usually the category under which a malady like Attention Deficit Disorder gets placed), or specific learning disabilities.

The purpose of this federal legislation since 1975 is to ensure that all children with disabilities have available to them a FAPE that emphasizes special education and related services designed to meet their unique needs and prepare them for employment and independent living. It also ensures that the rights of children with disabilities and parents of such children are protected. It assists states, localities, educational service agencies, and Federal agencies to provide for the education of all children with disabilities. This education must be provided at the public expense, under public supervision and direction, and without additional charge to families.

It must meet the standards of the state educational agency and include the appropriate preschool, elementary, and secondary school education in the state involved.

This law states that children with disabilities will have a FAPE available to them between the ages of 3 and 21 (a few states qualify for an exemption & provide services only for children ages 5-18), including children with disabilities who have been suspended or expelled from school. Students with an Individualized Education Plan (IEP) may stay in high school until they are 21.

It is the responsibility of the school district to actively identify, locate, and evaluate all children with disabilities. Once identified and evaluated, an IEP must be developed for each child with a disability and reviewed at least annually. The child must be educated in the "least restrictive environment" (with children who are not disabled) to the maximum extent possible. Children participating in early-intervention programs will experience a smooth and effective transition into preschool programs.

Teachers in either public or private school are supposed to be adequately prepared and trained to manage student behavioral issues in a manner that ensures that children with disabilities are **not suspended or expelled at higher rates than their non-disabled peers.** If there are behavioral/emotional problems, a separate document addressing behaviors can be written targeting the specific behaviors. This is frequently called a "behavior intervention plan" or something similar. The BIP usually covers the same period of time as the IEP, unless the interventions are not working and it needs to be revised more frequently.

Special Education means specifically designed instruction at no cost to parents to meet the unique needs of a child with a disability, including instruction conducted in the classroom, in the home, in hospitals and institutions, and other settings. It also means specifically designed instruction in physical education. When an evaluation is about to be started, a notice will be sent home with a permission slip for the parent(s) to sign giving permission for the evaluation. At that time you should also receive information on what your parental rights are under the law. Read this carefully and keep a copy of it handy.

Evaluations

- The school must conduct a full and individual initial evaluation in order to determine whether a child has a disability and what his/her educational needs are before the provision of special education and related services can be offered.
- Parental consent must be obtained prior to an evaluation.
- Reevaluations must be conducted at least every three years but may be conducted more frequently if the child's parent or teacher requests an earlier reevaluation.
- Evaluations must utilize a variety of assessment tools to gather relevant functional and developmental information.
- The evaluations must assess the relative contribution of cognitive and behavioral factors.
- Evaluations must assess the child in all areas of suspected disability.
- The assessment instruments must be selected so as not to be discriminatory on a racial or cultural basis.
- The instruments must be administered in the child's native language or mode of communication.
- Assessments must be validated for the specific purpose for which they are being used.
- The assessment instrument must be administered by trained personnel in accordance with the instructions provided by the producer.
- A child must have a reevaluation before changing or discontinuing special education.

The Individualized Educational Program (IEP)

The IEP must consist of the following:

- a statement of the child's present levels of educational performance
- a statement of annual goals and short term objectives
- a statement of services to be provided to the child or on behalf of the child
- an explanation of the extent to which the child will be pulled out of the regular classroom (the law states that the child MUST be educated in the Least Restrictive Environment possible)

- a statement regarding modifications to statewide requirements
- the anticipated start date, frequency, location, and duration of services
- a statement of how progress will be monitored, and how the child's parents will be kept informed

The IEP is a legal document, a contract, if you will, that MUST be carried out. It has the force of law.

The IEP team consists of:

- the parents of the child with a disability
- at least one regular education teacher of the child
- at least one special education teacher
- a school representative who supervises special education (frequently an administrator, due to monetary issues)
- an individual who can interpret the instructional implications of the evaluation
- other individuals who have knowledge or expertise regarding the child, invited by the parents
- the child with a disability, whenever appropriate, but especially as the child gets older

Parents have the right to:

- review all of their child's school records
- obtain an independent educational evaluation for their child
- be notified in writing in their native language whenever the school proposes to initiate a change to the IEP (this one may be tricky as school districts are limited in resources of people that may speak the native language as well as monetary resources for translating and printing materials in several languages)
- due process if they feel that an IDEA violation has occurred, such as their child's educational rights being compromised. In this case, they must file a complaint with the school district, with a copy to the state, describing the nature of the problem, along with supporting facts and a proposed resolution.
- mediation to settle disputes between the family and school.

Related Services

Related services means transportation and such developmental, corrective, and other supportive services as may be required to assist a child with a disability to benefit from special education. This can include speech-language pathology and audiology services, psychological services, physical and occupational therapy, recreation including therapeutic recreation, social work services, counseling service, orientation and mobility services, assistive technology, and medical services. There must also be early identification and assessment of disabling conditions in children.

Specific Learning Disabilities

Specific learning disabilities means a disorder in one or more of the basic psychological processes involved in understanding or in using language, spoken or written, which may manifest itself in imperfect ability to listen, think, speak, read, write, spell, or do mathematical calculations. This includes perceptual disabilities, brain injury, minimal brain dysfunction, dyslexia, and developmental aphasia (a language disorder that affects a person's ability to communicate). It, however, does not include learning problems that are primarily the result of visual, hearing, or motor disabilities, cognitive disability, emotional disturbance, and cultural or economic disadvantage.

Transfers Between School Districts

If a student who has been approved for special education services and has an IEP must move to another school district, the new school district is obligated to provide services comparable to those in the previous school district. These services must continue until the previous IEP is adopted or a new IEP is developed, adopted, and implemented, in the case of a transfer in the same state or until a new IEP is developed, in the case of a transfer outside the state.

Discipline

A student with a disability may be removed from his/her regular educational placement if there are serious violations of the school code (i.e., drugs or weapons) just as a non-disabled student would be. In the case of a student with a disability, he/she may be educated in an alternative setting, such as 1:1 with a substitute special education teacher at the local library. Usually if there are behavioral problems, a Functional Behavioral Assessment must be done. If the behavior is found to be part of the child's disability, a treatment plan is written in conjunction with the IEP.

For disciplinary reasons, my younger son was asked not to come back to school for the final two weeks of that particular year. He had an IEP, so I knew that the school district had to offer him something in an alternative setting. The assistant principal dropped Aaron off at home with a stack of worksheets for each of his classes that he was supposed to complete and, then, I was to bring them back to the school. The assistant principal knew that I was a special education teacher in another school district. I looked at him and said, "Now Bob, you and I both know that what you are doing is illegal because Aaron has an IEP and must be educated until the end of the school year." He acknowledged that I was correct and offered a substitute for a couple of hours a day at the local library to help Aaron work on his packets. Since this was high school, I decided to let Aaron decide how the material would be completed. Aaron chose doing them at home with me answering any questions that he might have, thereby letting the school district off the hook for the rest of that school year.

Many school districts use a time-out room or quiet room when a student gets out of control. It is usually a bare room with four walls (usually of concrete block to resist damage), the door, and perhaps a window in the door. (This kind of seclusion room is different than a sensory room, where there are weighted blankets, music, big balls to roll on, etc., to help the child calm down). If your student has a behavioral plan, the use of this room on an as-needed basis may be mentioned in the plan. Please, please, please, monitor the school's use of this room for your student closely. Your son or daughter should not be left in there for long periods of time. It should be a matter of minutes, not hours. (Solitary confinement for long periods is psychologically harmful to anyone, especially a person with mental health issues. It is such a critical international issue that the United Nations has stated that solitary confinement in prisons for more than 15 consecutive days is considered torture.)

The seclusion or timeout room is no different. Especially for people with mental health issues, solitary/seclusion can make matters worse. It may NOT reduce negative behaviors. Used inappropriately, it could amount to punishing the student for having a mental illness. It should be used for the purpose of trying to calm the student's behavior by removing stimuli, and restoring peace to the classroom so that teaching can take place for the other students.

If the behavioral plan includes physical restraining, the same considerations apply. It should be monitored closely. Seclusion and restraint can be options for any student whose behavior is out of control. However, the vast majority of students who require these techniques are special education students (see Chapter 32, Jails and Prisons as Institutions for the Disabled.) If your son or daughter is experiencing these behavioral techniques frequently, I urge you to read through the Parent's Rights brochure that you will get at an IEP meeting. You should then request a meeting with the principal, special education teacher, and district officials to discuss better options and modifications to existing plans. In some cases, you may even need to consider filing due process on your child's behalf. The school needs to find positive behavioral modification methods rather than placing your child in restraints or in a seclusion room. Taking the time to understand the anxiety that triggers a student's outbursts in the first place goes a long way toward lessening the use of seclusion and replacing it with positive behavioral interventions.

Educating a student with severe behavioral issues is about three times more expensive than educating a child in regular education. In the absence of federal legislation that sets minimum standards and strict monitoring and reporting requirements relating to student behavior, disability advocates and parents of students with disabilities warn that school districts will continue to set their own policies and procedures. There have been repeated attempts in Congress over the past several years to establish nationwide standards relating to school discipline, but they have gone nowhere.

If your school district has "zero-tolerance" policies regarding certain types of behavior, the inflexibility of these policies invites the involvement of the criminal justice system into the resolution of problems. This poses a great deal of peril to your child, especially for students with mental health issues. There is a fairness and equity issue here. You need to be a strong advocate for your child and ask that your child **not** be subjected to the school's or district's disciplinary policies if they contain "zero-tolerance." A Functional Behavioral Assessment needs to be done and the behavioral program prepared along with appropriate disciplinary measures. You should also make sure that all school personnel working with your child are trained in classroom management, conflict resolution, and approaches to deescalate classroom disruptions.

Transition from High School

Transition services should begin at age 16. Transition plans should include a statement of inter-agency responsibilities and any needed linkages. I used to invite the Division of Vocational Rehabilitation (DVR) representative to the IEP meetings of all the students on my caseload from age 16 through graduation. This gives parents time to complete DVR applications and gives DVR staff an idea of the needs of the students that will be applying to them for services so they can better manage and prioritize their funding. The DVR can provide funding for continued education at technical schools, community colleges, and universities, as well as for job developers/job coaches to work with your loved one to find full or part-time employment and support them on the job. They can also pay for workplace and equipment adaptations, assistive technology, and similar accommodations.

The whole purpose of transition planning is to provide for smooth and continuous services from high school to the adult world outside of education.

Life After High School

At the postsecondary educational level (college) the institution is required to provide students with appropriate academic adjustments and auxiliary aids and services that are necessary to afford an individual with a disability an equal opportunity to participate in a school's program. However, postsecondary institutions are not required to make adjustments or provide aids or services that would result in a fundamental alteration of a class/program or impose an undue burden upon the institution/instructor.

Postsecondary students can get special services after they "self-disclose" that they have a disability and request these services. This falls under Section 504 of Civil Rights Law as once a student graduates from high school, they are no longer under IDEA. Usually a postsecondary school will want a copy of a high school IEP if the student is coming directly from high school. If the student is coming from the work world and has had some sort of disabling accident, the school may want medical records or a report from Division of Vocational Rehabilitation (DVR). Services provided can be something as simple as extra time on tests and/or testing in a different location, or technological assistance such as a textbook uploaded to a computer that will read the textbook audibly.

The really scary part of life is when your loved one "ages" out of the K-12 school system and enters the adult system. The transition from a structured day to having little or nothing to do in the adult world can cause the young adult to start regressing. It is imperative that transition services are talked about and parents do their homework about what adult services their state offers for whatever challenges their loved one has. Depending upon your loved one's needs, the adult system in your state may or may not have the services that are needed. If there are services, frequently there are long waiting lists for those services. As a special education teacher, I always invited the Division of Vocational Rehabilitation (DVR) representative assigned to our school to attend the junior/senior Individual Education Plan (IEP) meeting so she could explain to the parents what services DVR would pay for in the adult arena and give the parents a packet of other information.

A FINAL NOTE OF CONCERN

Parents of students with disabilities need to remain vigilant concerning their child's education. If an older high school student's disability is making education too difficult, or their mental health issues are causing problematic behaviors that are interfering with learning and/or getting them into trouble, he/she might want to drop out of school. It is not uncommon for students with disabilities to drop out of school if the going gets too tough and they are not being supported adequately to be successful. Parents need to do everything they can to make their students' educational experiences as positive as possible and be a tireless advocate for them, in their IEP meetings, with classroom teachers, and with the school district administration. My older son, Eric, told me that he almost dropped out of school due to the challenges he faced, especially with bullying.

CHAPTER 24

SOCIAL SITUATIONS

Social situations with children can be challenging. Many a parent has carried their kicking, screaming child out of a social gathering. A disability can add complex dimensions to social situations and sometimes serious problems. Depending upon what the disability is, social situations may be very difficult for the child (or adult). He/she is out of his/her normal realm being asked to interact with others in *socially appropriate* ways. Children are expected to *play nice* with other children and *share*. The social time may interfere with their normal nap/sleep time or their meal schedule. The food being served may be totally different from what they are used to. And mom and dad are trying to have adult conversations with the other adults and not paying as much attention to the kids.

Some people are very uncomfortable being around a child with a disability because the child's behavior may be problematic. Sometimes comments are made about the child's disability or their behavior that can be very hurtful to the parents. I have met many parents who were feeling as isolated as my husband and I were because we were not invited to social events, or asked that we not bring our children when we were invited. Sometimes we even were specifically asked not to participate at all in some events. We were told that the behavior of one of our sons would be a bad influence on the other children. That really hurt. That was a church-sponsored event. With whom should my son associate to learn appropriate behavior if not people from church? Several years later, we were asked to be adult leaders for this event; I could not say yes because I was still hurting. Maybe that will change in the future.

We have encouraged our son, Aaron, to join some groups that we thought would be of interest to him and offer positive social relationships. His brother and sister-in-law are involved in one of those groups, so we thought that might make it more comfortable for him. Another group is composed of formerly incarcerated people, like him, but he only knows one person that belongs to that group. He has been reluctant to join any of the groups we have recommended to him. He is once again incarcerated.

Social events can be challenging even for adults with disabilities. Our oldest son, Eric, suffers from high anxiety. He also suffers from irritable bowel syndrome with vomiting. He was not able to complete post-high school education and training because the social interactions in class, with fellow students making comments about his clumsiness, made him anxious, upset his stomach and his esophageal ulcer, leading to him throwing up, sometimes in the classroom wastebasket! This, of course, created more of a social stigma, so it became a vicious circle. One class met every day for three and a half hours. If he got sick in the first hour and sent home, he missed a lot of school. Consequently, he didn't get very good grades.

Many times, a person with a disability needs to be coached as to what is appropriate behavior in a group, such as:

- Don't dominate the conversation
- Give the other people a chance to talk
- Look for social cues such as other people trying to make a comment, or a person needing to go on to another task
- Notice if someone to whom you're speaking seems to be lost trying to follow your conversation
- Be aware of appropriate personal spacing

Eric and Natasha belong to a group that is made up of people with disabilities. They are supposed to be quiet when it isn't their turn to talk and pay attention to the person speaking. Sometimes they find it very hard to focus when someone else in the group is being disruptive by talking loudly or laughing, or perhaps kicking one of them if sitting next to them. They get so agitated that they leave the group early because they are about to *blow*. Learning how to deal appropriately with and tolerate these situations is important for all people, but especially challenging for those with disabilities. Everyone needs to be given a chance.

CHAPTER 25

EMPLOYMENT OF OTHER ABLED

Title II of the Americans with Disabilities Act (ADA) of 1990 prohibits discrimination on the basis of disability by state and local governments.

The largest unemployed segment of the population is people with disabilities. People with a disability may have a difficult time landing a job. Because they often have less work experience, they may not even get an interview, especially if an employer is just looking through applications.

I remember Dr. Temple Grandin telling that she had to have a portfolio of her work to show and always had to go in to talk to employers because she didn't feel that she would be admitted to college or jobs just based on the paperwork alone. That is how she got all of her degrees and all of her employment.

Many people with disabilities find it difficult to work a full time job. Their disabilities are just too limiting. However, most want to work up to their abilities. They want to feel valued. They want to use their talents to be a contributing member of society. They want to be given a chance. And they should be able to. Companies that are proactive in employing people with disabilities say that, although it takes a lot of initial work to include them, and there were times that they didn't think it was going to work out, they are glad they persevered. The analysis of 140 companies showed profit margins 30% higher for those that had taken a focused interest in inclusion of workers with disabilities. Employers with disability inclusion practices were also found to have revenues that were 38% higher than those without.[26] For every dollar spent to rehabilitate a person with disabilities for employment, ten or more dollars are returned to our economy.[27]

Hiring people with disabilities sometimes takes a great deal of understanding. "If you take an individual—any individual—and give them the opportunity and the support they need, they're going to succeed," said one employment manager. Once they had the understanding, employers found that people with disabilities were marvelous workers and a valuable asset to their companies. The people were totally integrated into the company and formed friendships with others in the company, both abled and disabled.

A marvelous quote from film studio executive Victoria Alonso is, "People with autism have a remarkable talent *we* need. *They* need a place they can have a future. And we [as society] need to make change. It was a perfect symbiosis. I was 100% in."[28] Other employers are starting to give people with disabilities a chance, but there are still great strides that need to be made. Many people in power need to be educated about what a person with a disability can offer them and their business. While some with disabilities are making inroads and being employed, others with disabilities who have successfully held a job for years are suddenly being terminated by a new owner of the business who doesn't understand the person with the disability or what this person can provide to the business.

People with physical disabilities usually know what their limitations are and can advocate for themselves regarding any accommodations that might be needed to successfully perform their job.

Each state's Division of Vocational Rehabilitation usually has job developers and job coaches that can be helpful in advocating with employers, setting up appointments, and "greasing the skids," so to speak, about a person's abilities and talents for a particular job. There are frequently county human service agencies that may do the same thing, especially for people with developmental disabilities. There are for-profit as well as

[26] Anna Gouker, "Hiring People with Disabilities Makes Good Business Sense," *The Cap Times* (Madison, WI), January 8, 2020.
[27] Jennifer Weir, *CODI: Cornucopia of Disability Information*, http://codi.tamucc.edu/index.html.
[28] S.C. Stuart, "At This VFX Studio, Artists with Autism Make Magic for Marvel," *PC Magazine*, August 23, 2017; https://www.pcmag.com/news/at-this-vfx-studio-artists-with-autism-make-magic-for-marvel.

non-profit private companies that also do job coaching. In some locations, cooperatives have been started to provide work for people with disabilities.

A job developer is a person that works with an employer to develop a customized job for a person with a disability. They usually start by finding out what the person is interested in, what they are good at, and what types of tasks they could see themselves successfully doing on a job. They ask the person what areas they might like to work in. The job developer then makes cold calls to specific businesses on behalf of the person with a disability. They may ask the owner/manager what tasks don't get done because everyone else is too busy. These are usually such things such as emptying the wastebaskets, filing, stocking, general cleaning, etc. In restaurants it could be wrapping silverware, making some sauce, cleaning tables, doing dishes, doing the laundry, or folding laundry. The job developer then introduces the possibility of this specific person working for this company. The job developer explains what the person's disability is, what the individual can do for the employer to increase operational efficiency, usually for some amount of money around minimum wage. They may even have a copy of the person's resume to show the prospective employer. If the employer is agreeable, there is usually a *meet and greet* set up so the employer can meet the individual and do an interview. This meeting is valuable for both the employer and the prospective employee; the employer gets to meet the person and the person with a disability can see the physical layout of the business and meet some of the employees. Both parties can gauge whether there is an appropriate employment opportunity here.

A job coach is a person that assists a person with a disability learn and settle into the job. The job coach and the employer may make up a list of tasks the person is expected to do and then the job coach is responsible for training the person with a disability in these tasks. The job coach serves as an intermediary between the employer and the new employee. Sometimes a job coach will even do the job if the person they are supporting is ill and cannot report to work. The job coach remains with the employee until they can successfully complete the tasks to an acceptable standard by themselves. The job coach then continues to check in weekly, then monthly, until their oversight is no longer necessary. The job developer and job coach may be the same person or they may be different people.

There is a presumption by many employers that everyone has certain basic reasoning and people skills, and they expect those skills to be used. Most people usually pick up these skills in their family, in school, or by osmosis. These assumptions disadvantage many people with disabilities, especially those with developmental disabilities. People with these challenges often need to be specifically taught many of the *soft skills*— being on time to work, calling in when ill, interacting appropriately with coworkers, completing all tasks, and similar skills. Without a job developer or job coach, a person with disabilities may not succeed because they lack these fundamental work skills.

Without a job coach, a person may be fired because they don't remember all the tasks they are supposed to do or are too slow in completing them. A young woman I know wasn't fired from her job but, because she was too slow in doing her job, her employer kept reducing her hours until she wasn't being scheduled to work at all. I strongly suggested that her parents contact our *bridge builder* who had helped develop a job for and coach our son. The last time I talked with our bridge builder, she said she was going to start working with the young woman to see if she could help lay a foundation for the young woman to be successful at her current job and, if not, to find another job she would enjoy and at which she could be successful.

Our daughter-in-law, Natasha, got a great part-time job at a veterinary clinic doing filing, laundry, and sweeping and mopping. She is very good with animals and loves the job. She has successfully transitioned to not having the job coach check in more than quarterly and is doing nicely on her own. In fact, they have increased her hours on the job.

Our bridge builder helped our son, Eric, get a job as a garage attendant at an auto repair shop specializing in foreign cars. He struggles with sticking to a task until completion and has difficulty with monitoring and evaluating the quality and thoroughness of his work. One day, he blew up at his job coach and walked off the job. His employer, who was semi-retired, had made a special effort to come in early that day to work with Eric and now Eric was leaving. For most people, this would have been the end of their job. The value of having a job coach is that this person can run interference with the employer and explain that sometimes things like this happen with a person with disabilities, that this is a temporary setback. It just cannot become a pattern.

When Eric's employer suddenly sold the business to one of the mechanics, Eric lost his job. We had known that this was a possibility. Since we were going on a planned vacation trip, we decided not to worry about it until we got back. While on vacation, the job coach met with the new owner and asked if he had noticed a difference in how the shop looked with Eric doing clean-up work, and did he want to continue having Eric perform these tasks so he and the other mechanic could focus on the revenue-producing repair work. The new owner rehired Eric.

There was a lot of uncertainty concerning job tasks as another person was taking over. Eric can successfully perform his tasks. However, he sometimes feels overwhelmed and afraid that he isn't doing a good job (even with reassurances from everyone). The money ran out for Eric to have his job coach with him all the time, so his dad coached him for a while. This initially consisted of going to work with Eric, sitting there doing other things while Eric performed his tasks, and periodically checking-in with Eric. A few times when his dad needed to run errands, leaving Eric alone, proved to be too challenging psychologically for him. The anxiety would cause Eric to throw up and need to leave work. However, now that the business has moved to a much smaller, nicer facility, Tom is still taking Eric but does not stay. Eric successfully completes his tasks independently. There still are issues with Eric throwing up when his anxiety gets the best of him, but we are working on that and it has lessened greatly. Next step: get him to go to work on his own when we are out of town.

A fantastic program in British Columbia has started fourteen (to date) cooperative working programs. They find out what people with disabilities are interested in making or doing as work, do an analysis to see if there is a market for the product or service, and secure capital. They have also started an artisan workshop and store. They have people with disabilities who are very creative. The group secured a spot at the local farmers' market. They were well received and able to sell a fair amount. They decided the artists would spend the winter building up inventory. They did and now have a retail store. One painting artisan has done so well that he has outgrown the cooperative and is getting ready to show in a local gallery.

Another employment scenario for people with disabilities is job sharing between or among people. For instance, a movie theater might hire a team of two or four people with disabilities to work shifts to clean up popcorn, candy wrappers, and beverage containers once a movie is over. If one person can't make it to work, they can call one of their team to fill in. Sometimes even the best of plans don't work out; a person with a disability may lose his/her janitorial job because a janitorial company is hired to clean the business where they had worked.

It is often easier for a person with a cognitive disability to get and keep a job than it is for someone with a mental illness. While people with cognitive impairments may be hired to do more lower skill level jobs, they seem to be able to remain happier in their jobs for longer. Individuals with mental illness or anxiety issues, like our son Eric, seem to have a more difficult time sustaining their employment because of their mental health issues. As discussed above, they may be more apt to *fly off the handle* about something and walk out or not show up.

I taught with a lady who had bipolar disorder. She was able to work full-time for most of her career. However, there were a couple of times when she would have to go on short-term disability leave because her bipolar disorder was not under good control. She needed to stay home from work to simplify that part of her life until medication adjustments were made and she could fully function again in all arenas.

CHAPTER 26

HOUSING

Depending upon a person's specific disability, living arrangements could be *dependent*, such as an institution; *semi-independent* such as a foster or group home, a house/apartment with a care-giver, or with a family member; or *independent*, such as a house, condo, or apartment.

Most young adults think about living on their own, even if they might not be capable of doing so. They want to be like their non-disabled peers and do the same things they are doing, moving out of their parents' home and into their own. They just want to be given a chance.

Eric's first foray into *independent* living came with answering an ad for subletting an apartment for five months, from November through March. The apartment was about six blocks from our house. We had an available twin bed so Eric took that along with his dresser, night stand, desk, entertainment center, and TV. I had some outdoor furniture that was about to come in the house for the winter so Eric took two Adirondack chairs, a love seat, and a couple of end tables. He had a card table, four chairs, all the kitchen equipment he needed, and a vacuum cleaner, so he had all the basic furnishings he needed. We bought a shower curtain liner and he used an old shower curtain and hooks that we had. All in all, he was pretty well set.

It was a good experience for him. His girlfriend, Natasha, frequently took the bus or drove her mom's car to visit Eric at the apartment. Sometimes she even stayed overnight, or tried to. Because we had co-signed for the apartment, we had the extra key and when either Eric or Tasha wouldn't answer their cell phones, we would go over to the apartment to check on them. In their early twenties, they longed for the opportunity to live like their non-disabled peers and were enjoying a measure of freedom.

Freedom and independence is wonderful, to a point. Eric found that while he was enjoying some freedom, he was also extremely anxious and throwing up almost every day. He had never been responsible for opening important mail that needed responses, making repairs in living situations without a lot of guidance, deciding what to eat and preparing it, or living in close proximity with anyone but his family. Needless to say, there were a few interesting relationship issues with neighbors, having him call us with a maintenance problem, or finding out after the fact that the landlord expected something that hadn't been accomplished. After his five-month experience of being independent, Eric asked if he could come back home to get his life together while trying to decide what he wanted to do.

If your loved one with a disability cannot work full-time, he/she is probably on SSI and/or SSDI. Neither of these programs pays a lot and it is difficult to rent an apartment, pay utilities, and buy food and incidentals on that amount of money. Our son and his girlfriend live together. They are able to meet these basic expenses through combining the disability benefits each of them receives from these programs. They would like to get married, but cannot because they would lose one half of their SSI as well as coverage through their parent's medical insurance. For two people living together with a combined SSI income of only about $1,800 a month, losing half is devastating.

Mortgage lenders and landlords recommend that what you pay for housing should not exceed 30 percent of your gross income, no matter what your income is. So, if you are looking at a particular unit to rent, if it is more than 30 percent of your gross income, you probably will not be accepted. Eric and Natasha could qualify for Section 8 federally subsidized housing, but in our area there is a very long waiting list, which is probably true in many areas. With Section 8, apartment managers or owners agree to only charge one third of a person's income, regardless of the amount for which the unit normally rents. Therefore, if an apartment normally rents for $800 per month, in Eric and Natasha's case, they would not be charged more than $600 per month for a Section 8 housing unit because their combined income is about $1,800.

Some locales where people might want to live do not have landlords willing to accept Section 8 renters. Many landlords believe people on Section 8 are lower-class and/or trouble-makers and don't want to rent to them. Discrimination? Yes, but hard to prove. Often, if there is Section 8 housing, it may be concentrated in one part of a city where there tends to be higher public safety concerns or other issues such as limited access to public transportation.

We put in an application to one apartment complex that took Section 8. It had its own police sub-station because there were so many public safety problems. Believing that all low-income people create problems is just as stereotypical as believing that all people with disabilities cause problems. Neither is true. However, these patterns of housing are very real and challenging for those with limited incomes.

The federal Fair Housing Act of 1968 and Fair Housing Amendments Act of 1988 (42 USC 3601 *et seq.*) prohibits discrimination in the sale, rental, or the advertising and showing of available housing to prospective buyers or renters because of a disability or the disability of a person associated with them. The law protects people who:

- have physical or mental disability that substantially limits one or more major life activities/areas—including, but not limited to:
  o mobility impairments
  o hearing impairments
  o visual impairments
  o chronic alcoholism (if it is being addressed through a recovery program)

- o   mental illness
- o   HIV, AIDS, and AIDS-Related Complex, or
- o   cognitive disability
- •   have a history of such a disability, or
- •   are regarded by others as though they have such a disability

When a tenant or a prospective tenant has not asked for accommodation, the Fair Housing Act, as amended, prohibits the landlord from asking whether the applicant or a person intending to live in the rental has a disability or about the severity of the impairments. They cannot ask to read medical records. Landlords must treat disabled applicants and tenants in the same way as those without a disability.

However, a landlord may ask all prospective tenants, including disabled applicants, about whether they can meet the financial requirements of the tenancy, whether they abuse or are addicted to an illegal controlled substance, whether the applicant qualifies for a rental unit available only to people with a disability or a certain type of disability, and whether the applicant qualifies for a rental unit that is offered on a priority basis to people with a disability or with a certain type of disability.

If you or a member of your household have a mental or emotional health disability, or appear to such, a potential landlord may only evaluate you on the basis of your financial ability to pay the rent and your past history as a tenant, not on the basis of your mental health. The landlord may reject you only if he/she can point to specific instances of past behavior that would make you a threat to the safety of others (such as information from a previous landlord that you repeatedly threatened or that you harmed other residents). If you cannot meet the good-tenant criteria that the landlord applies to all applicants (such as a minimum rent-to-income ratio), you may be rejected on that basis, though landlords must consider a possible cosigner if you are otherwise qualified for the rental except for your income. In our case, my husband cosigned the lease with Eric and Natasha when they first moved into an apartment together which cost more per month than one third of their income. Since then, a new management company reduced their rent so that it was more in line with the one-third rule. However, my husband continued to sign each lease. My husband also managed to get written into the lease an MOU (memorandum of understanding) that accompanies the lease, a statement that Eric and Natasha can give as little as ninety-days' notice to break their lease with no penalty if they were ever eligible to get a house.

Landlords may not require tenants to be capable of independent living. Landlords must accommodate the needs of disabled tenants within reason at the landlord's own expense, such as installing grab bars in bathrooms. You can expect your landlord to reasonably adjust rules, procedures, or services in order to give you an equal opportunity to use and enjoy your dwelling unit or a common space. Accommodations can include such things as parking. Providing a close-in spacious parking space would be an accommodation for a tenant who uses a wheelchair. If you need a guide dog or other service animal, your landlord cannot say no just because the building has a no-pet policy. Landlords are expected to accommodate reasonable requests, but they don't have to make changes that would seriously impair their ability to run their business. For example, a landlord would not need to install an elevator for an applicant who uses crutches and prefers a third-story apartment. That expense would be unreasonable.

Landlords must allow tenants with disabilities to make reasonable modifications to their living unit or common areas at their own expense if needed for the person to live comfortably and safely in the unit. Modifying the space is acceptable as long as the modifications will not make the unit unacceptable to a future tenant, or if you are willing to undo the modification when you leave. Examples include lowering countertops, installing a ramp into a raised or sunken living room if you use a wheelchair, and installing special faucets or door handles for persons with limited dexterity in their hands. Obviously, any such modifications need to have prior approval from the landlord.

Landlords must tell you about all vacancies in their building and then let you decide which apartments are suitable for you. They cannot charge you a different amount of rent regardless of your disability.

Should you be in a lease and become disabled through an accident, or have a progressive illness that gets worse to the point where it is difficult to continue living in your current situation, and accommodations are not feasible, you may legally break the lease without penalty. Examples would be someone in a car accident who becomes a paraplegic, or someone suffering from Parkinson Disease or Multiple Sclerosis who was ambulatory before but now must use a wheel chair. If the door to the bathroom is not wide enough for the wheel chair to go through or the bathroom isn't big enough for the wheel chair to turn or maneuver, this would no longer be a safe and comfortable environment in which to live. Ripping out walls to make the bathroom bigger would not be considered a feasible accommodation. In this case, you would likely be asking the landlord to release you from the lease early or seeking to sublet your apartment for the remainder of the lease. A person who is physically disabled needs to live in a place that is safe and accessible.

Climate can be a big access issue as well. If you live in northern states that get snow, it is difficult to negotiate a wheelchair in snow, slush, and ice. You may be going out or coming home before there has been a chance to clear walkways and parking lots. Or the snow may have been cleared, but then plows came around and blocked a sidewalk egress that had been open.

I know several parents who have purchased a house or condo for their child with a disability so the loved one would have a place to live that is theirs and not subject to the uncertainties of a property management company. I also know of one family whose adult child needed a care giver. That family purchased a three-bedroom condo for their child and her care giver so the care giver was assured her own space.

Group homes, nursing homes, and assisted living facilities are all options as living arrangements depending on the amount of care needed by the person with the disability. I have known people in each of these living situations. Availability will depend upon the community where the person with the disability resides. I know of two individuals who were under 55 years of age and lived at my mom's assisted living facility. One had physical disabilities and the other had emotional disabilities.

In our community, there is a program called Movin' Out that provides down payment financial assistance to people with disabilities who are trying to purchase a house or condo. This funding is available as interest-free loans to adults with disabilities as well as to parents of children with disabilities, if purchasing a dwelling can somehow help the individual with the disability remain independent. For example, if a family living in an apartment had a child with a disability who did a lot of screaming and were asked to leave because of disturbance to other tenants, this family could qualify for this funding. The funding to purchase a home of their own would benefit the child and family by not having to move constantly because of the behaviors. Some of this money is federal, coming from the Federal Housing Administration; some is local, coming from cities; some is private, coming from banks that lend money for mortgages. Some of the loaned money is *forgivable* after the person has lived in the house for 5 years. Most of the money is a loan that only needs to be repaid if the house or condo is sold. These loans can be a substantial amount of money.

Eric and Natasha applied to Movin' Out for money to be able to get into a home of their own. My husband and I (and occasionally Eric and Natasha) looked at properties for about 3 years before we found something that we thought might be suitable for them. Now, with a property in mind, we learned that one of the requirements to get the money from Movin' Out is that they still needed to be spending 30-40% of their income for housing. The property was a condo which had a monthly Home Owners Association (HOA) fee, but in order to meet Movin' Out's guideline, they still had to apply for and take out a mortgage loan as part of the purchase. Here are two people living below the poverty level and the only way they can make things work financially is to *share* a dwelling and expenses and they are being told that they need to get a mortgage in order to qualify for the Movin' Out down-payment funding! They were approved for a $65,000 mortgage, but only needed $60,000.

While Eric and Natasha had found a condominium that they liked, I thought it was too small and was not in favor of a condo because of the HOA fees which were high and always go up. Nevertheless, they decided to put in an offer. It was accepted by the seller and agreed to by Movin' Out and the bank through which they were getting the mortgage. Both Natasha's mother and we gifted them some money to meet the purchase price. They were required by Movin' Out to attend some classes on home ownership and they chose to attend a couple others that were offered. They got the condo and moved in 2 months later. This made closing a huge "family affair" as not only were Eric and Tasha, the two sellers, and the title company there, but also Natasha's mom, me, our realtor, the bank providing the mortgage, and staff from Movin' Out. (And the HOA fee did go up between the purchase agreement and closing, and also every year since!) They are very happy in their condo now and, since getting a kitten, feel their life is complete. They still need a lot of assistance from the parents and their Bridge Builder to maintain their dwelling in a safe and sanitary manner.

CHAPTER 27

TRANSPORTATION

Transportation provides a vital lifeline for most people. It is essential for medical appointments, jobs, grocery shopping, and so many other activities of life. It is just as essential, maybe more so for people with disabilities. It allows them to live as independently as possible within their communities. In addition to The Rehabilitation Act of 1973, which provides protection for people with disabilities in the area of transportation, The Americans with Disabilities Act (ADA) of 1990, as amended, requires accessibility in public transportation by intercity and commuter rail and for public transportation other than by aircraft or certain rail operations.

Even with these two landmark federal laws, there may still be issues of accessibility for people with disabilities. Sometimes authorized programs and policies are not implemented or there isn't sufficient funding to implement them. Even if the transportation is available, sometimes there are other factors preventing peoples with disabilities from accessing the transportation, such as snow on sidewalks making walking or using a wheelchair not only extremely difficult, but also very dangerous.

PARATRANSIT

Paratransit is an alternative mode of flexible passenger transportation that does not follow fixed routes or schedules, and can offer door-to-door service that is particularly important for people with disabilities. These services often have modified vans that are equipped with lifts to accommodate passengers who use wheelchairs. Paratransit passengers must be certified as eligible to use the services, which usually consist of filing an application that describes the person's disability, explains why he/she is unable to use regular transit, and requires the signature of a health care professional. Eligible passengers usually receive a special card that allows them to purchase paratransit fares and schedule rides on the system. Paratransit services to medical appointments are paid for by Medicaid. A person eligible for services must use the Medicaid services as opposed to taxi services to get to their medical appointments.

Paratransit services must be provided by a public entity that also operates a fixed route service, so these services may be provided by a city, county or a state. They may contract out this service. The law says all new vehicles purchased or leased by these public entities must be accessible (retrofitting of existing vehicles is not required), and good faith efforts must be demonstrated with regard to the purchase or lease of accessible used vehicles. Paratransit services are frequently limited by budget constraints in most geographic areas. If the transit authority contracts out the paratransit services, it needs to closely monitor the reliably of the provision of the service. The public entity needs to track the number of complaints and find solutions so people with disabilities can get to the services and medical appointments they need in a timely manner.

I have heard many complaints about paratransit services. Their complaints are that the service doesn't come, it comes late to pick them up and then very early for the return trip, gets lost even on regular standing rides for the individual with a disability, or gets cancelled at the last minute. In just one area of our state, there were more than 4,000 paratransit no-shows and more than 55,000 late rides in about a 9 month time-frame. If multiplied across all US communities, this is a truly awful picture. No-show or late rides cause many medical appointments to be missed—appointments which may have taken the person weeks or months to set up. Having to try to reschedule and start this process all over again is a needless complication and frustration for people with disabilities. Medical services are an integral part of their lives and not being able to get there causes many problems.

OVER-THE-ROAD BUSES

Over-the-road buses are buses with an elevated passenger deck located over a baggage compartment. In 1998, the US Department of Transportation published a regulation requiring a large bus company's entire fleet to comply with the ADA's accessibility requirements by October 2012. Smaller bus companies must provide an accessible bus with 48 hours advance notice that a patron needs an accessible bus. The Over-the-Road Bus Transportation Accessibility Act of 2007 (PL 110-291) requires the Federal Motor Carrier Safety Administration to consider a bus company's compliance with the 1998 regulation when deciding whether to grant a company authority to operate in interstate commerce. In March 2006, the House of Representatives held hearings on *curbside* bus companies. These companies operate bus routes that pick up and drop off passengers along a road or street rather than at a terminal, primarily in the Northeast Corridor of the US. These companies were often ignoring compliance with the ADA and this was one factor leading to the 2007 law.

The enactment of the 2007 law helped to enforce the provisions in ADA that apply to over-the-road buses. By now, the entire fleet of large bus companies must meet accessibility standards. Over-the-road buses must not deny transportation to passengers with disabilities, require or request a passenger with a disability to reschedule his or her trip, or require individuals other than the bus staff to assist with boarding a passenger with a disability. For small bus companies, accessible services must be provided on 48 hours advance notice, and passengers should be aware of their rights if an over-the-road bus company does not comply with the law.

AMTRAK

Amtrak has increased its ridership by 32 percent between 2002 and 2008. Within that ridership, 288,000 were passengers with disabilities. Although all Amtrak trains meet or exceed the requirements of ADA, not all stations are accessible. Currently, 94 percent of Amtrak passengers board at accessible stations. Congress mandated a deadline of July 26, 2010, for all stations to be accessible, but Amtrak does not have enough funding to make this a reality. It is estimated Amtrak will need $1.6 billion to complete this work, but Congress has only allocated $144 million.

AIR TRAVEL

The Air Carrier Access Act (ACAA) of 1986 was reauthorized in 2009 and ensures that individuals with disabilities can utilize aircraft travel. Like many other disability policies, enforcement of ACAA has been inconsistent. Airlines are required to provide assistance with boarding, deplaning, and making connections; they cannot count assistive devices against the number of pieces of carry-on baggage a person may take; and wheelchairs and other assistive devices have priority for storage in the baggage compartment. The reauthorization in May 2009 included a provision to apply the ACAA to foreign carriers, making international travel easier for passengers with disabilities. Nonetheless, airline staff are frequently inadequately trained to serve customers with disabilities, and many passengers are treated unfairly, abandoned on the plane upon landing, or are returned broken wheelchairs or other equipment. It is important for passengers to know their rights before going to the airport to ease the flying process.

CHAPTER 28

SEX AND OTHER
FUN STUFF

It is not realistic to think that your child will not want to have sex when the hormones start raging. While individuals with developmental delays may not understand what is going on in their body, the hormones are still there and there is a desire for sexual gratification, even if it is not comprehended. You as the parent need to be ready for this and equipped to deal with it.

We talked with both of our sons about sex, protection, and responsibility. We even bought a package of condoms. That didn't mean that they always used them however! The image of my son's bare bottom in the air humping his girlfriend when I walked in on them on Christmas afternoon will remain in my memory for a very long time.

We had some friends who adopted a couple of cognitively challenged boys. One of the stories they told us was that one of the boys found a girlfriend through the sheltered workshop they attended. She would come over to the house and he would go over to her house. One time our friend found them engaged in sex and was absolutely horrified. Our friend went to his priest to talk to him about it. The priest very wisely counseled our friend that the two of them were doing what came naturally. It didn't matter that they had a disability and really didn't understand what was happening. This was a normal part of physically maturing and they were just doing what their bodies told them to do. He suggested that our friend talk to the young man and provide him with some condoms and that they talk to the girl's mother and perhaps get her on birth control, but not make the young people feel as though they had done anything wrong. Wise counsel.

I had a student in high school that during his freshman year got five girls pregnant. This young man with a 72 I.Q. (just barely above the cognitively disabled range) would never be able to financially support or be a parent to one child, let alone the vast number he could procreate in his long reproductive years. Social workers from school and the county talked to him. The police talked to him because the girls were all freshman too (13 years old). Nothing seemed to get through to him that this was not acceptable. When these adults told him that he needed to wear a condom if he was going to engage in intercourse, he replied that it "didn't feel as good" when wearing a condom so he wasn't going to do it!

One day I received a call from my younger son who had just gotten out of jail after about 90 days. He had been calling his friends to tell them that he was out. One of his female friends informed him that she had contracted an STD (sexually-transmitted disease), probably from him, which meant that he had contracted it from someone else. He was calling to say that he probably needed to see a doctor. When I hung up, I burst out laughing. My colleagues asked what the phone call was about that made me laugh. When I told them, they asked how I could laugh at that. I replied, "What else was I supposed to do?" I guess this is one example of being able to compartmentalize our lives. For us, it was just another thing to deal with, but ultimately of no earth shattering importance.

People with disabilities frequently cannot legally marry without jeopardizing disability benefits they may have. Our son, Eric, and his girlfriend of fifteen years, Natasha, wanted to get married but they would have lost one half of their SSI. Each of them would also have lost coverage under their parent's health insurance. In 2006 they got an apartment together and split the bills. However, they wanted something more formal.

I started researching commitment ceremonies. Natasha's mother said her church had done some commitment ceremonies. We pursued having a commitment ceremony, i.e., a wedding-style ceremony and reception without the state paperwork, for the two of them. Friends and family were most supportive of both *the kids* and of us parents. We set a date and made all the arrangements. Friends and family came from near and far to witness their commitment to each other. A *real wedding* couldn't have been any more special than this ceremony was.

Eric and Natasha belong to a bowling group for individuals with disabilities. The group decided to have a *bridal shower* for them. Eric and Natasha registered at a few stores and got a lot of the items for which they registered as either *shower* or *wedding* gifts. The whole ceremony experience was very special. Eric, who usually throws up when he gets really nervous or anxious, was like a rock. I asked him if he was nervous. He said, "A little, but this is the best day of my life. I am *marrying* my best friend!"

Again, people with disabilities have the same needs and desires for their lives as people without disabilities and should be able to pursue their dreams just as anyone else can. They want to be *like others* in activities in their life and be able to pursue the same milestones—to be given a chance.

CHAPTER 29

SSI/SSDI

Only a minority of people with disabilities actually qualifies for SSI or SSDI (disability income) since "total disability" or inability to work is a requirement to qualify for such income.

Supplemental Security Income (SSI) is a program for people who are either age 65, blind, or disabled with a medically determinable physical or mental impairment that prevents them from working and who also do not have other income or resources to meet basic needs. Social Security Disability Insurance (SSDI) is a program that pays benefits to you and certain family members if you have worked long enough, and recently enough, and paid Social Security taxes on your earnings. People who have become disabled and are no longer able to support themselves through working can draw on this Social Security benefit. Both of these programs generally provide an income that is below the poverty level. Both require extensive paperwork and investigation into and documentation of the disability. Frequently medical records have to be reviewed and sometimes even an appointment with a psychologist or physician of Social Security's choosing is a requirement.

Both of my children have qualified for SSI, neither having worked long enough to qualify on their own for SSDI. However, once I started drawing Social Security at age 65, both of my sons qualified for SSDI, based on the number of quarters that I logged while working. If the SSDI monthly benefit is lower than the monthly benefit a person would be eligible for under SSI, then they get both the SSDI and an amount of SSI to make up the difference for a total of what the SSI amount would be.

Medical services are paid for by either Medicaid or Medicare or both. Medicaid (or Medical Assistance—MA) is a joint program of the federal and state governments that provides payment for health-related services for people who fall into certain categories and who meet financial requirements for program eligibility. Medicaid or *EBD* Medicaid is for elderly, blind, disabled (EBD). It pays for medical, rehabilitation, and support services for people who are over age 65 or who meet the disability or blindness requirements for SSI plus limits on income and resources. Most people on who qualify for SSI also qualify for MA.

You may be eligible for Social Security Disability Insurance based on having a disability if you meet the test for having worked and paid Social Security taxes or you are an adult child of a parent who paid Social Security taxes, your parent is now disabled, retired, or deceased, and you have a disability that began before age 22. A person who receives SSDI benefits becomes eligible for Medicare coverage twenty-four months after they start receiving those benefits even if they are under age 65.

Medicare provides health insurance, but coverage is much more limited than that provided by Medicaid, particularly for long-term support services. Medicare also requires you to pay substantial premiums, deductibles, and co-payments. You can also buy private Medicare *supplemental insurance* to help pay the deductibles and co-payments. If SSI or SSDI is your only source of income, frequently, Medicaid and/or the state you are living in will pay the Medicare monthly premium because of your low income.

Whether a disabled child receives any of these benefits can depend on the total family income. If the family income is too high, the disabled child might still be able to get Medicaid and can then qualify for SSI once they turn 18, even if they are still living at home. I was advised by a Social Security examiner to write out a contract with my sons stating that if they received SSI and were still living at home, then they would pay a certain monthly amount for room and board. (Initially we chose $150 per month, however, I believe the current going rate for room and board in another's house is $300 per month.) Our having written out this contract was actually used by Social Security to give both of my sons the maximum amount. Social Security was interested in seeing that they paid that amount every month.

A person can work and still draw SSI/SSDI, but the number of hours worked is limited without drawing down the monthly SSI/SSDI benefit. You, of course, can choose to work more hours and get less in disability payments. There are yearly reports that have to be submitted to the Social Security Administration asking questions about continued disability and how the disability payments were spent. If a person is no longer disabled and can work full time, then that needs to be reported to the Social Security Administration so that disability payments are stopped.

Remember the players, procedures, and protocols that will drive you crazy? Dealing with the Social Security Administration is one of them. The number of visits to and hours spent at the local Social Security office trying to correct benefit changes and errors can be considerable. If a recipient is a minor, or if their disability is so profound that they cannot handle money, Social Security will ask for designation of a *representative payee*. If the benefit recipient seems to be capable of handling their own money, Social Security will pay the benefits directly to him/her, even if asked by the individual NOT to do this. It was only when checks started bouncing because Eric was spending money from the account that was needed to cover those checks did we persuade Social Security to make me his payee.

Our other son, Aaron, requested several times that I be made his payee. Without our knowledge, Social Security put $1,400 on a debit card. Not only was this expressly against our wishes, but Social Security decided that it needed to be paid back because Aaron was now in jail. However, since I was not his payee, bank officials legally could not talk to me, so the repayment needed to wait until Aaron got out of jail. This snafu could have put his SSI in jeopardy. Only after Aaron spent time in the county jail for having a mental health crisis while Social Security wanted their money back were we able to get me designated as his representative payee.

Fortunately, Eric is covered by my husband's health insurance because he has been designated a disabled adult child. This insurance becomes his *supplemental* or secondary coverage; Medicare is primary, and if there is anything left over, Medicaid is tertiary. My husband has tried to get Aaron covered under his insurance in the same way, but because he is so often incarcerated, it has been difficult getting required paperwork filled out by psychiatrists. When my husband did file all the paperwork, he has been frustrated by non-responsiveness from the federal Office of Personnel Management that is supposed to process the request. This is another *drive you crazy* experience.

If you are on SSDI, there is no limit on the amount of money you can have in the bank. If you are on SSI, however, you are limited to two thousand dollars. This includes all of your accounts. The rules for Medicaid are almost the same as SSI, with a few variations. Check with your local office. There are some resources that are not counted against those limits:

- Land that you own and are legally prevented from selling.
- A home that you own and live in.
- Household goods, clothing, and personal effects, furnishings, and equipment.
- One car or van if it is used to provide you with transportation.
- Property of a trade or business, or required by an employer such as tools, a computer used as part of your work or business, and funds that you need to run your business.
- Life insurance with a total face value of $1500.
- A burial space and prepaid improvements such as a marker, burial container and vault, and a contract for opening and closing the gravesite.
- Up to $1500 plus accrued interest that you have set aside **in a separate account in your name for burial expenses.**
- Money from a grant, scholarship, or other gift that you set aside for educational purposes (other than room and board costs). These funds may be held for 9 months without being counted as a resource.

In 2012, Eric received a bill for five thousand dollars from the Social Security Administration saying he had been paid too much from the time I had started drawing Social Security–in 2011! So they were recalculating what Eric should have received out of the SSDI pot of money back to when I started drawing, and they were also reducing his monthly benefit amount without realizing they needed to supplement the difference from the SSI pot of money. I was suddenly scrambling to pay his bills with $106 less per month than what we had been receiving. Not only did I again have to make several trips to Social Security with documentation, but also had to get a waiver for not paying back the five thousand dollars with the accompanying documentation for that. You can't realistically pay five thousand dollars back when you get less than twelve thousand dollars per year, especially when the issue was an accounting error made by the Social Security Administration. Another *drive you crazy* experience.

When Eric got his job in 2013, after getting a couple of checks, I took his pay stubs into Social Security to tell them that he had gotten a job. Even though he was barely clearing one hundred dollars a month, Social Security was going to reduce his monthly SSI by substantially more. Again, I had to argue with them about the amount of money he was getting, especially since he was paying a job coach much more than the one hundred dollars a month for coaching. I was finally able to talk to a representative who looked for and then cited in Eric's record, the rule for people with disabilities to not be penalized for having/paying for a job coach. The gentleman asked me if Eric's having a job was worth it since the job coach was being paid more than Eric was making. My answer was "not monetarily, but definitely in Eric's self-esteem".

That was the second time in two years that we have had major issues with Social Security recalculating benefits and then telling us we needed to repay money. The first time, it took me 6 months, at least 20 hours of my time, and about $100 in photocopying fees to get the benefits restored. The second time was probably as long and more complicated since the representative I ended up working with was not even in our state so I sometimes had to advocate for my son with the local examiners and tell them to read the notes that the Ohio examiner had put in Eric's record. This is a definite problem and frustrating, requiring lots of time and energy.

There were three years when there was no cost of living adjustment (COLA) in Social Security because the government said there was no inflation. However, people's expenses were still going up, such as rent, utilities, and food costs. While COLA amounts aren't much, every little bit helps. Eric and Tasha had an increase in their condominium fees, insurance premiums, utilities, food, and other expenses, yet got no more money than they did the year before. It is very hard to live on these incomes. It seems this is precisely what many politicians want so that people will *get off their butts* and get a job. They seem to have no concept of being disabled and unable to work. From time to time, we find ourselves receiving messages from friends promoting such policies, apparently forgetting we have disabled adult children who desperately need these benefit programs. We try our best to respond kindly and offer a different perspective, but you need to keep advocating for your loved one.

The coronavirus pandemic has wreaked havoc on people's jobs and living situations, including those on SSI or SSDI. Wisconsin and maybe other states have a rule that if you are receiving SSI or SSDI and lose a job, you are not eligible for unemployment benefits. The politicians consider this *double dipping*, yet sometimes this is the only way a person with a disability can stay afloat. The job that they lost may not have been full time, but the income from the job made a huge difference in being able to pay bills and remain independent. Politicians and the government are so shortsighted because a person living independently with or without a disability costs far less than a person who can't live independently. This is another instance of a law or rule made by people not giving those with disabilities a chance.

CHAPTER 30

GRASSROOTS GROUPS AND SUPPORT ORGANIZATIONS

Grassroots groups and support organizations usually spring up because there is a lack of services or access to those services that needs attention, or because there is a public policy or injustice that needs to be corrected. Group organizers are unsatisfied with the status quo because they cannot find or access existing services they need; the waiting list for these services is so long that a person might wait years to be served; the services may have been discontinued due to budget cuts; or perhaps the services never existed in their locale. Grassroots organizations may spring up because a group of people do not like how public funds are being spent for needed services. Services utilized by people with disabilities can be sponsored by government (federal, state, and local) agencies, private nonprofit organizations, faith communities (churches), or individuals.

A group in our area was started by one of the local television news anchors. With the help of other parents of children with special needs, nurses, and community activists, she started a nonprofit organization to fill a gap in respite services for children and their parents. Every year she and her husband host a couple of fundraising events to fund the respite service that she started.

Several years ago my husband and I joined a group that had been started in our area by parents frustrated with long waiting lists for services for their children or young adults with special needs. In other cases, their family member *fell through the cracks* of eligibility requirements for services, so there was no amount of waiting that would result in services. The group is facilitated by two community organizers who have siblings with special needs and are clients for services. We were encouraged to join by the mother of our older son's girlfriend (Natasha) who had joined the year before. Living Our Visions, Inclusively (LOV, Inc.) is a grassroots organization of individuals with disabilities, families, and community members building fulfilling, community-centered lives for all. To achieve this goal, LOV is engaging in collective action, mobilizing individual and community assets, increasing civic engagement, building reciprocal relationships of caring and mutual support, and developing inclusive and sustainable employment, recreation, and living opportunities. Their motto is "doing together what we cannot do individually."

This organization has provided social contacts for the children and young adults as well as a network of other parents facing similar challenges. After a few years it became apparent that more services could be offered to the young people if there were staff beyond the two community organizers that were running the program. The parent representatives figured out that together they would have enough combined purchasing power to hire a staff that could work directly with the young people as *community connectors* to pave the way for the young adults to become involved in various community-based organizations (church choir, local travel club, etc.) or as a *life coach* to help them realize some of their goals in the area of daily living skills (cooking, cleaning, time management). Although the organization started out with one full time employee, they quickly added a part-time employee. Currently, there are two full-time employees called *bridge builders* in addition to the two community organizers.

The LOV, Inc. staff periodically assembles the entire group (parents and young people) for activities. They also held separate activities for the parents and young people. The *bridge builders* have expanded their services by becoming job developers and job coaches. Parents have occasionally taken on responsibility for getting the young people together for social activities. There have been amusement park outings, bowling leagues in winter months, boating, attending minor league baseball games, cooking groups, hikes, gardening, computer gaming, movies, a book club, a travel club, mindfulness meditation, and pottery and other craft classes. There is a women's group, and a men's group among the young people, and a mom's group. The women have gone to see plays and had beach parties. The guys have done computer gaming get-togethers, and watched sporting events.

A group of parents initiated a discussion about their hopes and fears regarding their young person with a disability being able to move out of the parents' home and live independently. They spent several weeks meeting with people and entities knowledgeable about housing options, such as representatives of Movin' Out (see the chapter on Housing). Parents who thought their loved one would never be able to live independently found themselves looking for apartments or conferring with other parents about their young adults living together as roommates. These were parents who feared their loved one would end up in some type of a group home or having to live with a married sibling rather than living independently. This initiative was a great success.

I read a story about a similar group of parents in southern California who pooled their resources and formed a nonprofit to start an educational/vocational workshop for their young adults. The students go to "school" for 3 years and learn not only the information they need to know for a vocation, but also learn important social skills such as introducing themselves, how to conduct themselves in an interview, being on time, complete assigned tasks, being patient when someone is critical, letting bosses know where you are at all times, how to dress, and appropriate hygiene habits.

There are grassroots organizations fighting for social justice issues relating to disabilities. We became involved with one several years ago when disappointed by the lack of mental health treatment options in our community. People having a mental health crisis were ending up in our jails and prisons, and our county sheriff was advocating building a new jail. We and others asked, why not spend that money on the front end for treatment alternatives instead of putting them in jail or prison. We have become active members and speak out on treatment of people in jail and prison, especially those with a mental health diagnosis. We talk about the lack of treatment options in the community, the opportunities for closing prisons (like many other states are doing) and transferring that money to community treatment options. We highlight the impact on families and communities when a person is incarcerated, the punitive probation and community supervision rules that often send a person back to prison because they broke a rule, not because they have committed any new crime.

Grassroots organizations can be a support group for you as you experience challenges and frustrations concerning your loved one and *the system*. Becoming involved in such organizations and efforts can actually result in changes that will help your loved one and others. Becoming involved can also help you not feel helpless or hopeless about the challenges you face.

CHAPTER 31

SPECIAL NEEDS TRUSTS

Who is going to support or take care of your loved one when you are gone? Will that person care even half as much as you did? What about those special times like birthdays or Christmas, when you would do something special to make their day special? Will anyone do that after you are gone?

There is no one who is going to care for your spouse, son, daughter, brother, sister, or other relative with a disability just like you would, so forget that notion. The best you can do is to make arrangements for their financial well-being and care when you are no longer available to provide it. Two very important components of such arrangements are (1) setting up a *special needs trust* to help insure their financial security and (2) completing a *lifestyle assessment* or *life care plan*. There are various templates with different names that will help you come close to putting down in writing everything you would want someone to know about your loved one and how you made life work for them in a meaningful and satisfying way while you were alive. It should help guide how you would like some of the money you leave in a special needs trust be spent to continue a lifestyle to which your loved one has become accustomed.

A special needs trust (also called a supplemental needs trust) is a financial trust set up so that the parents', spouse's, or partner's assets are safely protected for the use of their loved one with a disability. The trust is written and managed in such a way so the person with the disability does not loose public disability benefits, such as SSI or MA or other long-term support programs that have resource or income limits or cost-sharing requirements. This trust should be written by an attorney familiar with

165

special needs trusts in accordance with your state laws governing the trusts. Once established, it is important that your will and the beneficiary designations for any type of account that you may have (IRAs, 401Ks, life insurance, pensions, etc.) be carefully revised to direct the assets, or a portion of them, into the special needs trust account set up for your loved one. If married, you can still have your spouse listed as the primary beneficiary, and then the special needs trust account for your loved one as the secondary beneficiary.

The trust is used to maintain the highest quality of life by leveraging public benefits with trust funds to pay for special needs not covered by the public benefits. It is to help each participant develop his or her full potential and enjoy as comfortable and happy a life as possible. It ensures that each participant pursues activities and associations that prevent isolation and loneliness and helps each participant remain in the least restrictive living arrangement appropriate to his or her needs for as long as possible, rather than being institutionalized. It uses government programs, appropriate private programs, and funded supplemental services to meet each participant's special needs, reducing duplication and overlap of services. The trust preserves the integrity of funds left by the family so the funds may enrich the life of the person with a disability, without jeopardizing their eligibility for continued public disability benefits. It provides participants, their families, and care givers peace of mind related to the future care of the person with disabilities.

These trusts are usually managed by a nonprofit organization approved to manage a special needs trust program. There are costs for drawing up the will (which usually states that any assets are to go to the trust), the cost of setting up the trust itself, and then an annual fee for administration.

The trust manager is responsible for receiving and deciding on requests for spending money in the account on your loved one's behalf. The trust may request that the family set up an *advisor* so when your loved one wants something, the trust would check with the advisor to see if they think this is an appropriate use of the funds. The trust cannot give cash directly to your loved one as this could put their public disability benefits in jeopardy by altering their eligibility. They can however spend trust assets to buy a wide variety of goods and services for your loved one. Special needs trust funds are commonly used to pay for personal care attendants, vacations, home furnishings, out-of-pocket medical and dental expenses, education, recreation, vehicles, and physical rehabilitation.

When we set up the special needs trust accounts for our sons, knowledgeable people recommended that we also complete a *lifestyle assessment* or *life care plan* using available templates. This document addresses numerous details about the life of the trust account beneficiary (your loved one). The templates ask for information and preferences about food, clothing, shelter, health, finances, family life, entertainment, employment, retirement, etc. It tells who the loved one's relatives are, how typical holidays are celebrated, how they usually celebrate their birthdays, provisions for medical treatment, funeral, burial, etc. You can include things like religious affiliations, sports interests, hobbies, other interests, housing, vacations, spending money, etc. All of this information helps guide an advisor or the trust manager in allowing your loved one to live a life similar to when you were around and in control. As likes, wants, and needs change; the lifestyle document will need to be updated.

While most of our sons' needs will be met when my husband and I die, there are some things that will be different. Both like to have a cash allowance. That will no longer happen unless the trust manager would allow the advisor to dole out cash to each of them or place a small amount of money into a special checking account every month from which they could draw cash.

Food is considered a necessity and is therefore supposed to be paid out of SSI. We have a membership at a wholesale club. When we go once a month, we ask the *kids* what they want from there. Anything purchased there should technically count against them and their SSI benefits, but even a Social Security examiner told me that "parents are supposed to help their kids!" If we were gone, they would no longer have access to that food anymore unless the trust paid the yearly membership fee.

Right now, my husband and I take the three of them (two sons and a significant other) on vacations and pay for most things. The trust funds can be used to pay for vacations and other trips they want to take (See Able Trek Tours). There would also be money for them to celebrate birthdays by going out to dinner or ordering holiday meals from a local grocery store. Birthday presents is another matter.

The person you select to be the trust account advisor can be a family member, such as a sibling, or a trusted friend. This person should know your loved one or be willing to get to know your loved one so they are able to advocate with the trust for a continued lifestyle. It is ideal if the advisor lives in the same area as your loved one. However, with the mobility of families these days, that may not be possible. We have selected one of my husband's older sisters who lives an hour away from us to be the advisor. Whoever it is, please have an alternate person in mind, as unforeseen circumstances could necessitate a change. Everyone's life is very busy so make sure the person is completely willing to take on this added responsibility.

CHAPTER 32

JAILS AND PRISONS AS INSTITUTIONS FOR THE DISABLED

I could write a whole book just on this subject. It is heartbreaking that many people with cognitive disabilities and/or mental illness are now housed in our jails or prisons by a broken legal system. We often hear it called the *criminal justice system*, but many of these people are not true criminals, and incarcerating them for long periods of time because through their disability they transgressed a behavioral norm of society, often doing nothing more than scaring people, is not justice.

More and more people with developmental and mental health disabilities are ending up in our jail and prisons because in the late 1970s and the 1980s we Americans closed and emptied out our state (mental) hospitals and failed to keep the promise of redirecting the funding for those institutions into the communities to support them. While most of the following information is regarding American jails and prisons, it is interesting to note that other Western countries are also experiencing some of the same issues with the same poor outcomes. And none of them give people a chance.

THE OVERALL PICTURE OF INCARCERATION IN THE US

The United States has the largest prison population in the world and the highest per capita incarceration rate. In 2018, the US incarcerated 698 out of every 100,000 people. While the US has about five percent of the world's population, it incarcerates around twenty-five percent of the world's prisoners. American prison sentences are much longer so the total incarceration rate is higher than other developed countries. The level of incarceration in the US exceeds the average incarceration levels in the former Soviet Union during the existence of the Stalin Gulag system, when the Soviet Union's population reached 168 million and 1.2 to 1.5 million people were in the Gulag prison camps and colonies.[29]

Between 1990 and 2005, a new prison opened in the United States every ten days. In the last 30 years, the US prison population has skyrocketed by almost 800%, due in large part to the mandatory minimum drug sentences and *three strikes* laws that passed in the 1980s and 1990s. It is only in the last five years that some states have started reversing the policies that have fueled *mass incarceration*, resulting in the closing of prisons. Prison construction and operation of prisons by private corporations has resulted in a *prison-industrial complex*—the business interests that capitalize on mass incarceration, making imprisonment profitable.

Millions of dollars were spent lobbying state legislators to keep expanding the use of incarceration to respond to just about any problem. Incarceration became the answer to everything—health care problems like drug addiction, poverty that had led someone to write a bad check, child behavioral disorders, and managing those with mental challenges who are also poor. Even immigration issues generated responses from legislators that resulted in sending people to prisons or detention camps run by private corporations. Never before had so much lobbying money been spent to expand America's prison population, block sentencing reforms, create new crime categories, and sustain the fear and anger that fueled mass incarceration than during the last 30 years in the US.

According to the US Bureau of Justice Statistics, 2,162,400 adults

---

[29] Wikipedia contributors, "Incarceration in the United States," *Wikipedia, The Free Encyclopedia*, https://en.wikipedia.org/w/index.php?title=Incarceration_in_the_United_States&oldid=974430858.

were incarcerated in federal and state prisons and county jails in 2016. Additionally, 4,537,100 adults were under community supervision, on probation, or on parole. In total 6,613,500 adults were under correctional supervision (community supervision, probation, parole, jail, or prison) in 2016. This equals 2,640 people out of every 100,000 US adults or 1 in every 38 adults. In addition, there were 48,043 juveniles in juvenile detention in 2015. The US incarcerates more of its youth than any other country.

Significant racial disparities exist among those who are incarcerated. In 2016, the incarceration rate per 100,000 people was 222 for Whites, 1,206 for Blacks, and 585 for Hispanics. One in eleven African-Americans is under correctional supervision today. More than one in three African-American males will likely spend some time behind bars.[30] Wisconsin has the highest rate of incarceration of African-American males in the US and the county I live in, Dane, has the highest county rate within the state. Today there are more African-American men behind bars or under the supervision of the criminal justice system than were enslaved in 1850.[31]

Although debtor prisons no longer exist in the United States, residents of some US states can still be incarcerated for debt as of 2015. According to the Vera Institute of Justice in 2015, jails throughout the US have become warehouses for the poor, the mentally ill, and those suffering from addiction because these individuals lack the financial means or mental capacity to post bail.[32] Those involved with criminal justice reform efforts across the US are trying to eliminate money bail, which unnecessarily keeps many people in jail and serves to further impoverish the poorest in our communities.

There seems to be deliberate indifference for prisoners' physical and mental health. Inmates have died and nearly died because they were not provided with necessary medical treatment in a timely manner. They have suffered miscarriages, unnecessary pain, and amputation, and have died of cancer or other maladies because they have been denied necessary medical treatment. California had such an "extensive and disturbing history of violating of prisoners' constitutional rights that a district court forced its

[30] Ibid.

[31] Michelle Alexander, *The New Jim Crow: Mass Incarceration in the Age of Colorblindness* (New York: The New Press, 2012), 180.

[32] Wikipedia, "Incarceration in the United States."

medical services into receivership. At the time, it was estimated that an inmate in California's prisons died needlessly every six to seven days due to grossly deficient medical care."[33]

CHILDREN IN ADULT PRISONS

Everyone knows or should know that our brains grow and develop just as our bodies do. If the body is not yet grown, why do legislators, police, attorneys, and judges believe that the brain of 16 and 17-year-olds is fully grown and has the capacity to understand all manner of issues to make correct and wise decisions?

For males, the executive brain function is not fully developed until age 25. As stated earlier, executive brain function is responsible for cause and effect thinking, and problem solving. Children do not belong in adult prisons. Fourteen states have no minimum age for trying children as adults. Children as young as 8 years old have been prosecuted as adults.[34] Again, the US has the distinction of incarcerating more of its youth than any other country in the world. Some 10,000 children are housed in adult jails and prisons on any given day in America. Children are five times more likely to be sexually assaulted in adult prisons than in juvenile facilities and face increased risk of suicide.

There seems to be no taking into account that many young children in America suffer abuse, neglect, poverty, and domestic and community violence on a daily basis. Children with any form of disability are 3 times more likely to experience abuse when compared to children without disabilities. Without effective intervention and help, these children suffer, struggle, and fall into despair and hopelessness. Some young teens cannot manage the emotional, social, and psychological challenges of adolescence and eventually engage in destructive and violent behavior. Many states have ignored the crisis and dysfunction that creates child delinquency and have subjected kids to further victimization and abuse in the adult criminal justice system.

[33] Paul Elias, "High Court OKs Early Release Plan for California Inmates", KPBS, San Diego State University, August 3, 2013. https://www.kpbs.org/news/2013/aug/03/s-court-oks-early-release-plan-for-calif-inmates/.
[34] Equal Justice Initiative, "Children in Adult Prison," https://eji.org/issues/children-in-prison/.

Around the time of puberty a dramatic increase in dopamine activity in the brain drives the young adolescent toward increased sensation-seeking and risk-taking behaviors. They have an underdeveloped capacity for self-regulation and responsibility, vulnerability to negative influences and outside pressures, and a lack of control over their own impulses and their environment.

There are nearly 3,000 children in the US who have been sentenced to life in prison without parole. The US is the only country in the world to sentence juveniles to life imprisonment without parole. They are in adult prisons at least after they turn 18. Children as young as 13 years old have been tried as adults, typically without any consideration of their age or circumstances of the offense. The US Supreme Court has now banned death-in-prison sentences for children convicted of non-homicide crimes. In 2012, in Miller vs. Alabama, the Supreme Court struck down automatic life sentences with no chance of release for teenage killers.[35] In 2016, the Supreme Court has said that even those teens convicted long ago of life in prison must be considered for parole or given a new sentence.[36] [37]

According to Angelo Pinto of the Correctional Association of New York, "putting a young person (less than age 18) in an adult system increases their chances exponentially of reentering the system."[38] There is evidence that juvenile detention is a counterproductive strategy for many youths under the age of 19, because many of these young people will not graduate high school, and that raises the chance that they will commit more crimes later in life. Juvenile detention seems to create criminals, not deter them.

---

[35] Ibid.

[36] Susan Haigh, "States Revisit Mandatory Sentences for Juveniles," *The Morning Call* (Allentown, PA), August 18, 2013, https://www.mcall.com/sdut-states-revisit-mandatory-sentences-for-juveniles-2013aug18-story.html.

[37] Robert Barnes, "Supreme Court: Life Sentences on Juveniles Open for Later Reviews," *The Washington Post*, January 25, 2016. https://www.washingtonpost.com/politics/courts_law/supreme-court-juveniles-sentenced-to-life-have-option-for-new-reviews/2016/01/25/06e3dfc2-c378-11e5-8965-0607e0e265ce_story.html.

[38] Barbara Herman, "Kalief Browder Suicide: Did Solitary Confinement Kill Him? Advocates On The 'Torture' Of Juvenile Detainees At Rikers Island," *International Business Times*, June 10, 2015. https://www.ibtimes.com/kalief-browder-suicide-did-solitary-confinement-kill-him-advocates-torture-juvenile-1960575.

WOMEN

In the United States, the number of women sent to prison increased 646 percent between 1980 and 2010, a rate of increase 1.5 times higher than the rate for men. With over 200,000 women in prisons and jails in America and approximately 1.25 million women under correctional supervision in the community, the number of women under the control of the criminal justice system has reached record levels.

Three-fourths of women in Wisconsin prisons suffer from mental illness. In 2009, a survey of mental illness among jail inmates in five jails in New York and Maryland found a total of 16.6 percent of the population suffered from a mental illness such as schizophrenia, schizoaffective disorder (schizophrenia and bipolar disorder), bipolar disorder, and psychotic disorder. The rate among women (31 percent) was much higher than that among men (14.5 percent).

DEVELOPMENTAL DISABILITIES

Developmental disabilities are a group of conditions due to an impairment in physical, learning, language, or behavioral areas. These conditions begin or manifest during the developmental period, may impact day-to-day functioning, and usually last a lifetime. They can include autism spectrum disorder and intellectual disabilities caused by such things as Down syndrome and fetal alcohol spectrum disorder.[39]

Until the 1970s, many people with cognitive disabilities were housed in private or state institutions (*state hospitals*). Then during the social movement of the 1980s, patients were released from institutions to the community, which were frequently ill-prepared to deal with them. Because they were ill-prepared to deal with them, there were few services or programs to support and assist these individuals. If they were living with family, there were few services to help families understand how to cope with their family member's challenges or even a place where they could be supervised or cared for during the day while people worked (day treatment or respite care).

People who experience forms of cognitive, intellectual, or other developmental disabilities become involved not only as victims of crime

---

[39] "Facts About Developmental Disabilities," Centers for Disease Control and Prevention, https://www.cdc.gov/ncbddd/developmentaldisabilities/facts.html.

but also as suspects or offenders more often than people who do not experience this form of disability. While they comprise two to three percent of the general population, people with intellectual disabilities represent four to ten percent of the population in adult prisons and an even larger portion of the population in juvenile facilities and jails.

When people with developmental disabilities are having a crisis and the police are called, most of the officers responding do not have any idea about how to deal with someone with diminished mental functioning. Their usual tactics of shouting at someone to "drop your weapon" or "get down on the ground" doesn't work with people who have abnormally slow mental processing and may be out of their element, scared, and upset about something. A woman in our state with developmental disabilities had picked up a hand ax in a local store. She didn't want to go back to the group home where she lived just yet. She became agitated and was damaging items in the store. The police were called. They told her to drop her weapon and then shot her when she refused to comply with their shouting and moved toward them. She died later in the hospital. Our society's *one-size-fits-all* police response does not work when dealing with the myriad of people and personalities that we encounter on a daily basis.

There are people with developmental disabilities in our jails and prisons who have been arrested for crimes they committed, not even understanding what was wrong with their actions or behavior. Florida courts declared Freddie Hall "retarded" in both 1992 and 1999. Yet despite the US Supreme Court's 1999 ruling in *Atkins v. Virginia* that executing mentally retarded individuals violates the Eighth Amendment, Hall was still facing the death penalty. Why? Because in Atkins, the Supreme Court left the process of defining who is mentally retarded up to the states. In Florida, where individuals are required to prove they have an IQ of 70 or below, Hall was found to have an IQ of 71 on a test with a margin of error of five points. In 2012, the Florida Supreme Court ignored that fact and ruled Hall eligible for execution, but in fall 2013 the U.S. Supreme Court agreed to hear Hall's appeal. In *Hall v. Florida* on May 14, 2014, the high court ruled that states must look beyond IQ scores when inmate tests are in the range of 70 to 75. They must consider other factors.[40] Subsequently,

---

[40] Andrew Cohen, "The Court's Emphatic Ban on Executing the Intellectually Disabled," *The Atlantic*, May 27, 2014. https://www.theatlantic.com/politics/archive/2014/05/hall-v-florida/371662/.

on September 8, 2016, the Florida Supreme Court reduced Hall's sentence to life in prison.[41]

People with intellectual disabilities are vulnerable to becoming involved in a crime or being a victim of a crime. A person with intellectual disabilities is frequently used by another criminal to help with illegal activities without understanding that their involvement is a crime or the consequences of their involvement. They might also have a strong need to feel accepted and might agree to help with criminal activities to gain the friendship of others. Also, because of their disability, these individuals might provide misunderstood responses to police officers, something that can increase their own potential to be arrested, incarcerated, and possibly even executed—even if they have not committed a crime.

Factors that can make a person with an intellectual disability more vulnerable to involvement in the criminal justice system are:

- A desire to hide their disability
- Confessing even if they are innocent
- Feeling overwhelmed by police presence
- Not understanding instructions or commands
- Confusion about who is responsible for the crime
- Saying things they believe the police want to hear
- Pretending to understand their rights when they do not
- Difficulties with describing details or facts of an offense
- Feeling upset at being detained or attempting to run away
- Being the first to leave a crime scene and the first to get caught

People with intellectual disabilities are often further victimized in prison. They are less likely to receive parole or probation and usually serve longer sentences because of an inability to understand and adapt to the rules of prison.

Intellectual or borderline intellectual disability and acquired brain injury are different disabilities from mental illness. However, they are poorly understood by staff members in the criminal justice system, so they are frequently treated the same as someone with a mental health problem.

---

[41] Brendan Farrington, "Florida Reduces Freddie Lee Hall's Death Sentence," *The Gainesville Sun*, September 8, 2016. https://www.gainesville.com/news/20160908/florida-reduces-freddie-lee-halls-death-sentence.

There is the need for special supports for those with cognitive disabilities and for those with dual diagnoses or co-morbidity.

Those individuals with borderline intellectual disability (IQ of 70–79) face particular difficulties because they are not recognized as having a disability for the purposes of receiving support and assistance from the state agency providing disability services. These folks are significantly over-represented in the juvenile and adult prison populations.

In 2002, there were still about a hundred people with mental retardation facing execution when the Supreme Court banned the death penalty for people with intellectual disability. In 2005, there were fewer than seventy-five juvenile offenders on death row when the Supreme Court banned the death penalty for kids.[42]

Special efforts should be made to educate children, teenagers, and adults with intellectual disabilities about how to behave when interacting with a police officer as well as how to speak up if they are being victimized. Parents may want to contact their school's special education department and request that relevant training be provided to their child as well as to all school staff. They may also contact their local police department to advise them of their child's disability and also find out if their officers receive training on working with people with intellectual disabilities (different from training on working with individuals with a mental illness disability). Parents may also want to create a card for their child to carry that explains their disability and instruct their child to show that card to authorities if they are ever detained.

MENTAL ILLNESS

Until the 1970s, people with mental illnesses were usually treated in private and state-operated psychiatric hospitals (commonly known as *insane asylums*). Numbers of people confined in these institutions continued to increase through the 1950s. Then in the 1960s, amidst the civil rights and social movements, thinking about the treatment of people with mental illnesses began to change. This was spurred on by institutional abuse

---

[42] Travis Waldron, "Rick Perry's Execution Record Includes the Deaths of Juveniles and the Mentally Disabled," *Think Progress*, September 2, 2011. https://archive.thinkprogress.org/rick-perrys-execution-record-includes-the-deaths-of-juveniles-and-the-mentally-disabled-67d0adf2b1e/.

scandals in the 1960s and 1970s. Changing public attitudes about mental health and mental hospitals, introduction of new treatments with new psychiatric drugs, and states' desires to reduce the costs of running state hospitals led to a *deinstitutionalization* movement. A series of federal court decisions in the latter 1970s restricting states' abilities to confine people involuntarily also propelled this movement. States started closing hospitals in the 1980s. In 1955, there were 340 psychiatric hospital beds for every 100,000 US citizens. By 2005, that number had dropped to 17 beds.[43]

As you may remember from an earlier chapter, the money states had spent on these institutions was supposed to be redirected to follow the patient with mental illness into the community. People were supposed to be served by community mental health centers. However, the money didn't follow them. Community mental health treatment centers weren't set up in a timely manner, if at all. Many people ended up on the streets where they became involved in petty criminal activity such as disorderly conduct and loitering. These *crimes* frequently led them to places like the county jail. Homeless people with mental illness are more likely to be incarcerated than non-homeless. The Los Angeles County Jail is actually the largest mental hospital in the US. Called the Twin Towers because of its design, one tower houses 1,400 people with mental health issues. Many of these people committed their crimes as a result of their mental illness, so now they are being punished for being mentally ill. Because there is no other place to put these individuals, they end up in jail. Jails have said they are drowning in mental health *patients*. It is a *Catch 22*, a revolving door of jail; being released with no access to proper mental health services, no money or employment, and often no place to live; then re-offending in some manner that sends them back in jail. We are criminalizing mental illness. Is this really the kind of society we want?

In the US, the percentage of inmates with mental illness has been steadily increasing, with rates more than quadrupling from 1998 to 2006. Meanwhile, between 1982 and 2001, the number of public hospital beds available for the mentally ill decreased by 69 percent in the U.S. The Bureau of Justice reported in 2003 that an estimated 16 percent of the two million prisoners in the US are mentally ill. That figure has now climbed to about 20 percent. Some disorders tend to be more frequently associated

---

[43] Wikipedia contributors, "Deinstitutionalisation," *Wikipedia, The Free Encyclopedia*, https://en.wikipedia.org/w/index.php?title=Deinstitutionalisation&oldid=974250687.

with criminal behavior such as schizophrenia, delusions, organic brain disorder, antisocial personality disorder, and major affective disorders. There are now more than three times more seriously mentally ill persons in jails and prisons than in hospitals. In some locales, one third to one half of those in jail take some kind of medication for mental illness. When NAMI (National Alliance for the Mentally Ill) queried families, they found that 40 percent of individuals with serious mental illness have been in jail or prison at some time in their lives.

Not only do people with recent histories of mental illness end up incarcerated, but many who have no history of mental illness end up developing symptoms while in prison! In 2006, the Bureau of Justice Statistics found that a quarter of state prisoners had a history of mental illness, whereas three in ten state prisoners had developed symptoms of mental illness since becoming incarcerated. According to Human Rights Watch, one of the contributing factors to the disproportionate rates of mental illness in prisons and jails is the increased use of solitary confinement which reduces socially and psychologically meaningful contact to the absolute minimum, to a point that is insufficient for most detainees to remain mentally sane. Another factor is that most inmates do not get the mental health services that they need while incarcerated. Due to limited funding, prisons are not able to provide a full range of mental health services and thus are typically limited to inconsistent administration of psychotropic medication or no psychiatric services at all.

Human Rights Watch reports that corrections officers routinely use excessive violence against inmates with mental health issues for non-threatening behaviors related to schizophrenia or bipolar disorder. They may be shackled, pepper sprayed, or electrically shocked with various devices such electrified batons (prods) or stun cuffs. We hear about abusive incidents in prisons from our son or others. One young man with bipolar disorder told of the guards purposely throwing his lithium medication on the floor, crushing it with their boot, and telling him to "snort" it off the floor. Another guard urinated in the young man's food before he passed the dinner tray into the cell. There have been inmates who have had seizures, been checked by medical personnel who said, "We don't need to call an ambulance; it'll save money." Our son reported another seizure incident happened just before the inmate died. Yells to the guards by other inmates to come and help him went unheeded.

On occasion our son has asked to go into segregation because he could feel himself becoming agitated while not on optimal medication. He would ask to see the psychiatrist, psychologist, or social worker, but be denied. He then *flips out* and gets more consequences. This is not humane treatment for anyone. These are human beings in need of healing, not *trash* as they are viewed in the cultures of some institutions.

A recent news article about the Fresno County, California, jail corroborates what our son has told us.[44] The inmates there spiral deeper into *madness* because jail officials withhold their medications. If the inmates do get medications, they are often at a lower dose or a cheaper substitute that doesn't work as well. Faced with budget deficits, state prison systems and county jails have drastically cut back on psychiatric drugs. They have also cut back on medical personnel who tend the inmates. This leaves care in the hands of the correctional officers who are not trained to provide such care, nor do they, in some cases, care what happens to an inmate.

The most astounding comments in this article are that Fresno County jail officials say they meet their legal obligations for providing psychiatric services! Really? Withholding medications, giving inmates lower dose medications or substitute medications, and not having trained staff available at all times is "fulfilling their legal obligations?" However, Fresno County has sent four hundred inmates to state mental hospitals since 2007 because of their deteriorated mental conditions, more per capita than all of California's largest counties. With such deficient care, inmates sometimes aren't even competent to assist in their own defense because of inadequate medication treatment. These are not isolated incidents. I have articles in my files from many states on prisoner abuse by guards, especially prisoners with mental illness. Mentally ill inmates are more likely to commit suicide. Approximately one half of inmates who commit suicide are seriously mentally ill.

Some counties and states are building facilities specifically for inmates with chronic and severe mental illness. Wisconsin has one such facility; my son has been there twice. While I commend the desire to be more humane and better deal with the problem, building special prison facilities is the wrong solution. More money should be allocated to diverting these people from the criminal justice system, or certainly from incarceration.

---

[44] Marc Benjamin and Barbara Anderson, "Without Proper Medication, Fresno Inmates Locked in Terror," *The Fresno Bee*, August 11, 2013. https://www.mcclatchydc.com/latest-news/article24751948.html.

Treatment Alternatives & Diversions (TAD) programs rather than brick and mortar warehouses, as well as more community mental health services, are what is needed and give a better outcome for the money.

Having people with mental health issues in prisons deprives them of their right to proper treatment and care. Most of them are not violent. It leads to maltreatment and stigmatization. Prisoners with mental illness frequently endure violence, exploitation, and extortion at the hands of other inmates. An inmate recently released from the prison in which my son is incarcerated persuaded him (tricked him into) signing a Power of Attorney for Finances, giving that person power over all of our son's assets—automobile, bank accounts, personal property, etc. Fortunately, my husband and I were intelligent enough to resist his attempts to collect our son's assets when he showed up at our front door unexpectedly and showed us the document.

The needs of people with mental health issues far exceed anything our jails and prisons can provide. The Madrid Declaration of the United Nations states that mental patients should be treated by the least restrictive methods. Incarcerating mental patients is a violation of this and a possible violation of patients getting adequate treatment.[45] Jails and prisons were not created to be mental hospitals. They are not structurally appropriate for patients, the staff is not trained in psychiatric care, and disciplinary methods typical for the general population are not appropriate for them and can exacerbate their mental illness. Imprisonment is counter-therapeutic for such persons and increases their chances of a psychiatric breakdown. Mental health treatment in the community is far less costly.

The recently retired executive director of Colorado Department of Corrections (CDOC), Rick Raemisch, used to be the Secretary of Wisconsin's Department of Corrections, and before that, sheriff in our county. Rick could see what was happening to people in solitary and kept abreast of current literature regarding best practices for inmates with mental illness. He knew that solitary confinement was not good for anyone's mental health, especially for someone who already had mental illness. He and the previous executive director of the CDOC had written articles on the use and detriment of solitary confinement. That previous

[45] Ahmed Okasha, "Mental Patients in Prisons: Punishment versus Treatment?" *World Psychiatry*, Vol. 3, No. 1 (February 2004), 1. https://www.ncbi.nlm.nih.gov/pmc/articles/PMC1414650/.

executive director was subsequently killed at his home by a former inmate who was discharged from a Colorado prison directly from a period in solitary confinement, never having gone back into the general population at the prison before discharge. Shortly after Rick took over at the CDOC, he decided to try solitary confinement in one of his prisons. He later wrote an opinion piece for The New York Times. He lasted 22 hours before asking to be let out. He stated that solitary confinement was "overused, misused, and abused."

Many prisoners have spent months, years, or even decades in solitary confinement–being by themselves in a 7- by 13-foot concrete box with concrete bed and metal toilet and sink for 22 to 23 hours per day. There is one hour of *recreation time*, but that could be at 4 a.m. or in a gym with no equipment. On any given day, almost 80,000 people across the United States spend almost 23 hours in total isolation, a practice described as torture by the United Nations.

In solitary confinement, a person can experience visual and auditory hallucinations, paranoid thoughts, and regressive breakdowns that can cause him/her to curl up in a fetal position or engage in bizarre behaviors like throwing their feces at the walls and door. Solitary confinement causes PTSD and a person can develop panic disorders and claustrophobia from being confined this way. Solitary confinement accounts for approximately one half of the suicides that occur in prison.

During Aaron's first prison stay, he was in *general population* for a while. Then two days before his twenty-fifth birthday, he *lost it* and was put into solitary confinement (the Wisconsin DOC calls it *administrative confinement*). We visited Aaron every two weeks at the prison. On one visit, I was able to talk to the psychiatrist about Aaron's meds being inadequate, but he didn't seem to really care. I found out later that he changed Aaron's psychotropic medication without any consultation with Aaron (or us) about what meds worked for Aaron. He changed Aaron to another medication whose side effects were worse than not being on any medication at all, and produced horrible, graphic nightmares every night. At no time did the psychiatrist prescribe the psychotropic medications that worked for Aaron or that he had been on before becoming incarcerated.

One time when we went to visit Aaron, after he had been in solitary about two months, the guard said that he refused to come out of his cell. We had heard this before from the guards, but found out later that Aaron wasn't even being told that he had visitors. So, we asked the guard to go back to Aaron's cell and tell him that his *parents* were here to visit him. The guard kindly did so. When he came back, he said that he still refused to come out of his cell. Then he said, "You know, Aaron isn't in his right mind." It turned out to be two more months before we saw Aaron again. In the meantime, his privilege of having visitors was taken away, but so was his privilege or receiving any mail. So, while Aaron was descending into a psychosis, the prison system stripped him of *any* contact with the outside world. Now he really was in *solitary* confinement.

When we finally saw Aaron five months after he had entered solitary confinement and two months after we had last seen him, he was in a different facility—the one prison facility for severely mentally ill prisoners. This facility is operated by the Department of Health Services with security provided by the DOC. We were shocked to find Aaron delusional and paranoid—completely psychotic. He looked like a wild man that had just emerged from the jungle. He had long, curly, matted hair, his beard was long and scraggly, he was wearing a black padded suicide smock, and his eyes were wide, piercing, sunken, and wild. He had lost seventy pounds and looked like someone emerging from a concentration camp! He spoke in gibberish for the first ten minutes that we were with him. We finally got him to talk in English, but he was still paranoid and delusional. He didn't believe we were who we said we were.

Here was our son who, when he was losing his grip on reality, was kept by the DOC in solitary confinement, on incorrect medications, and cut off from contact with us and any sense of reality. Aaron has significant cognitive deficits and many mental health issues, but when he entered the state prison system he was a sane person. Inadequate care and the torture of solitary confinement pushed him over the psychotic edge. Once we related what medications worked for Aaron to the psychiatrists at this facility, they immediately put him on those meds, and he quickly became sane again, losing the paranoia and delusions. If all jails and prisons were run like this facility, we would have a lower rate of recidivism in this country.

SMART ON CRIME VS. SOFT ON CRIME

According to a 2014 Human Rights Watch report, *tough-on-crime* laws adopted since the 1980s have filled US prisons with mostly nonviolent offenders. This policy failed to rehabilitate prisoners and many were worse upon release than before incarceration. It has been shown that community-based rehabilitation programs for offenders are more cost effective than prison, especially alcohol and other drug abuse (AODA) programs.[46]

Through enactment of stricter sentencing laws, many state legislatures have continued to reduce the discretion of judges in both the sentencing process and the determination of when the conditions of a sentence have been satisfied. Determinate sentencing, use of mandatory minimums, and guidelines-based sentencing continue to remove the human element from sentencing, such as the prerogative of the judge to consider the mitigating or extenuating circumstances of a crime when determining the appropriate length of incarceration. Time off for good behavior no longer exists as an incentive. As a consequence of the *three strikes laws* enacted in 28 states, the increase in the duration of incarceration in the last two to three decades was most pronounced in the case of the life prison sentences, which increased by 83 percent between 1992 and 2003 while violent crimes fell in the same period.[47] Our punitive prison system is vastly different and less humane than those in European and other *Western* countries.

Most correctional officers are honorable people, but in US jails and prisons they work in an environment focused on punishment of human beings. It is an environment that can be toxic to maintaining good character and human compassion. I have heard attitudes expressed in statements like the following:

- "These people are here because they want to be here."
- "You need to instill fear in these inmates or they won't listen to you."
- "We don't have any way to control these inmates except with behavior modification—putting our hands on them if they get out of control."
- "If you don't scare the inmates, they will hurt you."

I have personally heard some of these statements as well as many others. With the extreme number of incarcerated people having mental health issues, perhaps treating others as you want to be treated might be a more appropriate approach. I had a sheriff's deputy in my kitchen

---

[46] Wikipedia, "Incarceration in the United States."
[47] Ibid.

threatening me that if I made any more comments about certain procedures within the department, my son would be put back in jail. I had about a hundred things run through my mind to say to this individual, but decided against it for my son's sake. Power and authority invite the methods of intimidation.

Some states do a better job than others providing mental health treatment to individuals in the community so they do not end up in jail or prison. Data from 2004 show the odds of a person with serious mental illness being in jail or prison compared to in a hospital are highest in the states of Arizona (9.3 to 1), Nevada (9.8 to 1), South Carolina (5.1 to 1), and Texas (7.8 to 1).[48]

The state ranking based on per capita expenditures by state mental health authorities for the above states are: Arizona–14th, Nevada–37th, South Carolina–33rd, and Texas–48th. Except for Arizona, the other states having the most people per capita in jail or prison versus in hospitals are all ranking in the bottom half of the states in terms of spending for mental health services.

There is broad consensus that people with serious mental health issue are overrepresented in US jails and prisons. The estimated number of prisoners with serious mental illness runs between 16 and 25 percent and is rising.[49] A 2010 study compared the number of people with serious mental illness in jail and prisons with the number of such people in psychiatric hospital beds. Nationally, there are three times as many such people in jails and prisons as there are in hospitals. In Arizona and Nevada, the ratio was 10 to 1. States with the lowest ratios were North Dakota (1:1) and Maine, Massachusetts, Minnesota, and New York (1.2:1) According to the study, California had 246,317 people incarcerated, of which 39,411 suffer from serious mental illness, while the number of patients in state and private psychiatric hospitals and psychiatric units in general hospitals is only 10,295, a ratio of 3.8 to 1. In Texas, out of 223,195 prisoners, 35,711 have

---

[48] E. Fuller Torrey, *et al.*, *More Mentally Ill Persons Are in Jails and Prisons Than Hospitals: A Survey of the States.* Arlington, Virginia: Treatment Advocacy Center (May 2010). https://www.treatmentadvocacycenter.org/storage/documents/final_jails_v_hospitals_study.pdf

[49] Wikipedia contributors, "Mentally Ill People in United State Jails and Prisons, *Wikipedia, The Free Encyclopedia*, https://en.wikipedia.org/w/index.php?title=Mentally_ill_people_in_United_States_jails_and_prisons&oldid=969882610

serious mental illness and 4,579 people are in hospital psychiatric beds, a ratio of 7.8 to 1.[50]

As long as communities do not make mental health services a priority, people with mental illness will continue to be deprived of access to treatment in a mental health facility rather than in a prison or jail, and the community will be paying more and need more jail capacity. Communities are safer when citizens have access and are treated, enabling them to live healthy, productive lives.

There are several options for treatment. One option is to use assisted outpatient treatment (AOT). This requires selected seriously mentally ill persons to take medication under court order as a condition for living in the community. So far, this has been very successful in reducing the arrest rate of persons with mental illness. Another possibility is to use mental health courts. This gives the offender the choice between following a treatment plan, which includes taking medication, or go to jail. This has also been effective. Obviously, if there are funds to build and operate jails and prisons, there are enough funds for mental health services because they are less costly. The monies just need to be shifted from the corrections budget to the budget for health services, both at the local and state levels.

Treatment Alternatives and Diversion (TAD), mentioned earlier, is another option. TAD programs keep people with addictions and mental health issues out of jail and prison by placing them in effective treatment programs. Studies show that treatment and diversion programs are less costly and more effective in reducing recidivism and lowering crime rates. Every dollar spent on TAD saves taxpayers $1.96. The state saves when prison stays are avoided; counties save money when jail use is decreased. Over the course of seven years, one TAD program saved $35,000 per person per year for a $9 million savings to taxpayers for individuals to participate in the TAD program versus going to prison.

Establishing effective diversion programs can be very challenging. Established patterns of budgeting in governmental jurisdictions are hard to change. Agencies tend to fight vigorously to protect their administrative turf, budgets, and allocated personnel. However, the benefits to be gained in terms of better mental health services, saved taxpayer dollars, and fewer people with mental illnesses behind bars is worth the effort. For jail diversion to work successfully, it needs a collaborative approach involving

---

[50] Torrey, *More Mentally Ill Persons Are in Jails and Prisons,* 22.

all relevant stakeholders in a community, with resources coming from general and mental health providers and programs, law enforcement (jails), substance abuse treatment programs, the community at large, and others. Judges and county prosecutors also need to be on board.

PRISON IN OTHER WESTERN COUNTRIES

An American warden was surprised to see well-stocked kitchens, pottery studios, and cells that looked like college dorm rooms when he visited a prison in Norway. The only person having a key to an inmate's room was the inmate. Rooms were just that– rooms with a bed, television, desk, and computer– not a cell. No one is incarcerated for longer than 25 years (compared to many inmates facing life in prison in the US). In Sweden, the longest prison sentence is 13 years.

A trip sponsored by the Vera Institute of Justice, a New York-based nonprofit that works with government agencies to improve courts, prisons, and other criminal justice institutions and the John Jay College of Criminal Justice took a group of prison officials, prosecutors, researchers and activists from the US to tour German prisons. The purpose of the trip was to expose American correctional representatives to other kinds of correctional institutions in other countries. They found that in Germany correctional officers are more like therapists than guards–they had no weapons and talked and interacted with the prisoners. After seeing this, one of the trip attendees increased training in communication skills for his employees, shifting the whole focus around humanizing offenders and lifting the expectations for officers, to get every staff member to feel some ownership over outcomes. He also increased mental health training because when people understand the root cause of behavior, they are more likely to not interpret something as disrespectful.[51]

Germany takes a different approach in the running of their prisons. They have a low crime rate overall and a low recidivism rate among offenders. In German prisons, prisoners can wear their own clothing and can have unsupervised visits with family once approved by a social worker. One German prison that was visited had a workshop where inmates built and repaired bicycles. There were other prisons that had animal therapy

---

[51] Maurice Chammah, "How Germany Does Prison," The Marshall Project, June 16, 2015. https://www.themarshallproject.org/2015/06/16/how-germany-does-prison.

wings where rabbits were raised. A unit reserved for the prison's most violent offenders had a music room outfitted with drums and guitars.

The philosophy of the German system is that public safety is the logical consequence of a good *corrections* system that rehabilitates the person. So by examining what is causing prisoners to commit crimes, you can determine how to make sure they're less likely to commit more crimes once they leave prison.

Guards in other prisons stated they were surprised that the US reinstituted capital punishment in many states. They said it was important to restore a person's human dignity. Treating prisoners with respect would help teach them to treat others with respect. Since most incarcerated individuals in these other countries will be back in their communities, Corrections' authorities know that treating people with respect will result in less recidivism and keep the communities safer. Capital punishment is the ultimate act of disrespecting a person's humanity.

It seems that we have come full circle from the days when people with mental health problems were jailed because of their behaviors. Then in the middle of the nineteenth century, states began to establish asylums to house them and provide treatment, such as it was in those times. The asylums evolved into, or were replaced by, state psychiatric hospitals.[52] Such hospitals proliferated in the first half of the twentieth century but then, for reasons stated earlier, most have now been closed. Once again, jails and prisons have become the mental health institutions. A hospital psychiatric bed may not be available because the individual experiencing a mental health crisis doesn't have insurance to cover the cost, or the beds are already filled by seriously mentally ill patients who are court ordered to be there. This leaves very few beds available for someone in crisis needing in-patient treatment, which happened to my son.

The federal government could help the funding for mental health care for people who are in jails and prisons if they would change the Medicaid rules. Federal/state Medicaid is the single largest source of funds for mental health services. However, a person receiving SSI or just Medicaid alone loses that coverage if he/she becomes incarcerated. Not only is Medicaid not available to provide for their care in jail or prison, it can be difficult, or take a long time, to get it restarted once they are out of jail or prison

---

[52] Wikipedia contributors, "Lunatic Asylum," *Wikipedia, The Free Encyclopedia*, https://en.wikipedia.org/w/index.php?title=Lunatic_asylum&oldid=972340761.

(6 months). Thus, reestablishing proper treatment back in the community can be significantly delayed, putting them at risk for having another mental health crisis and going back into incarceration. Our laws and program rules are very short-sighted.

There is a place for incarceration. There are people who need to be incarcerated because of the dangers they pose, but they are far, far fewer than the 2.2 million adult men and women we presently have encaged in these institutions. There are alternatives to incarceration that are being used successfully in some places, but they need to become more universal. These include specialty courts and treatment programs for drug and alcohol abuse, domestic and family issues, mental health issues, veterans, and restorative approaches to justice. As a society, we need to ask ourselves whether a person did something really bad or are we just mad at them and want them out of the way. We can improve public safety and turn offenders into contributing members of society by working harder to make them and our communities more accountable for creating and accessing alternatives to incarceration. It will require shifting the way public monies are allocated. Let's get started!

INSTITUTIONALIZATION

Institutionalization as defined by Webster is "accustoming a person so firmly to the care and supervised routine of an institution as to make them incapable of managing a life outside." Life in prison (or an institution) is very structured. The administration tells you when to sleep, eat, recreate, take classes, etc. When released from jail or prison, that same kind of structure is not there. Only if you transition from prison to a half-way house is life still somewhat structured. Jobs give our life structure, meaning, finances, networking contacts, friends, and education. But it takes time to get a job, especially with a prison record. There are many companies that will not hire felons. If you have a prison record because of a mental disability of some sort, that makes success on the outside even harder to achieve.

It will take a while to get connected when first discharged from prison. Before you can tackle anything, you need to have money. Most people do not come out of prison with a lot of money, certainly not the equivalent of first month's rent and security deposit to secure housing. Then there are the things that go with housing such as heating, electricity, water, food, furniture, etc. You will need some sort of transportation. Being on a bus line is great, but you also need money for bus tickets. There are agencies that provide services for people coming out of prison, including housing assistance, bus tickets, and other resources. However, you need to be able to connect with these agencies. That means you need to be a self-starter. If your life has been structured and you have been told when to do everything, it is very difficult to suddenly become proactive in structuring your own life and needs.

My son served a sentence of five years behind bars. He was released at the end of July 2015. The first month was very rocky. Even though his mental health appeared to be fairly stable on our visits to the prison and he relished getting out, being able to sleep in his own bed, having home-cooked meals, playing with our cats, etc., this new freedom was also difficult to deal with. His community supervision rules prevented him from participating in most of the family activities that we had planned after his release. After the first week, he was also kind of bored. Interests that he had before incarceration were no longer that important. Instead of playing his drums for 10 minutes, he played for two minutes. He would follow me around the house asking me what he could do. It was like having a toddler in the house. Probation agents run your life. Aaron applied for jobs and didn't get them, and was prevented from applying for other jobs that he was really interested in because his agent didn't think he should work at that particular facility. The lack of 24/7 structure took a greater and greater toll on his psyche. He cut himself and ended up in the hospital for 3 days. The longer he was out of prison and adjusting to unstructured time, the better his life and ours became.

Holidays are difficult for a lot of people. Aaron had been out of prison for almost 4 months. He was really looking forward to Thanksgiving and filled his plate. When I questioned whether he would be able to eat that much, he told me he was making up for lost time. That evening, he became somewhat distraught and called the police on himself, saying that he was thinking of harming others and needed to be picked up. The police picked him up and when they called the county mental health provider, they were told to take him to jail. He spent three months in jail while the DOC tried to revoke him back to prison—for being mentally ill and having a mental health crisis. A judge denied DOC's attempt to revoke him.

When he got out of jail, he said he was never going back because it was too hard on his psyche. Yet six weeks later, he again called the police on himself, telling them to take him to the hospital because he was afraid he would hurt someone.

Aaron told the police officer that took him to the hospital that he was finding it very difficult to not have the structure that prison provided. The police officer, who had been in the Marines, said that when he came home from being deployed and then discharged from the Marines, he also found it difficult to participate in society because there wasn't the same kind of structure as he had gotten used to in the military. We are *making* people disabled with our institutional treatment of them.

We were surprised that Aaron called the police again because he had gotten a job which he liked, was working as many hours as he wanted, had just started taking guitar lessons, was participating in therapy and required classes, and started woodworking projects with my husband. The DOC again tried to revoke him back to prison for having a mental health crisis. After spending 10 months in the county jail, a judge again denied their request. But that didn't last long. When Aaron ended up in jail on a probation hold after his girlfriend overdosed, he was sent back to prison for four years for violating a rule of his supervision, not because he had committed any new crime. What a waste of taxpayer money and human capital! The list goes on. Once incarcerated and *in the system*, a person faces a mountain of issues that must be overcome to avoid going back to a cage, whether or not he/she has disabilities.

CHAPTER 33

DEATH AND DYING

Sometimes when a child is born with a disability, there may be complications that limit a child's life expectancy. The parents may be told immediately that their child will not live to majority. I had a relative whose child was born with only a brain stem, no brain. The baby lived only about an hour.

Later in life there may be circumstances that result in premature death. These might be connected with drug or alcohol use or mental illness or may be due to a vehicular accident or suicide. Death is an enemy. As stated earlier, people with disabilities die 25 percent sooner than their non-disabled peers.

We all abhor the thought of our children dying before us. Kids are not supposed to die. As a high school special education teacher, I had the unfortunate experience of attending several wakes for students I had taught. They died from car accidents, accidental gun shots, and suicide. It never gets easier to attend these. The heartache this produces for the parents is immeasurable. I recently attended a memorial for one of my sons' former classmates. He was 26 years old. He took his own life. He was very talented, incredibly smart, but could not deal with his particular demons anymore. The wake had to be the second worst night of his parents' life. Another friend's son just got out of the hospital following his second attempt to end his life. Because of his schizophrenia, he believes he is evil. My son's half-sister just took her own life at age twenty-five, leaving an eight-year-old daughter. Mental illnesses' chemical imbalances in the brain can really play havoc with being able to think things through and see light at the end of the tunnel.

The great majority of people who experience a mental illness do not die by suicide. However, of those who die from suicide, which the CDC says is more than forty-one thousand people per year, more than 90 percent of those have a diagnosable mental disorder. People who die by suicide are frequently experiencing undiagnosed, under-treated, or untreated depression. Worldwide, suicide is among the three leading causes of death among people aged 15-44. Across the US, suicides account for 60 percent of all gun deaths—far outnumbering gun homicides.[53]

An estimated 2 to 15 percent of people who have been diagnosed with major depression die by suicide. An estimated 3 to 20 percent of people diagnosed with bipolar disorder die by suicide. Suicide risk is highest in these individuals who feel hopeless about the future, those who have just been discharged from the hospital, those who have a family history of suicide, and those who have made a suicide attempt in the past. Thirty to 70 percent of suicide victims have major depression or bipolar disorder.

An estimated 6-15% of persons diagnosed with schizophrenia die by suicide. It is the leading cause of premature death for those with this diagnosis. Between 75 and 90 percent of these individuals are male.

Also at high risk are individuals who suffer from depression at the same time as another mental illness (co-morbid condition). Specifically, the presence of substance abuse, anxiety disorders, schizophrenia and bipolar disorder put those with depression at greater risk for suicide.

People with personality disorders are approximately three times more likely to die by suicide than those without. Between 25 and 50 percent of these individuals also have a substance abuse or major depressive disorder.

Sharing these statistics is not meant to frighten anyone. It is meant to heighten awareness to watch as best we can for any signs of trouble in this direction in our loved ones.

Anyone with a disability, regardless of age, can be vulnerable to suicide. My husband, whose depression was undiagnosed until his early 40s, confesses to two or three periods of suicidal ideation during his adult life. My older son, Eric, who is 35, relies on me a lot, both emotionally and to manage his life affairs. He has told me that he doesn't know if he can go on once I die. That doesn't make Tasha feel very good, but that is Eric's reality. We are working on making him more independent.

---

[53] Pew Research Center, "What the Data Says About Gun Deaths in the U.S.," https://www.pewresearch.org/fact-tank/2019/08/16/what-the-data-says-about-gun-deaths-in-the-u-s/.

None of us like to think about death but please be aware of the toll that grief can take on your body. Recent research shows that stress related to the death of a loved one can easily translate into a serious cardiac arrhythmia: atrial fibrillation. This is an irregular heart rate, often faster than the usual pulse, commonly associated with shortness of breath and fatigue. The risk for developing *A-fib* was 41 percent higher among those who had just lost a loved one, *within the first two weeks* after the death, than for those who did not. This is the time when people are most upset, planning the funeral, dealing with tying up the affairs of their loved one. This effect of A-fib can last for a year.

I am glad that I believe in the kingdom that God has promised when people will be raised from the dead, restored, and healed, when all sorrow, sighing, and crying will be done away. This doesn't mean that death doesn't hurt now. It does. It is an enemy.

When our youngest son was 17, we had been going through a particularly rough time with him. We were sitting in church on Christmas morning and he put his head down to sleep as he found the dramatization of the Christmas story *boring*. I told him that he needed to pay attention, which he reluctantly did. We had some family members with us at church and more arriving later in the day for Christmas dinner. At that point, I had a conversation with God. Things had been going so badly, that I acknowledged that my son may die and not make it to his eighteenth birthday, and that I was turning everything over to Him. I just wanted to have a nice Christmas without all the yelling and arguing and rule infractions that we had been having. We did have a good Christmas and Aaron is now 31 but incarcerated yet again. The revolving door of incarceration may be his lot in life, if he doesn't decide to end his life in frustration for not being capable of staying out of the institutionalized system.

We are all tested by life's challenges. When we or our loved ones have disabilities, it is that much more difficult. Only when others include us and give us a chance, an opportunity to be like others, can we forge ahead in this world.

CHAPTER 34

CONCLUDING THOUGHTS

In the last couple of hundred years, life for people with disabilities has both changed a great deal and yet not changed at all. When we were an agrarian society, family members with disabilities lived with the family and participated in family life and farm life as best they could. Once the industrial revolution was upon us, families moved off the farms and now it was not so easy to have a person with a disability to take care of. This was when institutions entered the picture.

Then in the 1980s, many institutions were closed and many people with disabilities found themselves out on the street. Although the money from the institutions was supposed to follow patients to community healthcare services, that didn't happen. People ill-equipped or unable to handle and manage life for themselves without any family or friends to assist them found themselves out on the street in a society that may have moved past them. These people with disabilities, physical or mental, weren't given a chance to realize their goals and dreams. They were made homeless by decisions made by politicians who didn't understand or care about them as human beings, and didn't view them as contributing members of society. This travesty has led to jails and prisons becoming the new institutions, but deputies and prison guards are also ill-equipped and need support. They have little to no training to deal with the people with disabilities that have been foisted upon them. A jail or prison environment often exacerbates cognitive and mental disabilities, but as in the age of public psychiatric institutions, it gets individuals we don't want to see or deal with out of our immediate vision.

I hope that from reading this book you now have a better understanding of people with disabilities and that I have succeeded in making you more aware of the simple accommodations that could assist a person with disabilities realize their goals and dreams. Just give them a chance.

The following section shares some of our family challenges with two sons with mental health disabilities and in the final section six individuals and families share their experiences with disabilities.

NO WONDER WE
HAVE GREY HAIR

Having a disability or being the parent of a child with a disability can be very isolating. People have told me that they know they can talk to us because we will "*get it*". They can tell us what their challenges are; we will understand and they won't feel that we are judging them. We are *safe* people with whom they can vent their frustrations with the world. Here are some of our experiences. We've had many that have allowed us a measure of understanding, yet without fully comprehending why people act the way that they do. While we wouldn't necessarily have chosen these pathways, we are eternally grateful for these experiences and how they have broadened our understanding of the human condition.

****

My mother desired to live independently for as long as possible. She was living in an apartment in the Chicago area after my step-father died. I was concerned that she wasn't eating nutritious meals. (Aging and the challenges that come with it are an acquired disability.) I talked to her about Meals on Wheels but she rejected that idea because she said their meals were too full of starch. I bought a bunch of plastic containers and when I would make dinner for my husband and myself, I would make extra and put it into one of the containers. I used masking tape on the lid to indicate what was inside and once a week I would drive the food from Wisconsin down to Illinois to my mom's. This way I knew she was getting at least one meal a day that was balanced with a protein, starch, and lots of veggies. This arrangement went on for about one and a half years until she needed more help.

My husband and I adopted both of our sons. We received a ten-day-old "healthy white infant" as our first son. Developmentally, everything seemed to go fairly well during the first five years. During the last two weeks of kindergarten and the first two weeks of first grade, we were told that our son had a hard time sharing, paying attention, switching from one activity to another, and so on. This was a kid that had no problems in day care and got along with everyone. My husband and I suddenly got even more involved in our son's education. We took him to a special pediatrician who did some testing, got information from both his teachers, his after school care providers, and us. Eric was diagnosed with Attention Deficit Hyperactivity Disorder.

My husband and I made the effort to educate ourselves about ADHD. We joined CHADD (Children and Adults with Attention Deficit Disorder) and attended the local parent support group, attended seminars on it, read books, and used recommended strategies to help Eric and us cope.

When we again applied to adopt, we looked at children that had ADHD and thought, "we know what this is all about, we have educated ourselves, and can handle another child with ADHD". We were told that there was a little boy that had ADHD, was taking medication for it, and had bonded with his foster parents so there was a high probability that he would have no problem bonding with us. His birth mother MAY have taken drugs and/or alcohol during pregnancy. Boy, were we naive. We happily welcomed 6-year-old Aaron into our home and family. God kindly shields our eyes from what is to come so we handle it little by little!!!

Right from the beginning of our visits with him, Aaron would run around our house checking things out, grabbing at everything, including big brother, Eric's, toys. We explained to Aaron that he needed to ask if he could use another person's possessions, while explaining to Eric that his new brother had been deprived all his life and Eric should cut him a little *slack*. Little did we know that these issues would continue on for many years to come with Aaron invading another person's space and using their possessions frequently without asking, many times losing or breaking the possessions and landing him in trouble with us, his brother, and other people. Aaron didn't seem to understand what the big deal was. Tom finally asked for a locking tool box for Christmas because he was tired of reaching for a tool, only to not have it available and nowhere to be found.

While on some levels Aaron seems bonded to us, on other levels he does not. (Professionals tell us that he is bonded to us, but not attached.) We learned after a few years of living with Aaron that he had what is known as Reactive Attachment Disorder (RAD). The normal cycle of an infant needing something (feeding, changing, being held), and being responded to by an adult, forms a trust bond between the infant and the adult. Aaron's early life was so chaotic that his needs apparently were not met and he did not form a trust bond with the significant adult in his life, resulting in RAD. When the needs of the infant are not met, he/she learns they cannot trust anyone outside of themselves to meet their needs so they develop reactive attachment disorder. Our house being Aaron's 9th placement didn't help any bonding either.

Somewhere along the line Aaron was diagnosed with Pervasive Developmental Disorder (PDD) which covers a lot of area, but basically tells you that the child is autistic or cognitively impaired, with developmental delays.

Although Aaron exhibited no physical facial signs or characteristics of Fetal Alcohol Spectrum Disorder, he seemed to exhibit some of the mental deficits that are associated with the syndrome. Aaron shows no cause and effect thinking and no problem solving skills and finds it difficult to modulate his emotions. He cannot be confronted with a situation, analyze it, and predict what outcomes of different behavioral reactions would be. This is a deficit in executive brain functioning.

We also suspect, along with his medical/mental health professionals, that at an early age, Aaron was sexually assaulted by an adult for a length of time. While we know many things about Aaron's early life, there was no mention of any suspected sexual abuse during these years. We did know of some physical abuse. If this is true, it probably has led to another probable diagnosis that Aaron carries, PTSD (Post Traumatic Stress Disorder).

When Aaron entered kindergarten, it was discovered that he had quite a few academic deficits in addition to needing speech therapy. Aaron went to kindergarten in the morning and Early Childhood Education in the afternoon. Even after one year of this programming, the kindergarten teacher recommended that Aaron repeat kindergarten. I was a special education teacher when we were adopting Aaron (retired now), so his state case worker, the social worker at school and the Early Childhood teacher thought if I worked with him during the summer and advocated for him in his new school district, he would be able to move on to first grade.

I did work extensively with Aaron not only that summer, but many summers and during the school year as well. When tested several times by several different professionals, Aaron scored in the normal I.Q. range; however, it was noted that his processing speed was so slow, he operated more like he was cognitively disabled, possibly due to suspected drug and alcohol use during his pregnancy. The suggestion for programming was to track him for vocational work as soon as possible because educationally he was on very shaky ground. One summer, Aaron and I worked on long division to bolster his math for the coming school year. During March of the following school year, Aaron was given a test that included several subjects. He scored very low in long division. I bought some workbooks for another summer of long division. When he sat down to do the math, it was like he had never seen the material before. Even worse than my refresher in Algebra—I at least had some recollection that I had seen the material before. Aaron had absolutely NO recollection of doing this same material the summer before. We had to start at square one. Again. Aaron's very poor memory affects many parts of his life, not just academically.

Another problem seemed to be how Aaron processed information or understanding the ramifications of what he was reading. An example of this is while reading a story on the Holocaust with his class, he started laughing. All the other children were puzzled and troubled by his behavior. The teachers were horrified and spoke to us. Aaron's explanation seemed to indicate that there was some free association going on in his head that led to some funny thought and he burst out laughing at this other thought. Who knows which of his co-morbid conditions or brain deficits caused this response. I later found out that this weird and inappropriate kind of response is called Pseudobulbar Affect (PBA). (This was not the only time that Aaron had exhibited this kind of emotional deregulation.) PBA is a neurological disorder of emotional regulation characterized by involuntary crying or uncontrollable episodes of crying and/or laughing, or other emotional displays that are disproportionate to the emotions being experienced. It is thought that the emotional outbursts are being generated in the brainstem impacting chemical signaling in the brain, which in turn disrupts the neurological pathways in the frontal lobes that control emotional expression.

PBA can occur in stroke survivors or people with other neurological conditions such as dementia, Alzheimer's disease, Lyme Disease, Parkinson's disease (PD), multiple sclerosis, Lou Gehrig's disease (ALS), attention deficit/hyperactivity disorder (ADHD), brain tumors, various encephalitides, or traumatic brain injury, as well as other lesser known maladies. It is thought to affect more than one million people in the U.S. PBA is often mistaken for depression, causing it to be under-diagnosed, under-treated or sometimes treated inappropriately.

All of this amounts to Aaron not understanding how the world works, trusting the wrong people and getting himself into a ton of trouble and not having any clue as to how he got there. It is very sad. The differences in the way Aaron thinks are not his "fault", but it affects his life very dramatically.

Aaron also has an incredible sense of entitlement that surprises everyone, gets him in a lot of trouble, and takes its toll on relationships. Aaron seems to have a skewed sense of money and possessions. It is nothing for him to wreck some possession (either of his or another persons') and state that he can always buy another one. Many of the things we have purchased for Aaron for Christmas or his birthday that were picked out specifically because he really wanted them, have been sold by him to purchase something else or pay someone off. At first we were hurt by his seeming callousness and lack of gratefulness for our getting him that cherished possession. Now we vacillate between not caring or being annoyed, but also not spending a lot of money on him for possessions.

A good example of a real disconnect in Aaron's brain is his fastidiousness for a clean body and what he considers stylish clothing so that people will think well of him, but not caring how he acts in public. There are times when he has a loud verbal meltdown in some of the most public places shouting swear words and thinks nothing of it. Or the fact that he has had "praying hands" tattooed on his neck, but can let loose with a string of swear words in his melt downs.

During Aaron's early school years he managed to get along fairly well in the regular education classroom with some special education pull outs. There were times when he was sent out of the classroom, or received either an in-school or an out-of-school suspension. During one in-school suspension when he was in third grade, Aaron had completed the work that had been brought to him by his teachers. After completing his work, he chose to write on the chalkboard. What he wrote encompassed our religious philosophy. For a child who even today has trouble articulating feelings, thoughts, and so on, and having only lived with us for two years at that point, he expressed himself very well. When my husband went to pick him up, the male principal was in tears, having tried to take a picture of what Aaron had written, but failed before the janitor washed it off the board. Aaron wrote that he was very sorry that he acted badly. He didn't mean to, but his brain was messed up and he couldn't help himself. He knew that there was nothing that could be done for his brain during this current time, but that God would fix his brain in the Kingdom and then Aaron would be able to act normal. It warmed our heart as well as the principal's heart.

Behavior changed a great deal in fifth grade (probably because educational concepts were getting too hard for him to understand and remember). He had 3 different teachers and classrooms; as he became more disruptive in one classroom, it was thought he might do better in another teacher's class. He even became aggressive with kids he had an otherwise good relationship with socially in other venues such as Scouts. One day he grabbed one of his fellow Scouts/classmates by the front collar and wrote on his face with yellow magic marker. What precipitated this no one knows. Aaron spent the last 6 weeks of 5th grade having an adult accompany him everywhere. When he got into middle school, a paraprofessional special education aide was assigned to him for 3 years. This aide and our family became fast friends because we spent so much time together and she had assisted our older son on occasion.

By the time Aaron graduated from middle school and went on to high school, there was no money in the budget for a 1:1 aide to be with him all day. Wow, what a difference these changes made. During the first semester of his freshman year, Aaron managed to get himself into so much trouble, including selling his Adderall (a medication prescribed for his ADHD) to other students. He was going to be in big trouble with the law. The assistant principal had our cell phone numbers on speed dial and we had his number memorized. The school was more than willing to work with us. I don't know how much of this might have been professional courtesy.

We also became well acquainted with the police department in our city and the local judge. During Aaron's high school years, he was given many municipal tickets and the three of us met with the judge on a 1:1 basis many times. Aaron could have purchased a great car with all the money he paid in municipal fines.

Aaron became a ward of the state during his freshman year, as we were exploring residential placement for him to try to get behavior under control so he did not get further into the juvenile/criminal justice system. We met with the head of a residential treatment facility and quickly made application. Aaron was in residence for five months. While he made some strides, he never got to the point of being really successful either in his placement or in his behavior. The county decided they didn't want to pay for him to be there anymore, so extensive home visits were set up and "family therapy" with the psychologist. On one occasion we were having therapy with the psychologist, and either he said something to Aaron or I did. Fifteen-year-old Aaron literally threw himself on the floor like a two-year-old and started tantruming. The psychologist was floored. He told Aaron to knock it off and take a time out outside on the picnic bench (about 5 feet from us, but outside). Then he proceeded to tell us "good luck" and "I hope you have a plan B for what to do with him when he gets home". My husband and I were stunned. Wow. Thanks a lot to the professionals. Nothing like cutting and running!

Aaron did come home that August after five months in residential treatment. The school year started out rocky and just got worse. In December we found a residential treatment facility in another state. We petitioned the juvenile court to relinquish jurisdiction of Aaron so we could send him to this facility. They gladly did so and gave us their blessing. Aaron was enrolled in early January in this facility about a 7 hour drive from our house. They operated on a level system. In 9 months, Aaron never attained the level where he could make home visits. We drove down to see him once a month and usually had a lovely time. His behavior and our relationship was the best during this time. School was computerized & individualized and Aaron had both academic core classes, as well as elective classes that he enjoyed. Construction was his favorite class. Very hands on at this school.

Aaron missed us very much while in residential treatment. He also was able to see some hypocrisy in the teachers not obeying rules the students were to obey. This really "bugged" him and after 9 months he just didn't want to do it anymore and got kicked out of the school for injuring a teacher. Back to square one.

****

As a parent, you want what is best for your child. If they are physically ill, you will take them to the doctor or hospital. When your child has what might be a mental illness, I am sorry to say that I, too, fell into the stigma of worrying about having my child hospitalized in a mental health facility. And this comes from someone who worked in mental health administration for fifteen years and had a K-12 license to teach special education. Not one of my stellar moments. Our older son, Eric's, sixth grade year was a really rough one. His behavior was changing dramatically. He was tried on a variety of medications, with no great results. He had gotten suspended from school a couple of times and both the school and we were at our wits end. When the decision to hospitalize Eric was made, I cried for three days. The hospitalization went well and life for a couple of years was o.k.

★★

After that first experience with putting my son into a psychiatric hospital, I never had a problem with it again. I learned a lot about a lot of things, including my own prejudices. Eric had a couple more hospitalizations, and Aaron also had several. One time the boys were going at it together and both were taken to the regular hospital and when beds had been arranged for them to be in-patient in the psychiatric hospital, two different ambulances had to be ordered to transfer them since they had been in conflict in our home. Life is never dull.

During the summer of 2000, our family of four and my step-mother took a trip to Alaska. We flew to Vancouver, B. C. and boarded the cruise boat there. It was Tom's and my 25th wedding anniversary. As an anniversary present, my step-mother had the boys in her cabin so Tom and I could have some privacy. We had a great time on the cruise and disembarked in Seward, Alaska. One half of the people on the cruise were starting the land portion of their trip in Anchorage, and the other half, like us, were taking a flight from Anchorage to Fairbanks where we would start our land package, eventually making our way to Anchorage.

When our flight was called, the boys were the first in line at the security conveyor belt to place their backpacks. Aaron was second in line and decided that he wanted to be first. He shoved Eric out of line and moved up to the conveyor belt. Eric shoved back. Before we could do anything about their behavior, Aaron took a metal medallion that the kids had gotten on board the cruise ship and swung it right into Eric's head. Eric was now bleeding from a gash to his head and people were lined up behind us. The TSA people were very gracious, helping get the kids settled out of line on a nearby bench while another came with a first aid kit. This was before 9/11. I am sure that if it had happened after 9/11, the police might have been called. The bleeding got stopped, a bandage applied to Eric's forehead, both kids given a mild talking to by TSA, the blood cleaned up off the floor. Then we were allowed to put our stuff through x-ray and board the plane (after everyone else had boarded).

The kids think of this trip fondly and as one of the best vacations we were on. They don't even remember this incident, but we sure do. We also remember overhearing parents saying to their kids to stay away from our two kids because they were "bad news". That hurts.

* *

There was some incident at our house where the police were involved. I thankfully have no recollection of what it was. However, I will never forget the kindness and thoughtfulness of one of my neighbors. This woman lived in the circle/court opposite ours. We had exchanged waves a couple of times, but I didn't really know her. After the police left (I think with the kids), she appeared at my door with a bouquet of flowers saying that she hoped the flowers might brighten my day a little. She said that she knew our younger son from school, and that her son also had disabilities and she knew how difficult parenting children with disabilities could be. We talked for a few more minutes about our elementary school, parenting children with disabilities and then she left. I had no further contact with her but appreciated the incredible thoughtfulness during a rather difficult time.

* *

One late summer day I got a call at school from my oldest son, Eric. I was a special education teacher at a high school in a different district than the one my kids attended and consequently, my school started two days before theirs did. The kids were about 9 and 13 at the time.

"Mom, the fish tank is leaking," declared Eric.

"Where is it leaking from and why is it leaking?" I asked.

"It is leaking about 2/3 of the way down because it got hit by the phone, and has a hole in it!" Eric confessed.

"Why did it get hit by the phone?" I inquired.

"Aaron was being a butt-head and threw the phone at me and it hit the aquarium," Eric declared.

Thank goodness I had a prep period starting right then. I told my colleagues that I had to run home for an emergency and took off out the door, dialing my cell-phone on the way. When my husband answered, using a few expletives, I told him I was on my way home and what the kids had done. He said he would leave work too and meet me at home.

When we got home, the ten-gallon tank was indeed leaking, more like pouring onto the floor. Fortunately, we had another ten-gallon tank in the basement. Running down to get it, it became very obvious that the problems were not just contained to the fish tank and the water on the floor on the first level. Water was pouring from the ceiling onto the basement floor. So, there was a bunch of clean up to do, as well as fish to save. Thank goodness this happened before we had the basement finished as water coming from the first floor into the basement after it was finished would have meant dry wall ceiling repair and a lot more money.

We gave everything a "lick and a promise" and returned to work, completing the task of putting our house back in order at the end of the day. I don't remember what we did with the kids. One of us may have taken the younger one with us to work so they were separated, or given them a huge lecture and threatened their play time. At any rate, we all got through it. The fish lived, and, miraculously so did the kids!

✶✶

There are times when life just seems overwhelming and there seems to be no light at the end of the tunnel. Recently my husband came across a copy of an e-mail that we sent to Eric's psychiatrist after a session with him in the fall of 2001. While Tom suffers from chronic depression and can tend to feel down quicker than I do, there are times I am right there with him. Most of the following e-mail is Tom's feelings:

"I feel like we're all about to tumble off a cliff. I feel like the family is about to just disintegrate and vanish—Poof! The heartache Jan and I are feeling is so great that I don't know how long it will be before we just all break down.

"I don't mean to sound so dire, but after leaving your office and getting supper at Taco John's, Jan ad I dropped the boys off at home, got them going on homework, and then headed off to Middleton High School "Back-to-School Night" (for Eric). It felt like one beating after another as each teacher told us how miserably poor Eric's progress, or complete lack thereof, is. He is just not turning things in, he is not completing work being done in class. He refuses assistance and accommodations provided for in his IEP. One teacher recommended he drop out of class, which will assure he will not graduate in 2003 unless he goes to summer school. On and on and on. . . the story is the same in all classes (with the exception of Drama where he loves the improvisation section they are in); however, he isn't turning in his journal writing in that class either although at least some of it is done. Several of the not-turned-in assignments are done and in his backpack. We spent hours working on these assignments only to have them never viewed by his teachers. Then there are the others which we do not know about and which he has tried to destroy our having any knowledge of (i.e., phone messages left by his teachers which he has erased).

"What is really getting to Jan and I is that we feel we are imprisoned from the life we really want to lead with our children, by the behaviors of our children. If Eric has to go to summer school, then we can't really go on those trips for which we bought our motor home this year. Even if we found someone to stay with him or with whom he could stay, it still would result in us not having the "family trips" for which we hope and long.

"It just seems like there is no way for us to succeed in going where we really want to go as a family. We feel imprisoned by these issues for which we can find no solutions. Hopelessness is what I feel; no way out; etc.

"When we got home, and after relating what we heard from his teachers, I said to Eric, "I have just one question: why are you doing this?" His answer?–the infamous "I don't know." In some follow-up he said,, "I just don't care [about anything]." As we worked on some of his homework, he repeatedly talked about poor self-esteem.

"Somewhere in the conversation, I made a reference to hospitalization. Eric said he thought being hospitalized might be a good idea (committed was the word he used). This is not the first time in the last few weeks that he has asked about or suggested that hospitalization might be a good option. We thought that he was just looking for another escape from the work he is supposed to be doing. But we're not so sure; maybe he really sensed the direness of his situation.

"When I reference hospitalization, I was thinking in terms of intensive psychotherapy, because I think his mental state is serious enough that hour-long therapy sessions even once a week would not be sufficient to help him sort out who and where he is. However, meds also may be an issue–they don't seem to be working and haven't seemed to work for this whole last year–since his blood draw in December, 2000. He seems very depressed and hopeless in his attitude about his life on one hand and on another level he is in fantasy land about graduating and going into the military, or buying things that cost a substantial amount of money when he doesn't even have a job.

"Where do we go from here? Is changing meds an option? (He cannot take Depakote.) Would changing meds need to be done on an in-patient basis, considering where we are at?

"We're not necessarily expecting an answer to this message (unless perhaps you have a reaction to the thought of hospitalization). It's just that this window into our gut-level frame of mind was opened this afternoon and I (we) needed to vent some more emotion out through it to in some small way relieve some of the pressure that arose this evening.

"Thanks for listening (reading)."

Well, after some reprogramming, Eric managed to get through sophomore year (and so did we!) and did graduate on time with his class. That was one of our prouder moments. Interestingly enough, this e-mail was written in the fall. It was a couple more years with problems in the fall before we started noticing a pattern. It seems that Eric has a seasonal affective disorder that happens in the fall rather than in the winter months when most people experience it. Light therapy seems to have some effect, but intensive talk therapy during this time has kept things at bay (at least no police contacts in the last couple of years).

✳✳

Eric was in the bedroom that housed his computer. I had asked him numerous times to do something and he didn't want to interrupt playing his computer game to do it. I was getting frustrated and was on his case. I had to get something out of the closet in that room, which meant that I had to walk past Eric. As I was backing out of the closet, all of a sudden I got hit in the left side of my face by something. I screamed. It knocked my glasses off and when my vision cleared, I noticed that blood was dripping onto the carpet. I yelled for Tom to call the police. Eric had hit me with his joystick. He went to jail and I went to the emergency room and got 7 stitches above my left eye. That was the beginning of his foray into the criminal justice system.

Eric was sentenced to the First Offenders program and was able to complete that with a glitch or two.

****

Parenting two children with not only mental health issues but also other disabilities can be a real challenge and sometimes we don't know which end is up. We just never know what life (and the kids) is going to throw at us.

Tom and I were out of town for a friend's 100th birthday. Our younger son who had been staying with his girlfriend, called us (at this point I wasn't sure if I was grateful for cell phones or not). Aaron said that the girlfriend's parents had kicked them out of the house and they had no place to stay. It was January! And we live in Wisconsin! He needed some help. At the same time, Eric was calling us to say that Aaron had been there saying they didn't have any place to stay and could they stay at his apartment. Well, Eric's place is usually a disaster area, the two girlfriends do not get along real well, and Aaron has stolen from Eric's girlfriend before. Not a great situation and we are an 8 hour drive away, except that we flew! Also, we really didn't want them staying at our house without us there, even though there was a key hidden outside.

We borrowed my brother-in-law's computer (this was before smart phones), got on line and found prices for some of the hotels in our area. We called Aaron back and told him that we would get them a hotel room for the night. We called the hotel and gave them our credit card number, explained the situation, and gave them a description of our son and his girlfriend. So now the kids had a place to sleep for the night, we didn't have to worry about the two girlfriends getting into a cat fight at Eric's and didn't have to worry about any of our stuff being abused if they stayed at our house.

****

Another time when Aaron was staying home, Eric and Natasha were going with us on vacation. We were part way to Virginia when we got a call from Aaron. He had just gotten a car and broken up with his girlfriend (the one from story above), so he lost his place to live because they were living together.

"Hey, mom. I'm stuck in Milwaukee. My car was stolen and I have no way to get back to Madison," announced Aaron.

"What in the hell are you doing in Milwaukee?" I questioned.

"Well, this guy needed a ride to Milwaukee and he paid for gas, but on the way he hit some cars and kept going. . ."

"WHAT?!! You let him drive your car and he hit other cars? Why did you let him drive your car?" I exclaimed. "Who is this guy?"

"I tried not to, but it wasn't . . . I didn't want him to but. . ."

This conversation is only one of the many that have taken place between my then 21-year-old adopted son and myself and/or my husband in the 24 years since we adopted the child. Many of our conversations consist of Aaron calling us in some sort of trouble and our incredulous questions/responses to his latest antics. He seems to have a sign on him that says, "Gullible." As it turned out, this was the beginning of a very long nightmare and incarceration for Aaron that started with this story but soon became very complicated, all because he decided to do some guy a favor and drive him to Milwaukee.

✶✶

There are times when I truly hate my kids. I think that their mouths' are the biggest problem. When they are angry, they are verbally abusive or bullies. Granted this may be part of their disability, but it doesn't make life any easier. Sometimes the behavior is because the afternoon meds haven't been taken or haven't kicked in yet. After a while, I just don't care what the reason is, I am tired of it and want it to stop. It takes a lot of emotional energy to continue to parent. There are times when I see the wisdom of animal parents who eat their young!!!!! Friends and relatives have commented that they don't know how we can keep going. There are some days when I don't think I can keep going, and/or I don't want to keep going. I just want to run away. And yet, keep going is exactly what we must do.

Finding someone who will care as much as you do when you die is a worry and challenge that every parent of a child with a disability faces. While there may be many times that we want to die because we just can't seem to take it anymore, dying for parents of the disabled is the scariest of all. Part of the scariness is due to the clearing out of the institutions that used to house/care for some of our loved ones. In other cases, the individual is not severe enough to have been housed in any kind of an institution. Many parents set up trusts for their children; however, that is only money.

That is not a loving, caring person that will do all of the same things that you as the parent do/did for your disabled child/adult such as answer the phone 20 times a day to give guidance or just be there as an emotional support.

(I have now completed a multi-page Lifestyle template for both Eric and Aaron, as well as a new document that the participants at LOV-Dane put together. I also completed a Functional Behavioral Assessment for Aaron should I die before he gets out of prison, so that hopefully he would be able to get IRIS or Family Care services). Eric, Eric's IRIS consultant, a friend, and a couple of relatives have a copy of this document for Eric. Eric has the copy of the document for Aaron.)

★★★

Navigating through 12 or more years of school can be challenging. When Eric was a freshman in high school, we found out during a teacher conference that he had been skipping his algebra class. There had been some other infractions where I felt a life lesson was called for. I had explained to Eric that dad and I had jobs. If we didn't go to our jobs, we would get fired. If we got fired, we wouldn't have any money to pay our bills and we would lose our home. I told him that his job at this point in his life was to go to school. Since he hadn't been going to school, or at least to this class, he was now homeless and would have to set up his tent in the backyard and sleep out there instead of in his bed in his room. This tactic had actually been pretty effective. So, when the algebra teacher said that Eric had been cutting class, I turned to him and said that he was now homeless. He knew what that meant but the teacher didn't. She asked for an explanation. We gave it to her.

Later that evening, while I was in the basement, the doorbell rang. Tom answered the door and there stood a policeman. The police officer said that he hated this part of his job but said that the police had been called because the algebra teacher thought that our having Eric sleep outside in his tent was abusive. It was March, but the temps were hovering around the freezing mark. The officer explained that if we made Eric sleep outside that night, the police would need to make a report to Child Protective Services (CPS) about us. Tom explained the "life lesson" strategy and while the officer thought that it sounded like a good idea, he was asking us not to follow through at this time. Tom then explained that both Eric

211

and he were members of the local Boy Scout troop and that the troop was going camping OUTSIDE this weekend. The temperature was supposed to be about the same as it was going to be that night. Tom asked if the police were going to refer to CPS all the Scout leaders, because the same equipment that Eric would have been using tonight was the equipment he would be using on the weekend Scout camp out. The officer agreed that there seemed to be a huge discrepancy but pleaded with us not to have Eric sleep outside that night. Tom agreed, saying he had no intention of going to jail over his kids.

This incident taught both Eric and Aaron a valuable lesson. If they didn't like something that we were doing, they started telling us they were going to call the police on us and get us in trouble. We started telling them to go right ahead. We didn't mind at all if the police came and removed them and took them to foster homes. While Eric had no recollection of being in foster homes because we got him at 10 days old, Aaron certainly remembered being in them. They usually settled down and cut the crap until the next time, but this showed us all that the incident stripped us parents of any authority. Now that they are older and more mature, they understand the extremely awkward position that we had been placed in while trying to find consequences for their misbehavior.

★★

After almost 19 years of parenting Aaron and trying to get through to him on many different topics, including that we love him, we received the following letter the other day from him from prison: (I have corrected grammar and spelling for the most part).

"I would really like to share my appreciation for you all for dealing with all the sh__ while growing up till this very day. It kind of took someone else who had a similar incident in his life to explain to me in a way that I truly could understand that you guys are my family and the ones who always showed that you care and love me. The fact that you have always committed to parenting and dealing with my life issues shows just how much you really accept me as your own son and that no matter what I have done in life, I know that I'm still accepted as family to you.

"I have made the decision recently to accept that this is how life is. I can't imagine how much I have hurt you over the years by pushing you away and destroying potentially great vacations such as Alaska, and others that would allow us to grow together as a family. For some twisted reason I've spent my life convincing myself that I belong to another family which clearly was me being delusional. Yes, I have (my birth family), but with all honesty, they are not my family by anything more than blood. I don't know them and they don't know me. And it's way too late in life to try and get to know them as family when it has been 20+ years. I will still speak to them, but I can no longer look at them as mom, sister, brothers, etc. What sense does that make? I am sending their letters/pictures back."

I read this letter first. Tom asked me who the letter was from. I told him that it was supposedly a letter from Aaron; however, it was a "who are you and what have you done with my son" type of letter because it was so out of character for him to write this. Tom read it next. He kept exclaiming as he read, having the same reaction that I did. I later read it to Eric. Eric verbalized "who are you and what have you done to my brother?" as I read. Eric has spent a lot of time being mad at Aaron for how he has treated us. According to Aaron, his cellmate is the one who got through to him.

★★

Life comes in all shapes and sizes with many twists and turns. The cellmate above seemed like a nice guy. After all he was able to get Aaron to see that we were more than chopped liver. Well guess what? Shortly after receiving Aaron's letter, we received one from the cellmate saying that two days before Aaron's 25th birthday, Aaron had gone "nuts" and started swinging things, yelling, etc., and got put in solitary confinement. When he was swinging things, Aaron had apparently broken a part off the cellmate's TV. We felt bad, so we paid to have the part replaced. A few weeks later, we received another letter stating that the TV couldn't be fixed and that a new TV was needed immediately and if it wasn't received, private information that Aaron had shared would be made public which would get Aaron in more trouble. Although put off by the extortion tone of the letter, we felt that if our son had destroyed the cellmate's TV, then we needed to make things right so we sent the balance of the money needed to purchase a new TV.

Life went on. About 3 months later, we received another letter. Although not signed, it seemed to be from the cellmate. It was again trying to extort money from us and was very threatening. Since we had been in contact with a sheriff's detective from the county where the prison is located, we called him and sent him the letter. He later told us that the cellmate was going to be charged with extortion and making threats to our lives.

I told my husband that we lead a crazy-assed life." He agreed.

During a meeting one time with a few members of our LOV Dane group, we were explaining some challenge and one of the members stated that the LOV Dane parents would step in as "parents" when we were gone. I was so touched. Here were people who had loved ones of their own with disabilities and challenges and they were kind enough to try to put our mind at ease by saying the parents of this group would look out not only for our older son, but his girlfriend as well since they are in a committed relationship.

✶✶

The day before his 25th birthday, Aaron took exception to taunting from the prison guards and "went crazy", swinging a sock loaded with bars of soap, putting shampoo on the floor of his cell, tying a thin mattress to himself, yelling and screaming. He was placed in Solitary Confinement. He had been in solitary (23 hours in a cell, 1 hour out) for a little over 2 months when we had a visit with him. There were marks on his face that he had put there by banging his head on the concrete wall or scratching himself. He stated that he was somewhat suicidal. Two weeks later, we went up to see him and were told that he refused to come out of his cell. We asked that he be made aware that it was his parents that were there to visit him. He still refused. The guard commented, "You know, Aaron isn't in his right mind."

We left on vacation. Aaron knew we were going on vacation and our usual protocol was to send him post cards and letters while we were gone to let him know of our activities and see some of the "sights" through the picture post-cards. He was able to call us on my husband's cell phone. We found out later that he was not given most of the post cards, nor some of the letters that we wrote! They all went through the U.S. Mail. It is a FEDERAL offense to withhold a person's mail, even in prison. The only reason to do so would be if it was determined that it was somehow dangerous to the facility. Since prisons open mail, it was obvious that letters about our travels were not dangerous or threatening to the facility. I believe this is a grave miscarriage of justice and violation of Aaron's civil rights.

When we returned, we again tried to visit Aaron. Through one excuse or another we were not allowed to see him.

After not seeing Aaron in prison for almost three months, we were finally able to see him in a facility that is run dually by the Department of Corrections and the Department of Health & Human Services. He appeared with long, dirty hair and beard, wearing a suicide smock. His eyes were piercing and strange. He was talking gibberish in a loud voice. We were shocked, but not surprised. One of the medical personnel asked if we wanted to terminate the visit. We said no, not yet. We wanted to try to get through to Aaron. Finally after about 10 minutes, we were able to get him to take a breath so we could get a word in edgewise. Aaron started speaking English finally, but was suspect of everything we said. He was tapping his index fingernail on the counter to a "heartbeat" rhythm and kept looking over his shoulder as if someone was there. He sometimes responded when looking that way, perhaps responding to voices in his head. He stated that he had died 3 times and knew he was being watched.

Aaron had been in solitary confinement for about five months, not with the proper medication, with the last month or so cut off from us completely in like a super solitary where he could not even receive mail from us. The United Nations has deemed more than 14 days in solitary confinement to be torture. So, the bottom line was that putting someone with mental health challenges into solitary and cutting him off completely from the outside world served to cause a psychotic break in our son. The really sad part is that the DOC (Department of Corrections) knew he was losing his grip on reality in May and they did nothing to stop his slide into psychosis until the end of July when he was in really bad shape. We had heard that guards didn't like to send people to the mental health facility as they felt it too "cushy" for these people. Stripped of all human dignity, people act out.

We sent a letter to the medical staff at this Wisconsin Resource Center. It listed the medications that Aaron had been on when he entered jail, prior to going to prison, as well as their individual efficacies in treating his maladies. The psychiatric staff immediately put Aaron on these medications. Every three weeks when we visited, we could see an improvement in Aaron's mental health. (Treatment with dignity goes a long way!) Although Aaron continued to test us with questions that only we would have the answers to, we could have intelligent conversations.

215

The delusions, hallucinations, and voices were lessening. This process took about three months.

* *

With the help of a job developer/job coach through LOV Dane, Eric was able to get a job in a foreign car mechanic shop. We will be forever grateful to the man that agreed to a "meet & greet" with Eric, was impressed by him, so hired Eric to do odd jobs around the shop, thus creating a job for Eric where none had previously existed. Eric worked two days a week for 3 hours/day. The job coach worked with Eric until the money ran out. It was decided that Eric would work without assistance and if he needed assistance or checking on, that his dad would provide that. Eric has Irritable Bowel Syndrome with vomiting. Eric was terrified that he would not successfully succeed in doing his job without the support of his job coach. The thought of going in to work alone literally made him sick. He was throwing up so that he could not go into work or had to leave work. This has actually happened a number of times which made us cringe and afraid that he would lose his job. Tom coached Eric for about a year. I make soup for them to take in every Tuesday. They eat soup (Eric's new boss who is one of the mechanics, the other mechanic, his old boss and another coworker and Tom) and then Eric starts work. Thursday's however just became untenable so Eric only works on Tuesdays now for 2 hours. Now he is able to work on his own for the two hours, but still will not go to work unless we take him. If we are out of town, he changes days that he works or just doesn't work. Not good financially or for proper employment skills.

Eric now has a Support Broker that is going to try walking with him to work and then Tom will meet them there with the soup. Tom has tried walking with Eric to work but that didn't work. We have also been talking about this a lot in therapy. So far, no progress has been made with Eric independently going to work on his own.

* *

After high school, Eric started taking classes at the community college. At first he wanted to major in animation, but due to limited enrollment and many people wanting to go into the field, he wasn't able to get in. Then during a 3 week hospital stay, he got interested in cars. He drew a number of cars and colored them while in there. After getting out, he used the internet and read books on cars. He became very knowledgeable about models, motors, accessories, nuances, etc. He decided to make his major auto mechanics. He was accepted into the program.

Eric had made contact with the Disability Resource Center at the college. He was given a note taker for each class, extra time to take tests, textbooks read to him through a computer program, and wonderful counselors looking out for the students to help them succeed.

For part of the time that Eric took classes, the Division of Vocational Rehabilitation (DVR) paid for the classes. When he was trying to decide what to go into when he couldn't get into Animation, he took a couple of semesters off. When he went back to school, he paid for the classes himself or we paid for them.

Somewhere during the time when he was taking the classes, I was still working, but Tom's schedule was flexible so Tom would drop him off and then one of us would pick him up later. We found out later that Eric would go sit in the cafeteria instead of going to class. He was doing no homework so consequently failed the classes and wasted our time, gas, and wear and tear on the car. We were very frustrated

By this time, he had all of his general education courses taken and started taking the auto classes. As long as his classes were the 2-3 credit variety, that met a couple times a week, he did okay. As he got further into the program and the classes became more intense, meeting for 3 3/4 hours every day, including some lab time, things got a bit tense for him. These courses lasted for 8 weeks and then another course started for the second 8 weeks during the semester. Apparently, some of the other guys would make fun of Eric in the lab because he isn't terribly coordinated. This irritated his irritable bowel syndrome and he would throw up, sometimes making it to the bathroom, sometimes using the trash can in the classroom. Protocol was to send Eric home so he wouldn't expose others to germs. It is hard to pass a class when you are throwing up every day or every other day and then are sent home and there is still 2+ hours of class left. We talked to the Disability Resources counselor. She suggested that we visit DVR again and get Eric's file reopened. She said that they had worked with DVR with other students to enable them to take the classes they needed with assistance. The counselor said that the college would set up course numbers that are specially used so that the student could take the course for the entire semester, taking an incomplete during the first 8 weeks, completing the course during the second 8 weeks, and make up the incomplete getting a grade in the class. The key was to have DVR pay for it because it would be costly to pay for each class twice.

When we discussed this with DVR, they told us that they would only pay for Eric's classes when he had a 2.0 GPA cumulative. Since he had failed some classes due to the Irritable Bowel Syndrome and other reasons, DVR wouldn't talk to us. When we tried to explain the circumstances, they still wouldn't budge. It didn't matter how many times we tried to talk to them about it or explain the diabolical nature of the requirement or to whom. So, here was a school willing to do whatever it took to help a student succeed, and a social service agency designed to help people with disabilities that wouldn't help a person with a disability!!!!

****

While Aaron was in prison, he apparently had the social worker get him the paperwork necessary for him to search for his birth mother. He had completed as much of the paperwork as he could, but needed me to fill in a lot of details. He had written his birth mother a letter. He asked if I would fill in the needed information, pay the required fee, and send it off to this agency which would attempt to locate Aaron's birth mom.

I had a great deal of information on Aaron's birth mom and half-siblings. Rather than pay some agency to try to find them, I decided to do it myself with the help of the internet. Success. My husband, Tom, and I wrote a letter to Aaron's birth mom, telling her that he desired to get in touch with her, perhaps have a relationship, and was currently in prison. We told her that if she chose not to acknowledge Aaron and his request, to let us know and we would break the news to him. Instead, she wrote to Aaron and eventually visited him along with some of his half-siblings. She called us to find out how to set up a phone account. She thanked us for raising her son!!

****

Eric is good with spatial things such as puzzles and he, Tom, and I enjoy putting puzzles together. Aaron has a very difficult time with jig-saw puzzles because he just can't get the spatial arrangement. However, like Eric, he is good with "creating" something with Legos. He is also a master at creating things with recycled materials, making *junk art*. He also has a good sense of rhythm and is a good drummer. Aaron also has a good sense of balance. He loves to skateboard. And he is good at it. While Eric can ride a bike and can roller blade, he just doesn't have the same balance and style that Aaron does when skateboarding. Aaron decided one day that he was going to teach Eric how to get some style and balance. Aaron was instructing Eric in a move where the skateboard gets flipped up and caught. Well, Eric got the flipping up part right but didn't catch it. He put a hole in his left cheek right under his eye. Time for the emergency room and stitches. That was the end of both Eric trying the skateboard and Aaron trying to teach him anything!

✶✶

When Aaron was much younger, he loved to "play with fire". He built a "fort" under our deck which is raised because we have a walk-out basement. While we were away and a friend watching him, he had a friend over and decided to make a snack. He took one of my 8x8 cake pans, put some bananas in it and took it outside where he had built a fire under the deck in the sandbox. When my friend who was watching him came to investigate, she said that she could see flames through the window that were reaching up toward the bottom of the deck–so the flames were approximately 6 feet high!!!! She got the fire put out, scolding Aaron along the way. Don't remember if the kids ever ate the bananas. I still have the cake pan. It definitely shows its wear and I remember having to scrub to get the "burnt" off of it.

Another time, Aaron was roaming around the court and since it was garbage day, he found an empty cardboard box. He also found some matches. Matches + cardboard box + neighbor's lawn = burned neighbor's lawn = Aaron in trouble again. He first had to apologize to the neighbor, then cut out the burned sod. He had to use his allowance to go to the store to buy new strips of sod to repair the lawn and then go over to the neighbor's about a block away every couple of days with the sprinkling can full of water to water the sod until it "took".

Sometimes I think it is a miracle that our pets survived living in our house. After seeing something on T.V., both Aaron and Eric decided to see if a lit match would actually become like a blow torch if a person farted with the lit match about an inch away. After trying this on each other, they decided to try it on the cats. Thank goodness I chose that moment to go see what they were doing and saved the cat from possibly going up in smoke.

For playing with matches, Aaron had to light 1000 matches (and singe his fingers a bit) EVERY time he used fire inappropriately and without supervision. He later told me he thought this was fun, not punishment!

★★

Aaron got out of prison on July 28, 2015. We were all excited. Aaron was transported back to the area by sheriff's deputies, directly to his probation officer's office. By this time it was late afternoon. We went out to dinner that night at a restaurant that Aaron had chosen, along with Eric and Tasha, and my brother and sister-in-law.

The next day, Aaron got a phone and started calling his birth family. One night, about 3 days after getting out, Aaron talked to either his birth mom or his half-sister (who were not speaking to one another at the time). After Aaron got off the phone, he was very quiet and melancholy. I asked him what was going on. He told me "nothing, that I was being paranoid". I knew something was up. I was lying on the couch watching TV. About 10 minutes later, Aaron came downstairs and said, "Mom, I'm bleeding". Even without looking, I knew that this was not an "I cut my finger chopping food" situation. He had taken a razor to his arm and made multiple superficial cuts between the elbow and the wrist. I got him cleaned up and cleaned up some of the blood that he had dripped along the way. I asked him why he had cut himself and he said to let the strong emotions out and feel alive. I told him that there were better and more acceptable ways to "let the emotions out" and if he did this again, he was going in to the hospital—with or without the police. He subsequently promised his half-sister that he would never do that again.

Things were going along fairly smoothly for about a month when he cut himself again. This time it was not only his arm but his chest as well. Tom cleaned him up while I made a phone call. A provider that had earlier in the day said that they had a 14-bed unit complete with nurses that was cheaper than a hospital as an option for Aaron's suicide ideation, was now turning us down and told us we needed to take Aaron to the Emergency Room. Told them thank you for nothing and hung up. Another example of resources that are supposed to be available but really aren't. I gave Aaron the option of going to the hospital quietly with us or my calling the police and having them transport him (any police contact had to be reported to his PO). He willingly went with us.

After spending about 4 hours in the ER and Aaron getting checked out by a psych doctor, they were going to send him home. I protested. I forcefully explained that Aaron had made a verbal contract with a therapist and me for "no harm" and now 9 hours later he was bleeding all over my house. Because of this, I didn't trust him to do/not do whatever he said. How was I going to be able to sleep, or was I going to have to stay up all night. They finally admitted him for 3 days, tweaking times he got his meds, but not his meds themselves.

Because of his fragile state of mental health, a church convention that our family has attended for 45 years was suddenly in jeopardy. Aaron was not allowed to take any trips this soon into his probation. Tom was speaking at the convention so he had to go. I didn't feel that I could leave Aaron home alone (even though my brother-in-law was living with us, he couldn't deal with this). Eric and Tasha opted not to go so maybe they could provide someplace else and something else for Aaron if they stayed home. That meant that Tom had to drive to and back from Michigan by himself on a holiday weekend. I was devastated and feeling very sorry for myself. But due to technology, I was able to hear what was going on at the convention via the internet connection. Not all bad.

Other church conventions that were normally attended during the fall were now not attended in person but rather via the internet.

****

Life seemed pretty good as Aaron was starting to get connected and take the classes which were required. However, jobs that he really wanted, he was not allowed to even apply for because they were forbidden by his PO. That was very degrading for him.

Normally, I host Thanksgiving for the whole family, however, this year my niece had moved into a duplex and wanted to host her mom, dad, step-mom, and brother. Tasha's mom decided to host the rest of us. Aaron was very excited because this was the first Thanksgiving in 5 years that he would be "on the outside" and with family. He only ate sparingly during the early part of the day so he could "pig out" at dinner—and he did too! After dinner, we watched vacation pictures from our East Coast trip. Not only did Aaron actually miss the trip because he was still in prison, but he also missed it vicariously because he fell asleep in front of the fireplace almost immediately after dinner!

Our state's national football team was playing that night and Aaron was looking forward to watching the game with his dad and uncle after we got home. He asked me if I would be willing to watch TV in the basement so they could watch the game in the family room. On the way home, Aaron announced that he was going to watch the game up in his room. I told him that he could do that if he wanted, but his dad and uncle would be watching in the family room.

About 2 ½ hours later, I came up from the basement and went up to bed. I was lying in bed reading when I decided to check on Aaron because I thought it a little too quiet down in his room. I was surprised to find that his room was empty. I went downstairs to ask Tom where he was since I could see that he wasn't in the family room. Tom said that Aaron had said something to him a little while ago and he answered Aaron but didn't know that he had left the house. I was about the check the front porch where Aaron goes to smoke when the doorbell rang. There stood two city police asking if we were o.k. We quizzically said yes and they explained that Aaron had called them making threats to do bodily harm to people so they had taken him into custody on a probation hold. They said that since this was a holiday weekend, his agent wouldn't be in the office until Monday, so Aaron would at least be sitting in the county jail for the weekend. While we were somewhat used to this kind of thing, we were also a bit shocked as everything seemed to be going pretty well.

On Friday as the gravity of Aaron's situation sunk in, Tom and I both felt like we had been punched in the gut–hard enough to knock the wind out of us. The police had explained that they thought this was a mental health crisis and wanted to take him to the hospital, however, whenever mental health issues are involved, the agency that has the county contract is called. They told the police to take him to jail. Thanks a lot. What kind of advocacy is that?

We conferred with Aaron's Probation Agent. She stated she recognized this as a mental health crisis and had no intention of revoking Aaron back to prison for rule violations (threats against self or others is a violation of their rules). The jail mental health staff stated that Aaron had been assessed by the contract agency and they found him not to be a danger to himself or others. The jail mental health staff concurred, so we expected Aaron to be released the next day. Another sucker punch. The Department of Corrections (DOC) had decided to revoke Aaron back to prison because there were no mental health beds to be found in any of the hospitals or institutions in the southern part of the state—even two hours away. Wow. At first, the DOC wanted to revoke Aaron back to prison for five years. Later they settled on one and a half years—for having a mental health crisis and not being able to be put into the hospital! Our tax dollars at work.

During the first 2 weeks of Aaron's jail incarceration we had no contact with him. Although we had put money on the phone account, there was some problem with the pin numbers the jail was giving Aaron so he could not call us and we could not go see him without him setting up the visitation. Thank God for friends in high places. A pastor friend of ours who we met through social justice reform was able to be Aaron's pastoral contact so he was our go-between for that first 2 weeks, and continued to see Aaron until Aaron was released. Jerry has continued to see Aaron for pastoral counseling every time he has landed in jail.

The man that Aaron drew as a public defender for his original case is a wonderful human being. During Aaron's incarceration we conferred with him several times pro bono. We had also contacted him after Thanksgiving weekend to let him know what was going on. Needless to say, we again contacted him. He immediately called the Public Defender's office and told them that when the paperwork came through on Aaron, he wanted it as he was taking Aaron's case. They agreed. David (the attorney) decided that rather than fight the DOC outright, he would advocate for Aaron's punishment to be the time that he already spent in jail as an "alternative to revocation". That would amount to about 90 days. David has continued to support our family and Aaron specifically through all of Aaron's ins and outs of jail/prison.

Court was before an Administrative Law Judge (ALJ) in the jail. It was much different than it a regular court of law. Aaron was present for the whole hearing, along with his attorney, probation officer, and the ALJ. Witnesses had to sit out in the hall and were called in one by one. The primary police officer for the incident on Thanksgiving night was "testifying" for the DOC. Tom, our pastor friend, Jerry, and I testified one by one without being able to hear each other on Aaron's behalf. The Administrative Law Judge then has 10 working days to make a decision. We won and Aaron was not revoked to prison. However, the DOC had 10 days to appeal. While they didn't appeal the verdict, they did keep Aaron in jail for 8 of the 10 days because they could.

Since getting out of jail, Aaron has participated in all of his mental health therapy sessions, in all meetings required by his probation officer, attended his required classes, and gotten a part time job. He has been working about 15 hours a week and loves it, so far. Getting this job was a real morale booster for Aaron and good to put on his resume. This is so important for anyone with a felony charge.

★★

Sometimes I wonder why I get up in the morning. It is a Friday. Eric has therapy with his psychologist. Whatever we were discussing put him in a "picked on" mood. He was rather disagreeable, in a 'kick the dog' kind of mood. After we were done with his session, we picked Tasha up and went grocery shopping. Things seemed to be going well. Since he had thrown up yesterday at work and gotten sent home, he was supposed to make up an hour today at work. Tom and I came to pick him up, but were tight on time. He called to ask where we were. We were just down the street waiting for the stop-light to turn green. He said o.k. We pulled into his driveway a minute later and sat, and sat. I called to let him know that we were in the driveway. He said he knew and would be out in a minute—he was now going to be late for work. When he got into the van, I ask him why it took so long when he was calling us 5 minutes before to find out where we were. He took extreme offense at my question and said, "Stop the car, I'm not going to work." Tom had already pulled out of his driveway and was heading toward work. He heard Eric open the door to the van. He stopped the van, told Eric to shut the door. He thought Eric was complying, but Eric was sitting behind him so he couldn't see what was happening. Eric made moves like he was going to shut the door, but instead, popped his seat belt and started exiting the van just as Tom was pulling away again. That knocked Eric down onto the street, scared us, and sent Eric into a rage. He then kicked the back of the van with his size 13 boot. Big dent. Do we call the police? Get him medical help? (This is not the first time that Eric has opened the door of a moving vehicle. He did it when he was 11-years-old, wearing shorts, and I was driving. He ended up with a plate sized laceration on his thigh. You'd think 20 years later, he might have become more discerning about opening the doors of moving vehicles.)

Tom took the van for an estimate. We told Eric he was going to have to pay for the damage he caused to the van. The first estimate was for $1349. He decided to get another estimate. Tom and the estimator were talking about how this happened. The guy said he has three boys and has replaced a number of hollow-core doors and patched the drywall in probably every room of their house. I don't know if he felt sorry for us or what, but the estimate came in at $953. Still a lot of money for someone trying to live on less than $12,000 a year.

Again, we felt as if we had been punched in the stomach. We couldn't even talk to Eric, we were so hurt and angry. We felt betrayed. We do SO much for both of these guys and then for Eric to cause us more hurt, anger, financial loss, etc., was just too much. And it was Aaron's birthday— the first birthday he would be able to celebrate with us in 5 years because of incarceration. We were all supposed to be going out to dinner. Eric and Tasha (poor Tasha) did not go out to dinner with us that night, they weren't there when Aaron opened presents, didn't get any of Aaron's birthday cake because we refused to reward Eric's bad behavior.

Eric calls me about 20 times a day, needing to hear my voice. For a little over 24 hours, I would not talk to him at all. I would text him and answer his texts, but not talk to him. He called Aaron on Saturday evening telling Aaron that he had a knife and was going to kill himself. Aaron asked me to talk to Eric. Great manipulation. I got Eric to put down the knife. I told him that if he wanted to use the knife on himself, he could go ahead. He would do what he needed to do and then other people would do what they needed to do. He asked me what I meant by that. I told him that if he drew blood on himself or anyone else, then the police would be called. His choice. After that I was basically talking to Eric again, although I told him that he needed to limit his calls to four times a day, once in the morning, afternoon, evening, and then before going to bed. Didn't happen, but calls are significantly less now on most days. Much of his debt for the car has been paid.

✴✴

We aren't over one shock yet, and Eric calls to tell me that his cell phone is broken. This is the cell phone that he has had for 7 months and there is still over $400 to pay on it. The screen is broken so while calls and texts are coming in, nothing can be seen, nor can it be transferred to another phone. The cat did it. (Lord, give me strength.) When Tom picks up the phone, not only is the screen broken, but the phone is bent as in probably having been stepped on. Cat my butt. Some days it's just not worth getting out of bed.

Aaron is again in prison. He did not commit a new crime but broke a rule of his supervision. The DOC revoked him back to prison for 4 years. It costs $30-35,000/year per inmate to keep someone in prison. The Legislature passed a law in 2014 to have DOC develop a list of short-term sanctions that they would be able to use to punish rule infractions rather than revoking someone back to prison for years. They have chosen not to use these sanctions. Tax payers need to revolt. Revocation breaks ties with family members and people lose jobs, housing, etc. There has to be a better, more humane way to deal with this situation.

✳✳

Eric was in Scouting from the time he was 5 years old until he graduated high school. He attained the Eagle Scout rank and was very proud of himself for doing so (as were we). Eric got away from Scouts for several years while Tom continued being involved. About two years ago, Eric decided he wanted to get back into Scouting as an adult leader so he has been helping new Scouts out learning basic camping and knot-tying skills, assisting Scouts with disabilities (and their parents), as well as assisting Scouts as they move through the ranks. He got notice about a week ago that he was getting an award for helping so many Scouts with rank advancement. That was a nice surprise and great for Eric's self-esteem. It was also great for us to be able to feel pride in our son's accomplishment. It also helped to reinforce that good things automatically come to those who do good work, help others for the sake of helping and not looking for a reward.

✳✳

As Eric's representative payee I take care of all of his financial activities. Recently I received his pay stub from his job. I knew that Eric had worked a little extra, but this check seemed a lot higher than what would be explained by that extra time. I noted that there seemed to be a rate increase. Another person had just taken over the accounting duties so I assumed it was a mistake and called the business. When I explained why I was calling, the new person told me he was going to connect me with the boss. When I again explained why I was calling, the boss told me that Eric was doing a fantastic job and so he gave him a raise!! What a nice surprise the positive comment and the increase in pay were. There was a time that

Eric was in danger of losing his job because he wasn't paying attention to detail and because of the IBS, was frequently absent or going home on the days he was supposed to be working. Through therapy we managed to get Eric thinking differently and he has been pretty consistent with his work attendance lately. This raise was affirmation that changing "the tapes in his head" and doing a good job at work were rewarded. Another win for both Eric and us.

✶✶✶

One of the reasons people with mental illness and cognitive challenges don't belong in prison is because they can be taken advantage of, exploited by others. Because of COVID-19 we have not been able to see Aaron in person for a number of months. Aaron informed us on a phone call from prison that he had sold his car to his cellmate who was getting out of prison in another month. Supposedly, the cellmate had put money on Aaron's release account. When we checked, no money other than what we had deposited had been placed on Aaron's accounts. When we told Aaron no money had been deposited, then he admitted the deal was that the cellmate would repay Aaron by buying a cheap car for him when Aaron got out of prison, figuring that he would have gotten a job and saved up enough money by then to do so. But there was no guarantee that that would ever happen.

Another inmate, getting out of prison the same time as the cellmate, managed to talk Aaron into signing a power of attorney (POA) for finances giving this person total control of Aaron's assets. The fill-in-the-blank form, which was not in Aaron's handwriting, also purported to designate this person as Aaron's Representative Payee for SSI/SSDI—a designation that I currently hold from the Social Security Administration. Then it said after ninety days Aaron wanted his birth mother, with whom Aaron has minimal contact, to become his Representative Payee. This inmate also alleged that he was starting a business and Aaron had committed to investing four thousand dollars in the business in exchange for 15 percent of any profits. What Aaron didn't know was that the inmate was only putting in two thousand dollars and making all the decisions. The two inmates were supposed to come to our house on a Tuesday when they got out of prison. No one showed up. On Friday, just as we were sitting down to dinner the doorbell rings. It is the inmate that was starting the business, asking for the car and the four thousand dollars. He had all the signed paperwork with him. My husband asked to see the papers and then told him that he was going to go make a copy. Upon closer inspection of the papers, Aaron had signed away ALL of his property to this person. We had just purchased new drums with Aaron's money. He could have taken those. Aaron has all kinds of birthday and Christmas gifts in his closet that he has not yet opened. The guy could have taken all of those.

We kindly explained to this person that I was Aaron's SSI Representative Payee and the paper he had didn't change that. It was Friday evening, banks were closed, and we didn't have Aaron's money here at the house. If, as Representative Payee, I turned over that kind of money to him, Aaron would lose his SSI, perhaps forever. And the car was supposed to go to the former cellmate. He wasn't the cellmate. So we weren't turning over a car nor were we turning over the four thousand dollars. The inmate suggested we call the police. We were glad to comply as we had already talked to our local police department about this matter and they were happy to come over. They explained to the guy that this was a civil matter and they were not going to try to enforce anything. He was told to go home. The officer later told us that if Aaron changed his mind about selling the car, all he had to do was say so and that was the end of the matter since no money had changed hands.

In our next phone call with Aaron, we explained what he had done in signing a paper that another inmate had written out, giving away all of his assets. He said that he didn't understand that that was what all of that meant. We asked him to write out a statement canceling the sale of his car and revoking the POA and get it notarized. He complied. About a week later, Aaron was able to get the paper notarized and mailed to us. We then mailed a copy to that person. So we think we are in the clear with other people trying to take advantage of him.

UNSUNG HEROS

People Experiencing Disabilities
in One Way or Another

Parents who have children with challenges have many challenges themselves and get very little, if any, praise or kudos for what they go through. Life is a balancing act. If you have a child or children with challenges (physical, mental, emotional), it is a super balancing act. These children take much more time than "normal" child(ren) take.

When thinking about having a child, most people think in terms of being responsible for that child until age 18 or through college and then the child being on their own. We have all heard stories about children coming back home, but these "children" are usually fairly self-sufficient. If you have a child with physical, mental, or emotional challenges, you are frequently looking at a life-long commitment of care for that individual. And worrying about who will care for that child/adult once you are gone.

Kids can be exhausting. Children with challenges are not only exhausting, it seems there is no let up to the exhaustion, because the care goes on and on and an opportunity at refreshing yourself never seems to come. Respite services are few and far between.

Marriage is a learning experience and stressful. If you have a child(ren) with challenges, the marriage frequently suffers. There may be denial or blame on the part of one spouse toward the other regarding the child's challenges. If only. . . seems to be a frequent thought on the part of one or both spouses. Or, 'there is nothing wrong with my kid', when it is obvious that there is. Couples have become estranged from one another or divorced, many times due to the challenges of parenting a child(ren) with disabilities. Somehow, the "for better, for worse, till death do us part" doesn't mean this or "I didn't bargain for this". What exactly was the commitment?

Having a child(ren) with any kind of challenge brings self-doubt, anxiety, and frequently depression to the parent(s). Many times there is a feeling of isolation. Friends and family seem to drift away or are somehow not around as frequently. There are events that your family is not invited to or perhaps the invitation is to only you and your spouse or significant other. Sometimes, even teachers do not understand and the parent perceives some blame from the teacher, especially if the child's challenges are behavioral/emotional. You talk to people but they do not seem to understand your challenges or your need to have some regular adult conversation that isn't focused on your child.

One unsung hero, is my friend Betty. She and her husband have a daughter who is blind, cannot speak, in a wheelchair, and has seizures. Aside from all the physical challenges, Betty has worked with her daughter so her daughter can be moved from bed to chair and back without using a lift. She frequently has her daughter in a "stander" so they can cook or bake together. They take her to concerts of her favorite groups and do other fun and educational things with her, as any parent might do with their child. As their daughter nears her 21st birthday and leaving high school, Betty is looking for possible work opportunities for her daughter.

Betty has been fortunate to be able to get outside help for her daughter. She puts ads in the college bulletin to get sitters so she can not only take a break for herself during the week, but she can also sometimes get away with her other daughter or her husband for the weekend or even a week. This gives the needed time to relax, refresh, and regroup to be able to continue on at a frenetic pace that never seems to end, and certainly didn't end when her daughter turned 18.

I have asked others to write about their experiences so you can get a first-hand look at what their life is like. Following are their stories.

Geoffery, Sharynlyn, and Marnye

Geoff and I had been married for one year and nine months. We were living in Chicago, Geoff was 29; I was 24 and four months pregnant. Geoff was in middle management overseeing three departments for a jewelry distribution company. I was working in accounting for a steel company.

We were very happy, still in the honeymoon phase of our marriage. Geoff's parents live in Michigan. We were going there for Christmas. We left after work on December 18, 1993, having about a four hour drive, plus we would lose an hour driving into the Eastern time zone. It was about midnight and we were four or five miles from Geoff's parents' house when all of sudden headlights were right in front of us. Geoff quickly turned the steering wheel trying to avoid an accident, but we were hit anyway.

The sound of crunching metal will stick with me forever. Then dead silence. I am aware of the seatbelt. I think that I am ok, but I look at Geoff and he seems unconscious. I get out of the car and go around to the driver's side and shake Geoff. He doesn't respond. I tip his head back and it sounds as if he is breathing through a straw and there are gurgling sounds. I thought Geoff may be having problems breathing so I put my fingers in his mouth to adjust his jaw to keep it open so that he could breathe. I don't know how long I was there like that but eventually a car stopped with a man and woman in it. The woman was a nurse. She called 911 and her husband went over to the other car. The man who hit us was drunk and had only scrapes and bruises and possibly a broken nose. Finally the ambulance got there and the nurse had to convince me that the emergency medical technicians could help Geoff and I needed to let them take over. I sat in the back of the police car with a blanket around me because I was cold, while they worked on Geoff and then I rode in the ambulance to the hospital. The nurse managed to call Geoff's family with the discombobulated information that I had supplied (but not phone number) and they came to the hospital.

We had not yet shared with his family that I was expecting. What was supposed to be a surprise with a cool Christmas gift indicating we were expecting, now turned into part of the trauma crisis that we were experiencing. The doctors started checking me out but then doctors for Geoff came in to say that they couldn't treat him at this hospital, but they had stabilized him and were med-flighting him to a Grand Rapids hospital that was equipped for traumas. Geoff's brother, his parents, and I left immediately for Grand Rapids, without me being medically examined. Looking back, I know that I was in shock, not thinking straight, not thinking that this is a car accident that has just changed my whole life forever, because it had, but I didn't know that yet. I thought that Geoff would be in the hospital for about a week and then be o.k. and we would go on with our lives as we had before.

We sat for hours in a room and more of Geoff's relatives arrived. I called a cousin back in Illinois and that is how my family found out. The doctors came in and explained to us that Geoff had what they call Traumatic Brain Injury, closed head, which means that when we were hit, Geoff's head bounced off the side window and support post but that nothing had punctured or penetrated his skull. It meant that Geoff's brain had bounced around in his skull and there was diffused bleeding all over his brain. This was termed the first brain injury. The second brain injury was when Geoff's brain started swelling and since this was a "closed head injury" it meant that there was no relief for the swelling pressure to his brain. It just so happened that the hospital was participating in a blind study of a new medication to reduce swelling in Traumatic Brain Injuries. It was a blind study, so there was no guarantee that Geoff would actually receive the medication, but we decided that it was worth a try. Geoff was moved up to Critical ICU and given the "medication". During this time they were worried about the brain swelling and the intra-cranial pressure (ICP). They drilled a hole in Geoff's head in which to place a monitor to watch/track the ICP. I slept in a room next to his ICU cubicle.

By lunch time the next day, my dad, sister, and brother and several friends from church in Chicago were there and many from the church in Grand Rapids were there supporting us. It felt good and comforting in some ways, but also somewhat awkward in that while they were there to comfort me, I also felt that I needed to be comforting them, which made me a bit uncomfortable.

It wasn't until the next night that I was finally examined. I really had to advocate for myself to get a medical check up because the hospital staff didn't understand that I had been in this accident too, that I was not completely examined at the first hospital and that I was pregnant. They finally did the exam which included an ultra sound. They said it was fine. I discovered during the exam that I was developing a bruise across my body from the seat belt restraining me. Not only that, I discovered that the seat belt had torn the sweatshirt and t-shirt that I was wearing along the line of the seat belt. No wonder I had been cold, with both my shirts torn open. I also developed bruises on my upper thighs where the lower part of the seat belt restrained me. I had no clothing beyond what I was wearing because not only was our car totaled, but it was impounded by the police as evidence so I couldn't get the suitcase out.

On Monday I called our respective jobs and explained what had happened to us and that Geoff was in a coma. Both companies were wonderful, assuring me that our jobs would be held for us. Each company took up a collection for us to help with whatever needs we had. The first of the year brought new health insurance for Geoff. The new insurance company was not going to covering as much as the old company. Geoff's employer made the quick decision to alter coverage for Geoff so that he would be allowed maximum benefits. They were able to make the coverage "maximum lifetime" benefits which Geoff exhausted in 1 ½ years due to his extreme needs. As time went on with Geoff still in a coma, it became obvious that neither one of us were going back to our current jobs in the near future.

One of the ladies from the Grand Rapids church worked at this hospital and got me a referral to a "high risk pregnancy" practice. Having been in an accident, and being pregnant, I felt very relieved that I was able to participate in and be monitored by a medical group whose specialty was high risk pregnancy. Who knows what this accident may have done to my unborn fetus.

Geoff was in Critical ICU for two weeks, in ICU for about a month, then a regular hospital room; each step-down lessening the number of tubes and wires protruding from him. However he was still in a comatose state. Comatose state is the correct medical term because usually a person wakes up gradually, like an old computer trying to boot up, not as portrayed on TV where all of a sudden the person wakes up. Eventually he went to a rehabilitation center where his coma lessened to the point that he was more "awake" and Geoff started to speak nonsense words.

So much had happened during the time he had been in the coma. In addition to the insurance issues, our lease was up on our apartment in Chicago. More church friends from Chicago had rented a storage unit, packed up all our stuff and moved it into the storage unit and paid for the storage unit for about a year. I had spent the first couple of weeks living at the hospital and then moved in with Geoff's brother and his new bride; and we were now both jobless, with Geoff having much work to do to become functional again. As the end of my pregnancy neared, I decided that I needed to get an apartment in the Grand Rapids area, so that I would be able to have my own space, have somewhere to call home for both my daughter and me, and to be able to have friends and family that were supporting us emotionally have someplace to stay while there.

Because Geoff was no longer hooked up to medical equipment, we were able to make arrangements for him to be transported to the hospital with a nurse to see our baby once she was born. Due to my situation my OB/GYN scheduled my induction and assured me that I would be having a caesarean section. Our daughter was born on June 3, 1994. We named her Marnye. Now I had two people to worry about and who depended upon me—my husband with a traumatic brain injury, and my infant daughter. We were almost 6 months post accident and Geoff had a lot of rehabilitation to do. He was given medication to help with frustration/help him cope while he was working on relearning things he had learned 29-30 years ago. We had celebrated Geoff's 30th birthday while he was in a coma.

After a few months, I had started noticing that something seemed a little "off" about Marnye. She didn't seem to be developing according to milestones. When I was "cooing" with her, as I brought her closer to my face, instead of her continuing to focus on my eyes, she averted her eyes either left or right. Some good friends were over when she was about 9 months old and when they tried to play "peek-a-boo" with her, she didn't react. At first doctors and we thought it might be a hearing loss but tests showed there was no loss. We waited. Marnye struggled with talking/language, socialization, and eventually cognitive concepts such as potty training. Geoff moved to 2 facilities in Grand Rapids, Michigan.

On Halloween, 1994, almost a year after the accident, Geoff's brain was healing and making new connections but it was like an infant with little to no self-control. We were given options of specialty programs in Texas, New Jersey and one with the U of M. At that point we moved to Ypsilanti, Michigan, where Geoff entered a "group home" run by the traumatic brain injury department of the University of Michigan Hospital. This was an intense program. There was approximately a 2 to one ratio of staff to patients. All had suffered traumatic brain injury as Geoff. They needed to be re-socialized and to learn strategies to cope as they were relearning the social skills they had lost. There were locks on everything. In some ways, it was a scary home to be in because the patients were all angry and yelling and locks and staff were everywhere. However, through group therapy, video taping, and individual therapy, as well as continued physical, occupational, and recreational therapy, Geoff eventually learned to control his behaviors. Interestingly, one of Geoff's issues was tactile defensiveness which he had not had in the past. During critical care and rehabilitation, he had grown a beard and mustache. Food would get caught in both and it was thought that it would be better to shave it off. Many hours were spent just getting Geoff used to having something touch his face before ever getting to the shaving it off part.

After completing this first group home, Geoff went to his second group home where skills were refined. This whole group home process took almost a year. Geoff's parents ended up paying for much of his time spent in the group homes as insurance had run out. We were thankful for their ability, generosity, and sacrifice. We moved back home to the Chicago area in September, 1995.

When we first moved back to the Chicago area, it was difficult. I had a toddler and an impaired husband, neither of whom could be left alone, or left alone with each other. I had to learn on the fly and with little instruction how to care for someone who could help himself and couldn't communicate his own wants and needs because he could not understand the concept of them. I broke down each task to re-teach Geoff, over and over. I planned our days around hours of therapies like the therapist had done. Every activity or journey out of the house took longer, was fraught with experiences Geoff couldn't tolerate and most ending in horrible failures.

A task, like opening a can of soup and heating it up could take an hour. Every movement every day was the same and yet Geoff's brain would not retain the information. Daily I was trying to assess if something was painful, if it was a sensory issue or if Geoff was not capable of processing things such as the sight of his own face and his own hand in the mirror and that it was his hand washing his own face. I went to the library and ordered books on Traumatic Brain Injury (TBI), TBI rehabilitation, and TBI family stories. There was surprisingly little on any of these subjects.

Because of both Geoff's and Marnye's individual challenges, there were times when neither could cope with the other one. And I had to advocate for both and cope with it all. Financially, we were sustained by Geoff's parents' unfailing support. My natural family understood little and though I tried to educate them, they could never understand that I was a single parent with two to care for with special needs.

A good friend of my father-in-laws was the head of the Rehabilitation Hospital of Chicago. Geoff received more "treatment" there. It was amazing to see how God guided just the right people into our lives when we needed them.

Eventually, I was able to get Marnye into the 3-year-old program of the local school district. Marnye is only 20 now, but it wasn't until she was about 10-years-old that we had a definitive diagnosis of autism for her. It seems that while autism has seemed to explode in the last 5-10 years or so, at that time the statistics were ten in a million children would be diagnosed with autism and nine of those would be boys. We were just lucky enough to be the one in a million girl with autism. Since the diagnosis, Marnye has received special programming and more than one person has wondered aloud about whether the car accident was the cause of Marnye's autism. I have had to advocate for her all the way and fight for a lot of the services that she has gotten. I had to educate myself on special education law and be "in your face" many times. Marnye will "graduate" high school in another year because in the state of Illinois, your education continues until the day before you turn 22 if you are in special education. After high school, Marnye will probably be in a self-contained workshop for part of the day and a day program through the special education park district. [Author's note: Geoff, Sharynlyn, and Marnye moved to Michigan just before Marnye turned 22 because the state of Michigan allows special education students to stay in school until they are 25.]

The dynamics of our relationship changed the night of the car accident. With his traumatic brain injury, Geoff could no longer be the primary breadwinner; that fell to me. Instead of Geoff making most of the decisions or us discussing a topic and coming to a decision together, now I made most of the decisions. As time has gone on Geoff has maximized his abilities and/or learned strategies for coping and can get along pretty well. He can be left on his own. And he can supervise Marnye while I am gone.

Geoff works part time at the local library. The Rehabilitation Hospital in Chicago found Geoff the job. He started working only two hours per week and eventually increased up to about 22 hours per week, being coached for a number of weeks by the Rehabilitation Hospital employees on how to do the tasks, interact with others, and get to and from work by himself. He takes a bus to work as he can no longer drive. He has worked at the library for 16 years, but because of his longevity, he is now one of the higher paid workers and due to budget cuts and minimum wage being much lower than what Geoff currently makes, his hours have been reduced to about 14 per week. I see the time coming when Geoff will either have to give up his library job and/or get another part-time job. The trouble is, most jobs are not close to our house and he would have to learn how to ride a different bus. When I contacted an agency to help with this, I was told that they could provide that service for Geoff, however, he would be on the waiting list, and it could take 6 months to 2 years before they could accommodate him. Just great.

Geoff ended up participating in a long term study with the hospital in Grand Rapids. They called me every six months for two years and then at five years and ten years post injury, asking me various questions such as how things are going, what improvements Geoff has made.

I have done several things since "losing" my accounting job following the car accident. I started back to work part-time when Marnye was about 6 and in first grade. I did accounting contract work. When Marnye was in Junior High, I did contract work full time. All of these were close to home with flexible hour so that if there was any type of crisis between Geoff and Marnye, I could run home, calm things down, get them both working on something and then go back to work.

Life continues to be a challenge, but I have been able to keep my sense of humor (most of the time), both Geoff and Maryne have learned strategies to delay gratification or to get along, and I have a big support system through church. Lately, we have been able to take more trips which broadens all of our horizons, is fun, helps us bond more as a family, and helps us see how others cope with life's challenges.

Craig, Megan, Hannah, Grace, and Matthew

We have 5 people in our family. My husband, Craig, daughters, Hannah (17), Grace (15), son Matthew (7) and myself, Megan. Craig and I married young, but we both had experience with disabilities before having 2 children with chromosome abnormalities. I had a neighbor that had Down syndrome when I was in elementary school and I would love to take walks by her house and talk with her. I also had a very close friend who was deaf and a small group of deaf friends in 3rd grade. One of my lifelong best friends had severe diabetes at a young age, and this has affected her throughout her life, and many times our play dates had to be cancelled. I was also attracted to the kids at school who had mental issues and I loved to befriend the children who others might not have felt as comfortable with.

Craig was actually raised for the first 5 years of his life by a mother with mild MR (mental retardation) and a step-brother with major MR. Sadly, his mother gave him love but could not provide him with some of the basic needs of life so he went into the Foster Care System and thankfully was adopted at the age of 7. Craig also had a close friend who had epilepsy, along with a step-mother and step-brother who also had epilepsy.

Craig and I started dating and got married young. Craig was 22 and I was 20. We knew with Craig's background that there was a good possibility of us having a special needs child. And even if we didn't, we had actually talked about adopting a child with Down syndrome. Special needs to us was not as scary as it might have been to someone else. Thankfully we both had our hearts open with love to those who had disabilities, because soon after we were married, we got fully saturated with it!

We loved our first years together and especially loved having our first daughter, Hannah. We loved everything about being parents. Hannah was so much fun and so easy to parent. Hannah was "normal" functioning, but we had a tough time getting her to eat at first. She also had many febrile seizures which were terrifying to us. We later learned that the Lord overruled and allowed these incidents to help strengthen and prepare us for what came next.

Craig and I absolutely loved being parents. The joy of everything Hannah did was just the best thing ever. It was a wonderful time in life, just being able to hold your baby and love them. Honestly, I wanted to do it again and again. I loved being a mom.

When Hannah was one, I became pregnant with Grace. During that time, Hannah had very scary seizures. During one of them, she tuned blue and I thought she had died. Three weeks after that, Craig's step-brother died from a seizure—so I was very shaken up. I noticed that Grace did not move inside of me the way Hannah had when I was pregnant with her, and I actually thought that my stress from the seizure incidents had caused a problem with Grace. I experienced major guilt that I had harmed my child.

Other than my fear that I had done something wrong and that something was wrong with my pregnancy, my appointments and ultrasounds were normal. Grace moved in me, but she was not as active as Hannah; she was more smooth and graceful, compared to Hannah who was a crazy kicker. I know now that her kicks were telling me something that the doctors did not pick up on. One thing I now know, is that God did give mothers intuition, and moms know best when it comes to their child, in most cases.

When Grace was born, we had our moment of glory—she came out simply beautiful. Even the doctor who delivered her told us that they could not give an apgar score of 10, but if she could, Grace would get it. We had our wonderful hour with Grace just marveling at her beauty. We are thankful for that hour because after that everything became crazy.

It all started when she tried to nurse. She could not suck. The Lord had prepared us through Hannah's eating difficulty to persevere through this. We discovered that she was tongue–tied [ankyloglossia–a congenital oral anomaly that may decrease mobility of the tongue tip, caused by an unusually short, thick lingual frenulum, a membrane connecting the underside of the tongue to the floor of the mouth]. Unfortunately we were in a research hospital–and the research study they were doing at the time was trying to fix tongue-tied babies by getting them to desperately want milk and to force the muscles in the tongue to stretch out and get it. But they wanted to do this by holding an eye dropper out in front of the tongue and dropping one drop of milk onto the tongue to try to get the babies' tongue to try to stretch out and get more. We tried this, but it was not working and was very frustrating and stressful to Grace. The hospital insisted we had to keep doing it this way. I was frantic because I knew this was not going to get my daughter to eat, but the staff did not want to allow me to help my daughter in my own way. They wanted to complete their research study and they threatened me if I did not continue the protocol. Thankfully, I had a wonderful pediatrician who literally signed Grace's life into her own hands to let us get out of the hospital so I could feed my daughter. For the next two weeks, we were literally feeding Grace around the clock. We had to cut off a nipple of the bottle and drip the milk into her mouth because she had no sucking ability whatsoever. It took hours to get through one bottle. Thankfully, our daughter Hannah, loved to just sit by me and "help her sister".

By the 3rd week of life, we had an appointment with an ENT who was supposed to be one of the best for children so we could get Grace's tongue cut so she could move her tongue, as nothing else seemed to help the sucking mechanism. During this time, I observed that something did not seem right with Grace's nostril; it seemed to be completely clean all of the time. I mentioned this to the ENT in our appointment. She stuck a utensil up Grace's nose and found out that Grace's nose hole was actually fused together so she could not breathe through one side of her nose. This was the reason she could not suck or eat. She was literally having to choose to eat or breathe because of this. At our appointment to discuss Grace's surgery to have this choanial atresia fixed in her nose, we were told by this top children's doctor that there was no other alternative that would keep the artesia from coming back except to have inch long tubes put in her nose. At that time, we did not know any better that we should question a top-ranking doctor, and just did as she suggested. We were told by this doctor that this would not be a big deal at all.

Grace came out of the surgery with hard plastic tubes that stuck almost an inch out of both sides of her nostrils. We no longer could hold her in most positions because the tubes would hit something and cause her nose to bleed or to hurt. She moved her hands a lot which then would hit the tubes and cause her to cry. She had a very hard time sleeping and she was a wreck. She was in pain, could not be held the way she wanted to. We had to clean the tubes every 4 hours which was a crazy process that she hated; our poor sweet daughter was very miserable and in pain for 6 weeks of this. It was awful. She cried almost the whole 6 weeks. I do not know how any doctor could have told us this was not a big deal. It was so awful for her that we thought that her delayed development and other issues came because of these nose tubes. The day that she got her nose tubes out was one of the most beautiful moments of our life. Seeing her face without those awful tubes took me to a faraway place of realizing what it will be like when God restores life to all of mankind when "there will be no more sickness or sorrow and all former things shall pass away." It was beautiful and I just cried with happiness.

We were not free and clear. We spent the next few weeks teaching Grace how to breast feed, and we were told that we could not do it–but we did do it! Once again, we are thankful for how the Lord gave us a small negative experience with Hannah's eating issues so we would stick to getting Grace to learn how to nurse.

Even though the doctor had told us these tubes were the only answer for her choanial atresia to not grow back, it did. We went to another ENT who said what the other doctor did to Grace was inhumane and he would not even think of sticking those tubes in a dog's nose, let alone an infant. He repeated the surgery with small little bandages up in her nose that did not cause her pain and discomfort–and we could hold and snuggle her any way we wanted. Oh what a difference that made!

On top of all of this, there were so many other things going on with Grace that first year that I could fill a whole book! She reacted negatively to vaccinations, had failure to thrive, soaring fevers up to 106F, a heart murmur, different fungal infections from the antibiotics she was put on, etc. The doctors suggested many things that could be wrong with her and we envisioned the worst. There were so many mistakes made with Grace. What I learned from this is to follow my intuition—a mother's intuition. I was so right; and either the doctors just did not know how to treat my daughter or they were just wrong. One example is that Grace was misdiagnosed with a severe hearing loss. A severe hearing loss means that she could never hear me no matter how loud I would scream. And they diagnosed her with this hearing loss in 3 different ways—but I knew she could hear—and the doctors just made me feel like I was crazy and imaging things. So, I listened to them and allowed them to put hearing aids in for 3 years that were set on "severe hearing loss". All along I was right, she could hear, her pathways were just not the same as ours so they pick up differently. When she was old enough for me to know for sure, we took them off. Grace is now 15 and unbelievable at phonics—yet a hearing test today will still say she has a severe hearing loss.

Grace's first year was extremely, extremely crazy and difficult. We had no idea what was wrong. Millions of questions went through our head. Why was Grace still like a newborn when she would be turning 1? Was it because of the surgeries, the nose tubes, the immunizations, the lack of air her first month? Was it an inherited thing, as we knew Craig's birth family had mental issues? I turned the guilt inward and wondered what I could have done differently; did I not speak up enough with the doctors, or was it because I was so stressed with Hannah's seizures when I was pregnant? Questions, questions, questions. It took a year of this wondering before the doctors finally gave Grace the test that had the answers.

When Grace was one, the test shows that she has a rare chromosome abnormality where she has an extra piece of a chromosome. So rare, they named it after her! Craig and I were then tested to see if we were carriers of this. I still remember the phone call when the doctor said that I was the carrier. I was shocked as we very much thought it was from Craig's side! It turns out that I have a balanced chromosome abnormality—which can lead to a normal child, a miscarriage, a stillborn child, or a child born with chromosome abnormalities. Throughout the years, I have experienced each of these scenarios, some of which is very sad.

The initial diagnosis for Grace brought much relief. Many people think it would be such an awful diagnosis to get as parents, but honestly, we were so relieved to finally know what was wrong. At the same time, it did not give us answers to many other questions as it was impossible to know what this diagnosis would mean for Grace. No one else has ever had what she has. The doctor and chromosome team originally gave Grace a life span of three years—but our pediatrician was wise—he didn't tell us this until she hit the 3-year-old mark and there was so much improvement in her that he said that he could tell us now that she would live! I do not know the exact percentage, but it is a very small percentage of children (outside of those diagnosed with Down syndrome) with extra pieces of chromosomes that live to a year, let alone be healthy after that! We are very thankful to have two children, Grace and then 7 years ago, we had Matthew with the same abnormality as Grace, to be alive and thriving. They are both huge miracles from the Lord.

The first year of Grace's life was definitely the hardest and the most touch-and-go as we did not know if she would survive. I am so thankful to the Lord that he gave me such a wonderful husband who could handle it, and a wonderful little toddler of a daughter in Hannah who was so content to be mommy's little helper—because there was no extra time for much else. Thankfully, I did have a wonderful support system; our families were close by and we had a wonderful church family. It was so obvious that prayers were being said and answered for us. I absolutely do not know how those without the Lord can possibly get through such challenges.

We also experienced the financial burden of a special needs child, as Craig was still in college and I had to quit my job to take care of Grace. Thankfully at that time Grace did qualify for SSI, which was a huge help, however, as time went on and Craig was able to get a decent job, as his salary increased, the SSI decreased. We experienced the conflict of wondering if it actually would have been better for us financially for Craig not to make more money, because then we lost the SSI and the benefits that went along with it. I can see how this would be a tough decision for many, to not want to try to earn more because you would actually get less financial help and less help for your child. Raising a special needs child is VERY expensive; with a lot of expenses that people do not even consider. Regular medical insurance can have high deductibles and high out-of-pocket expenses. It also does not reimburse for mileage. Most places offer free "Birth to 3" programs, which is extremely helpful. Where you live will determine what free programs are offered after that age. The school district we were in would cover basic therapy but not the kind of speech therapy that would cover apraxia which is what Grace has. They actually told me I would have to take them to court to get it. That might not sound like a big deal, but when you are struggling to meet your child's needs every day, a court battle seemed overwhelming at the time and just way easier to pay (or charge) your child's therapy payments. This adds up quickly, however!

When Grace was young, we lived in Ohio. In Ohio, the therapist seemed to stress ABA (Applied Behavior Analysis) therapy, a protocol for autistic children. Ohio seems to love this program, but some other states do not accept it. As I do not have an autistic child, I cannot say if it would be helpful to them or not. All I can say is that this program damaged my daughter. As Grace is nonverbal and does not fit into any category of special needs, it is easy to group her into the autistic category. She does share some of the same qualities, but this is not her diagnosis or how her brain functions. Many times professionals want to stick Grace into another medical group when they should realize she is on her own path with a separate diagnosis. The therapist would deal with her according to ABA protocol. Basically, Grace had to do something and then was given a reward, in a very straightforward manner, no fun to it. I hope with others who are given ABA that it is not this way, but this was our experience with it. It made Grace revert instead of moving forward, because she became fearful and hated the task. She would wave goodbye to the therapist the whole time they were there, as she just wanted them to leave. When she was 2, we had a bubble party for her because she loved bubbles so much, but then the therapists would use bubbles as s reward after the ABA and to this day, she is terrified of bubbles; to the point where she flips out and cries if bubbles are anywhere near her. Every therapist was very nice and I loved them as a person, but the way they were taught to handle teaching Grace was too strict and scary for her. We ended up taking a break from therapy for years because instead of helping, it caused her to be fearful and revert on already learned skills.

We were given huge lists of things we were to work on with Grace daily. Basically they wanted all day long therapy with her, and as a parent, it was impossible to do. I had another child to take care of, I had home responsibilities, we had to eat, etc., and my husband worked very long hours. It was just too much. But I felt like I had to do it all; that if I did not do it all then Grace would suffer for it. I had so much guilt because I could not do everything on that list every day. And these lists that I was given came from multiple sources. I felt the tug of emotions between wanting my child to enjoy herself vs. doing these things they wanted me to do. Finally, I was able to give it to God and just accept that Grace was a happy child and that what she needed most from me was my love and to help her to be the best she can be, but in her time frame and at a pace she and I could handle. Years later, as I look back, I never regret that decision. What a huge relief it was to break free from that guilt! She learned what she needed in her time frame when she was ready for it, not because anyone was doing therapy with her all day long. I will admit, the right kind of therapy is helpful, but in the correct dosage.

As stated earlier, Grace was misdiagnosed with a severe hearing loss, so she got American Sign Language (ASL) from a "birth to 3" teacher. She loved this because they were very play-oriented, but Grace did not pick it up then and she did not want her or us to sign. She would turn her head the other way when we did it. ASL was extremely hard to use, especially when Grace did not want us to use it and she did not have the motor skills in hands or face that is required. The methods to teach parents were extremely boring–which made it harder. When we were introduced to the Signing Time video series, that really made a difference for us all. Our family loved these, and Grace would watch it with love. When she was about 3-years-old, she started with her first signs. She no longer had her ASL teacher when she started to sign more regularly–partly because she did not qualify anymore as we realized she did not have a hearing loss, but also because the teacher along with other therapists, just did not work for Grace learning wise. After researching online, I discovered that ASL is not the best method for special needs children to learn for a few reasons: first of all, it is hard enough for someone with an average functioning brain to pick up sign language because unless signing one word, the sentences are backwards and not coordinated with spoken word. For someone with a compromised brain function, this is extremely confusing. Secondly, to those with limited hand and face movements, which my children have, the ASL signs are very complicated to use and my children simply cannot do most of the signs. I also found a drawback: depending on what region of the country we are in, people sign differently, which makes it even more confusing. Currently, we are sticking with the signs from Signing Time video because Grace loves these videos. I found that Signed English is more appropriate to use with special needs children who can hear. Signed English is signed word for word in an easier way. The problem with this is that there are hardly any references to this and it is not used much. Grace still does not use this very much–she uses a combination of her own signs, Signed English, and ASL. She still is very limited in what she chooses to use, but she has no problem getting her thoughts across to me. We have tried "talking machines", but both my children have yet to want to use them. Part of the problem is the way they are programmed which is not user-friendly, to what my children want to say. I have to reprogram it—I am still in the process of doing this and trying to figure out ways that my children might actually want to use it for communication rather than just a toy.

When we lived in Ohio we did have trouble getting services. I now know that the services that we were given had to do with what county you live in. Unfortunately the county we lived in denied every service for us even though Grace was developmentally delayed in all areas and was nonverbal. We could go through the school district to get some services, but even that was limited. We put her in a special needs preschool. There were pros and cons to that. One of the biggest problems was the "No Child Left Behind Act." This is a huge problem because that meant they wanted Grace in with children her own chronological age, and that did leave her behind because mentally she is years behind them. She learned best from those who were years younger then her—because they were her peers. But because of the law, the school would not allow her to be with the younger children. I felt the pressure from the professionals that worked with us to put her in school, like it was the best thing for her. When she was in preschool it worked out fine, because I could limit her time there, but she would get sick going there because she had so much anxiety She would also revert. She stopped using sign language and stopped being potty trained. Overall she did enjoy preschool in small amounts, but I could not send her to elementary school. There were just too many rules they wanted obeyed that I knew would cause problems with her. And being with children her age was too advanced; she needed the younger children to be with. She also did not perform for others the way she would be at home. Her special learning plans that the specialist set up were not followed, which I have heard from others that they have also had this problem. For us, the choice to home-school has worked great.

Grace overall really truly loves others and loves to make people happy. She loves her car. It is the topic of conversation and of picture taking all the day long. She also loves to go grocery shopping because she loves food and getting people presents. Grace gets upset very easily and nervous very easily. She has a huge temper that we are desperately trying to help control. We seem to find something that works for a few days, and then it stops working. She also does not obey well and interrupts us continually when Craig and I are trying to have time together or with Hannah. Her whole life she has had hard time sleeping and needs lots of comfort to fall asleep. But Grace has so much joy, and such obvious joy in life. One of our favorite things ever said about her was when she was in a choral group (where she jumped and waved) at a nursing home and one of the patients told me that the show could not afford to lose her in their act, as she was the center of attention!

Matthew came into our life 7 years ago. Grace was so sweet during the whole pregnancy; she just loved the idea of having a baby. My pregnancy with him was scary, as we knew the risks, but had to put it in the Lord's hands and it definitely helped us get through. Matthew is absolutely a joy and we are so thankful to have him. Other than not breathing at birth, his first year was easy in comparison to Grace's. We found out when he was 2 weeks old that he has the same chromosome abnormality as Grace. I have to admit, that was devastating and overwhelming. I just was done with life at that time; not suicidal, but done, where I just wanted us all to go immediately to God's Kingdom where there is no imperfection anymore. It was very hard, but the Lord lifted me up and taught me to take life day by day and to rejoice in the fact that Matthew did not struggle to live as Grace had done that first year. We also knew, because of Grace, what to do and what not to do and that was a huge relief. We knew from the experience with Grace that no matter what we did, Matthew would be in the baby stages a lot longer than normal and eventually he would walk, etc., so we could just enjoy him in each of the stages. He still had therapy but instead of feeling panic about when he would do things, we could relax and know that he will do most of them, but in his own time frame.

Our biggest issue with Matthew has been epilepsy. Epilepsy is a terrifying disease. Epilepsy to me is worse than almost anything else with which we have been challenged (other than having a stillborn). I have really had to learn to lean on the Lord to not have fear with this. His seizures can happen anytime, anywhere. He throws up in the middle of them and turns blue. He has them when he is sleeping face down, but thankfully it has always been obviously overruled that he has guardian angels and has not died. Epilepsy itself can cause learning issues, on top of what he has to begin with. The treatment itself also has side effects, including increasing seizures hundredfold. One of our experiences with a top Neurologist is that as we were switching medicine and Matthew was reacting negatively to it with increased seizures, the doctor would not listen to me. For almost a whole year, the neurologist would not speak to me, nor I to her. Everything would go to voice mail for a nurse to pick up, and then the message would be translated wrong, then the doctor would tell the nurse what to tell me. I even requested that the doctor call me a few times and the doctor never did. The nurse told me that the doctor did not believe me when I said Matthew's seizures were increasing. They then wanted me to hospitalize Matthew to see if they were seizures in fact, that he was having. So we put him in the hospital to prove he was having seizures. The neurologist then told me that she did not believe me that Matthew was having seizures before, but now she did after seeing the evidence. Thankfully, we were able to switch to another neurologist at a hospital that is not rated as high, but this neurologist calls me and listens to me, every time! That makes an unbelievably huge difference to have a doctor care enough to call. What a blessing!

After Matthew was born, we moved to West Virginia for my husband's work. We lost our wonderful support system we had in Ohio, but WV is unbelievably awesome to people with disabilities. It was definitely an overruling from the Lord to move here. The therapists in WV do not practice ABA therapy, and instead focus on play therapy. Play therapy is great and both Grace and Matthew love it. They also have this awesome statewide program for families of the disabled who have unmet miscellaneous bills. When you are experiencing a financial hardship, they will help pay bills, even a dance class, and it is not income-based. This is awesome in itself. WV's state Medicaid Waiver program for the disabled is based upon the child's income, not the parents', which is an absolutely huge help! If you medically qualify, it pays for respite, mileage, etc., and the biggest blessing is that it will pay parents to run home-based programs for their children. Every year the amount the child is given fluctuates, but this is absolutely huge at making everyday life easier and thus better for the whole family. This program has taken such a huge stress off our already stressful lives. In Ohio we would continuously go into debt, and there was not much we could do about it. There was no way I could work. WV gives us the tools to help our children and provide for them the way they need it. The money we get for them, we try to give right back to them. WV gives us the ability to buy them the organic food that their bodies need for their digestion issues and allergies. It gives us the money to help pay for all the natural things that we have found to help them that regular insurance does not cover. It even pays for our therapy bills and reimburses us for what we pay into my husband's work health insurance. Thank you WV! West Virginia finds paying these expenses is much cheaper than paying for people to be housed in institutions.

Matthew has an easy-going personality most of the time, thankfully. Unfortunately the medicine that helps his seizures is the one that causes behavior issues, like head-banging, breaking things, obsessiveness, etc. This is the battle we're in right now, but thankfully this is one we are figuring out and he has greatly decreased the head banging. We are on constant guard day and night for his seizures, as he has had hundreds this past year. We are in the middle of getting him off of Topamax, which we are pretty sure is triggering seizures—but because it is causing such an intense reaction in him, it will take a while to taper him off. We are very much looking forward to that day! I am one that largely depends on natural medicine, so prescriptions were a hard one for me to allow as it goes against my innermost being. But in this battle with epilepsy, I have learned why so many are scared to go the natural way, and why so many allow their children to be medicated. This has been quite a learning curve for me.

Matthew has not learned to eat by himself, partly because he has little desire to do so. The thought of trying to potty train him is overwhelming! The poor little guy does not understand sign language almost at all. He just does not get it.

One of my favorite quotes about Matthew is whenever he is at therapy, waiting in the waiting room, he waves and smiles at everyone. One of the patients said, "He is the best therapist, everyone comes or leaves smiles when they see him smile!"

Both Grace and Matthew are nonverbal and delayed in almost all areas. Almost every professional that has ever worked with them is dumbfounded. They fit in NO molds. The things that would typically help someone else does not help them or it backfires. They both are also allergic to a lot and their bodies are sensitive to changes. They both have experienced severe head banging, which is scary and heartbreaking. Not only are they stunted in their ability to do some things, they have no desire to do many other things. But thankfully what they do like, they love, and are happy a lot of the time. With them both being nonverbal, somehow we can understand them. Sign language is hard because they can hear, just not talk and ASL (American Sign Language) is not in the same sentence structure as English. Also ASL requires muscle movements that are impossible for my children. We have talking machines but they are not interested in them. And honestly, the way they are set up is not beneficial to my children and takes a huge amount of programming. It is overwhelming. Grace communicates with me very well through signs and gestures and simple words and I almost always can figure out what she is saying. Matthew has a lot to learn in this area!

Our daily life has definitely changed since having Grace and Matthew—for the better, and for the worse. We do not like to talk about the bad as we want everyone to love and appreciate our children. We do not want people to feel sorry for us as so many do. We want others to know how much our children are blessings to us and that they are worth everything. Their good side is so good. Their cute side is so cute. They are both so happy when they are happy—it is almost impossible to be as happy as them. We just love taking them to the carousel, as they jump up and down and dance to it. They are delighted as can be and have earned many free rides because of their excitement. They absolutely love music; it moves them in a way it does no other.

But everyday life is crazy, most every day, all day long. Granted, our family and daily life has changed. Going places, almost anywhere presents a challenge. Grace does not like to go most places and that is obvious. We are humbled by the way she acts in public, and sometimes feel there is little we can do to help the situation. We try not to allow our children to stop us or to change how we live—we just have to adapt differently, and expect that others might not react positively. We have experienced our share of negativity, but most people are compassionate. But we go most places anyway. . . I think this helps with resentment some feel towards their special needs children, because we do not feel like we can't do what other families do. We just know it will be crazy doing it!

Hannah is an awesome girl who has a huge heart. It is a joy to parent her. She is partly awesome because of having special needs siblings as she sees life in a different perspective. Sometimes she feels alone amongst her friends with normal siblings, and we feel sad about that. She has overcome some of those feelings and her love for others is so deep. Craig and I also try to find lots of time to be with her one on one, and that truly makes a difference. Craig and I thankfully both love being parents together and that has helped our relationship since we do not get much one on one adult time. We try to go places together frequently as a family, places that the whole family loves. For example: trips to the ocean, our relatives, church gatherings, friends, etc., and this really makes a difference in our life as a couple and a family.

Life is crazy and some days it is a battlefield. Things getting broken all around you. We have had to replace 3 windows, unmentionable numbers of phones, dishes, etc., that get broken when the craziness hits! But I am thankful for the most part that this is taken out on objects as compared to people! One child laughing uncontrollably and the other cannot handle it, so they knock something over. Not stopping, but passing a hotel or something on the way home that Matthew wanted to go to and you have to literally pull him out of the car screaming because he wanted something and we did not go there or do what he wanted. A battle to get a child to eat, to use the restroom the correct way, to brush their teeth, etc., etc., etc. A battle to tell a child to wait just one minute, and it is impossible for them to do so, so they decide to rip up something or destroy the phone. Thankfully, this battle is not all day long, just parts of the day, so a person can get a break and breathe and then go on! The battle is against a child not hurting themselves or others. It is a battle to try to keep them in time out. How do you do this one? And some of it is because the seizure medicine that was given caused rages as a side effect. This is our life.

I could continue about these areas, but I honestly do not want the whole world to know all our struggles. I want the whole world to see how wonderful our children are, how much of a blessing they are. But to other special needs parents out there, I do want you to know—I get it, I get the craziness, the heartache, the lack of sleep, the fearfulness, the overwhelmingness of it all. I also get that these children are truly gifts from God, and this has made me a crazier, yet a better person. And overall, each of our children have been our greatest joys in their own unique way. We truly love each one of them and are so thankful they were given to us to raise and cherish. Having a first-born such as Hannah, who has been such a pure loving child of God, has shown us how the Lord helps make life better each day. Grace has truly taught us God's grace through her experiences, and her laughter lights up the room. Matthew is just simply a sweetie; his smile brightens up anyone he comes into contact with. Our life is a crazy life, but definitely a blessed life, as God shows He keeps His promises to us each and every day. To other families, His love might not be so obvious, but to ours, it is extremely obvious each and every day. For that we are thankful.

Alice

My name is Alice. I am a single woman. I have several degrees in biochemistry, including a Ph.D. I used to teach and do research at two universities in the Midwest. I was involved in research on several subjects, but the last was discovering the sticky substance & nerve bundle in brains that leaves a person with Alzheimer's Disease called Tau. I was also involved in teaching and yearly training, testing, and certifying of staff for work in various hospital departments. The training/certification was for CPR (cardiopulmonary resuscitation) now called CCR, stroke symptoms, concussion symptoms, etc. I had a very rewarding and challenging career, making many friends among my colleagues.

When Hurricane Katrina hit the Gulf Coast, I went to help out in any way I could. I found a black Labrador that didn't seem to have an owner and we took a liking to one another. I ended up bringing him back to Wisconsin and he was a faithful companion. We liked to hang out together and go for walks. While I may have saved his life back then, he helped to save my life later.

One day after I got home from work, I suddenly felt like someone had hit me in the head with a baseball bat, my head hurt so badly. I knew what it was—a brain aneurism. I had specifically told my students that people who have a brain aneurism typically describe their headache as feeling as though someone had hit them with a bat. Well, now I was experiencing it for myself. I slid down the wall but knew that I had to get to the phone. My dog, Barc, had come to me immediately and I crawled and used Barc to get myself up to where the phone was on the wall to call 911. I was not able to make it to the door though to unlock it. The paramedics found another way in and took me to the hospital. Thank goodness for Barc. Without him I wouldn't have even been able to get to the phone.

I immediately underwent brain surgery to find and close off the vessel that had ruptured. As the surgeon was working, he found that I also had a brain tumor so they had to cut away even more of my skull to try to get at the tumor. The tumor, which was not malignant, but can grow back, was in the front of my skull, basically behind my forehead. The surgeons had to move various parts of my brain and other things around to try to get all of the tumor. Getting at the tumor was hampered by my optic nerve, my sinuses, etc. By the time the surgeons were done in my head, I had metal plates and screws that now made up my skull to keep my brain protected.

However, now when I touch my head, I can feel the metal plates and most of the screws. I now have no sense of smell because when they were doing the surgery, the center for smells area in my brain got nicked by the scalpel as they were trying to get the tumor out.

I was in the hospital for some time recovering and then in a rehabilitation facility relearning basic skills and how to care for myself again. The struggle was difficult, but I really wanted to get home to Barc again. Fortunately, my father, who lives in Milwaukee had become good buddies with Barc so took him home to Milwaukee to live with my parents while I was recouping.

There was much destroyed by both the aneurism and the tumor, and not just in my head. I had to quit my job, a job I loved, and go on disability. Now, not only did I have a life that was different from the one that I had had before, but I now had to get used to a whole different financial lifestyle. I made a good salary when I was working. My monthly disability check was only a fraction of that. Now I had to find living quarters for Barc and me, pay for those, plus all utilities, insurances, gas and wear and tear for the car, and food for both Barc and me. Then there was the occasional vet bill, too.

I have come to accept the "new normal" of my life. While I would rather be doing what I was doing before my aneurism, I have come to accept my new life and try to make the best of it. One of the side-effects of my ordeal and my "new normal" is almost constant severe headaches that make me nauseous and vomit frequently. So much for worrying about my food. If I have to make a choice about paying bills or buying food for Barc versus myself, it is a no-brainer. Because of the headaches and how physically crummy I feel much of the time, I don't want to eat anyway, so I don't purchase much food. I do buy diet pop because that helps settle my stomach. I do have anti-nausea medication that I take but it doesn't always work. Recently, I started a series of botulism shots in my head that are supposed to take away some of the pain I experience. I am also getting a steroid shot in my neck at the base of my skull. Insurance doesn't want to pay for these things but the doctors have worked it out with them.

My life used to consist of researching, teaching, and playing with Barc when I got home from work. We would go for long walks. Now, because of the headaches, I frequently have a hard time thinking. This makes planning and carrying out a task difficult. My day now consists of getting up, feeding Barc, letting him out in the yard, watching TV and occasionally going on errands to grocery shop, to see the doctor, or take Barc to the vet. Barc and I were still able to go for walks when my headaches weren't too bad. I was still able to drive. I was still able to get together with family and friends.

In January, 2015, I was taking the trash out to the curb when I slipped on ice on the driveway and broke my right foot. Great. Now my activities were cut down even more. I couldn't walk Barc, couldn't go down my basement steps to do laundry, couldn't drive. And to top it all off, Barc was diagnosed with cancer. I was devastated. Barc was my best friend, my rock. Now he was really sick.

There is an agency in town that not only runs a pantry, but also provides rides to appointments, or people to do chores. I needed someone to do my laundry, someone to walk Barc, someone to take me to the doctor, and to pick up a little something to eat. While my foot was healing and nice people were doing my chores, I was worrying about Barc. I started sleeping out in the living room because that was where Barc was. Sometimes, Barc wouldn't move from his bed, so I would lay on the floor and sleep with him. Just before I got the o.k. from the doctor to be able to wear shoes again on my right foot, Barc passed away. I was now in emotional pain as well as physical pain. I missed him so much. As a shut-in, I relied on Barc for companionship and to help my life feel somewhat normal because I had to feed and walk him, take care of him (while he took care of me). Now he was gone.

As I try to continue my life without Barc, my car which sat out most of the winter after I slipped on the ice, now had a cracked block. On disability payments, I couldn't afford to fix it. I was going to need to continue to rely on other people to take me to my appointments. What appointments? Just after my foot healed, I had two different episodes where the doctors thought that I had cancer. Really. How much more was this body supposed to be able to handle. Fortunately, both of the incidents turned out to not be cancer. Along the way, I have met some pretty nice people who have taken their time to help me out. I am very appreciative and getting used to this new life.

Mary, James, & Jose

Our family initially consisted of my husband, James and me. I come from a large, boisterous, dysfunctional family and James comes from a small family. Our life together seemed to be going well. We both had jobs that we liked. We were able to save enough money to purchase a house. We both enjoyed working in the yard. When we found out I was pregnant, we were very happy. However, in preparing for our future as parents, reading books on pregnancy and delivery, I soon realized that the person inside me was not following protocol. I knew that there was some problem. When Jose was born, he looked like a perfect infant. Nothing looked out of the ordinary. Were these just pre-parent nerves that told me there was a problem?

Initially, we were very happy being new parents. We had the same challenges any new parent does; little sleep, running on auto pilot, but being excited about our new son and accepting whatever came with that. James had some difficulty relating to an infant. Most of Jose's care fell to me. Life was moving along o.k. for us. James couldn't wait until Jose got older so that they could play ball together and do other "guy" things. As Jose grew, he accomplished milestones at the right time, however, he cried a lot. It also seemed that he was constantly moving. Jose would play quietly with his toys for only short periods of time and then he was moving around, throwing toys everywhere, breaking some things, including toys. This bothered James a great deal. He was troubled by the frequent crying, the sudden throwing of toys and breaking of objects, not the least of which was the toys. We quickly learned that anything that we considered valuable needed to be moved to a higher shelf or put away, out of sight. This was much more than "baby proofing" the house.

One thing that James really liked doing was watching sports on TV. He was anxious to be able to share that with Jose. So, when Jose was throwing toys and other objects around the room and screaming, it kind of freaked James out. He didn't know what to think. Who was this little terror? How was he going to be able to participate in sports and watch sports on TV if he couldn't sit still and was throwing things all the time? What was wrong with him? This is not how life was supposed to be going. This was not how a child was supposed to act.

As a mother, you love your child unconditionally. NO MATTER WHAT. That doesn't mean that sometimes life doesn't get hard. But you keep loving your child. And you advocate for them with everyone. I felt like I was constantly defending Jose, saying this was just a phase he was going through. I was defending Jose to James. I was defending him to people in our circle of friends and at school. However, I was busy checking the baby books to find out if this was normal behavior and what I should be doing about the behavior. This was the start of a rift between James and me.

Jose was in preschool and seemed to do well there. He as well liked by the other children and was able to be redirected to activities that the teachers had in mind. When Jose entered public school, life started changing. Jose was still "antsy" and the teachers were constantly calling us about him not being able to pay attention in school. Jose was eventually diagnosed with Attention Deficit Hyperactivity Disorder. I tried to learn as much about ADHD as I could. I shared my knowledge with James. He was mildly interested but I'm not sure he ever really got over having a child that "was different", because by that time James had decided that Jose was different. While still too young and unable to do "guy" things and toss balls that easily, this behavior/life wasn't what James had hoped for and imagined. I became very involved in Children and Adults With Attention Deficit Disorder (CHADD). It was so helpful to be able to talk to other parents of children with ADHD and even some adults that had ADHD.

James was able to teach Jose to throw a ball but for a long time, Jose had trouble catching the balls. Finally success. This helped somewhat with the relationship between Jose and James, however, the constant calls from schools and Jose's increasing desire to do things differently was the start of another wedge between them. They were able to still watch ball games together, although Jose's constant moving around drove James crazy. And, as the calls from the schools came in, this increased James' anxiety and relationship with Jose, and as I was defending Jose, it took a toll on James' and my relationship.

High school was a nightmare for all of us. Jose would get in trouble at school, I would get calls at work (not James as I knew he wouldn't be able to handle it emotionally). Then with consequences for misbehavior happening both at school and at home, life at our house became very stressful. James withdrew into himself. Jose either wanted to be out with his friends or was at home arguing with me about wanting to be out with his friends. We no longer did things together as a family, or even as a couple for that matter, not even meals. James would come home and if I didn't have something already made for dinner, he would make himself a sandwich, take it into the living room on a TV tray and watch TV.

I am sure that I was suffering from depression with my marriage on the rocks, my son wanting to drop out of school, all while trying to hold down a full time job, keep house, etc. Eventually, Jose was able to get into an alternative high school program and was able to graduate. After fighting so many battles, that was fine with me. Jose was good with his hands and was able to get a part time job.

My marriage, however, could not survive all the stress and the disappointment that James had in not having an "ideal son". This meant selling the house and splitting up the contents. There was some talk about Jose living with me, but he really wanted to be off on his own, living with friends. I decided to get an apartment big enough that he could have some space if he did live with me, if it didn't work out with his friends.

Having a child with a disability is hard on a marriage and we became one of the statistics. Knowing while I was pregnant with Jose, that thing weren't going to be "normal", James and I had chosen not to have any more children. Probably a good thing as that would have added more chaos and stress to our lives, and more children affected by the divorce of their parents.

Mark

Hearing the words 'You have Multiple Sclerosis' came as a shock, especially since all I was dealing with was a bladder urgency issue. Being in my upper 40's explains many bladder issues that wouldn't surprise me. But, suddenly, I have a disease with no cure. Sinus infections go away after taking antibiotics for 10 days. Colds go away after feeling lousy for about 4 days and then life returns to normal. But a disease for life, that's different, really different.

Now I had to answer some *really* tough questions: Can I continue to work and bring home a check to meet our financial needs? Do we need to make plans to sell our home and move? Are our daughter's dreams of a college education still possible? Will I become one of those people that can't even dress themselves? Who might be ashamed to be seen with me? How rapidly will this disease progress? No answers are good at the start of any disease or disability.

Ways of dealing with having a disease are different for everyone. Denying or ignoring it only works for a while and doesn't help anyone. Additionally, precious time can be lost dealing with a disease later rather than sooner. At my neurologist's recommendations, I started taking medication immediately but only told my wife and sister who is a nurse about my diagnosis. I didn't share the news with anyone else, no one. Not even our 10-year-old daughter, my parents, co-workers, church friends, or employers. That worked for about 5 years until it was evident that my walk was noticeably clumsy.

My sister, the nurse, offered to take me to the best clinic for another look. And off we went for a week. Perhaps they would discover something else. Maybe there was a research program that I could become part of. With the greatest brainpower in medicine at this clinic, surely they knew how special medicines would help. No such luck! In fact, they recommended taking no medicine at all because nothing was FDA approved to have an effect on the disease. Now what?

So, little by little, I let the word out. First to family and closest friends for a couple of weeks and then to everyone that asked. Much to my surprise, everyone offered help and compassion. Other people's thoughts and intentions should never be presumed even though feelings about myself are mixed. Trying to stay positive while letting the 'Bad News' out was difficult at times. There is much help available for anyone that makes their situation known and decides to take action to address their disease or disability. For me, it was important that I took an active role in gathering information and learning. MS affects each person differently, and how you and/or your spouse deals with it. Staying intimately involved with neurologists, general physicians, chiropractors, physical therapists, local support groups, and several that I'm forgetting, helps maintain perspective and provides a sound base for a positive attitude.

I found that most people are respectful and considerate toward those dealing with disabilities and diseases. My parents helped us financially to make ends meet when I couldn't continue working after 7 years into the journey. This, along with Social Security Disability Income (SSDI) has helped delay answering the questions about selling our home and moving. Delaying delivery of 'Bad News' to our daughter until her later high school years kept her from worrying. Having one less thing on her mind helped her to maintain excellent grades which led to academic scholarships. These answers to pressing questions may seem coincidental, but more on that later.

Young children and young adults are very perceptive, and that shows in their comments. When our daughter learned, her first comment was, "Will I get it?" Since she studied basic genetics in high school biology class she understood inherited characteristics. At least I was able to comfort her by letting her know that chances are very remote that MS would affect her. The "Y" generation are less concerned about traditional lifestyles and marriage than us Old Folks are. Our daughter hasn't taken an interest in guys; her focus is on figure skating and schooling. There's been no mention of her getting married someday. That may change as life progresses, but, I expect her independence to prevail. So, her decisions will be accepted by her mother and me.

One of the most difficult tasks I faced was changing daily pace and activities when I quit work and went on Social Security Disability Income (SSDI). While working for 30 years as an engineer and manager in the 24 hour-a-day world of printing, the pace was exhilarating and rewarding. I actually looked forward to work on Monday mornings. Interacting with people, decision-making, problem solving, and an occasional emergency made for a really interesting job. I kept it up for 5 years after being diagnosed with MS. But then when it was clear that I couldn't keep up the pace of getting up at 6 a.m. and getting home at 6 p.m. I knew it was no longer reasonable to be on the job. Staying home and collecting SSDI was the new norm. The next challenge was what to do for 8-10 hours a day at home, especially because I had all my faculties about me; I just didn't have physical endurance to keep pace.

Since I had a lot of time on my hands, I decided to dig in and learn as much as I could about MS. It was like being back in college doing research papers. There is much written about MS on the internet and I love to research topics that were previously unknown to me. Learning more about my disease helped me to come to grips with it and settled my mind that I was taking the best route to stabilize my condition. There's a saying in the MS world, 'I have MS, but, MS doesn't have me'. This sounds obvious and is a powerful reminder to me that I can either be controlled by my limitations, or, take control and make the best of each day.

Reaching out to a local MS support group created more contacts then I would have ever predicted. Being open to establishing new relationships didn't come naturally to me. But, there are many people willing to share loads of information as soon as I struck up a conversation. Many are much smarter than myself and have more experience with MS. Clearly, I wasn't the only one dealing with MS, while feeling poorly and confused about myself and my future. Staying active with the local support group has been rewarding in that I can help the newly diagnosed understand some of the mind-boggling terminology, changes, and experiences that will surely come their way.

Learning new and different things about a disease is exciting, especially when they are deemed to be positive things, albeit untested. In the 1990's MS research and understanding was on the cusp of many miraculous discoveries, much as cancer research was in the 1960's. Look at what is understood about many cancers now. In the '60's, some types of cancer that typically had very dreadful results in the short term are now being treated on an out-patient basis with positive, lasting results. Much MS research, testing, and advancements are leading to discoveries and successful treatment. The 2000's have produced many significant understandings about MS and many more are on the horizon. Genome identification of autoimmune diseases has opened the way for identifying specific paths for treating MS.

Through my support group contacts and reading, a new procedure came to light in 2008 known by the acronym of CCSVI standing for Chronic Cerebral Spinal Venous Insufficiency. First tried in Italy and rapidly spread to the US, it was initially reported as a major discovery in MS treatment and possibly a cure. Many patients had the procedure done with mixed results from miraculous to nothing at all. The basic premise of returning restricted blood flow to and from the brain back to normal caught my attention and made good sense even though there had been no organized testing or FDA approval.

And so, I learned more about CCSVI and with the encouragement of my neurologist, I found a site to have it done within 30 miles of my home. No trip to Italy for me! Without any grand expectations, the procedure was done as an outpatient, with no hospital stay or extensive recovery period. During the course of the next six months, I experienced four lasting improvements that continue with me for the three years since the surgery. Now, I wake up alert, earlier than before the procedure. And, that mental clarity stays with me all day. There is an increase in my physical stamina that my physical therapist noticed during my weekly sessions. Digestively, I am consistent with bowel movements all 30 days of the month, instead of unpredicted bouts of diarrhea or nearly constipation. But the best of all is improvement in eyesight that I can readily see the minuscule date on my wristwatch. Learning and being willing to try a new development can have positive results.

Maintaining a positive attitude through thick and thin as life presents a variety of circumstances sends a signal to others, but most importantly keeps one steady. This usually requires good mental health as well as good physical health. That's where trained professional help comes into the picture. Choosing good physicians and clinicians requires years of practice and endurance. Calling on those in similar circumstances is helpful such as support groups. Remember, you are the customer, and until the customer is satisfied, the search for the most helpful people in the field needs to continue. This should be everyone's priority in getting a handle on their disability.

Most people that work diligently and have reasonable control of their lives plan to enjoy life when they're approaching 50 and planning for a comfortable transition into their 60's. Then retiring! When that plan fell apart for us as a family, we had to come to grips with some plan we never thought about. Not only is this change a mental shift for me, it is a disappointment for most spouses. Fortunately, my wife provides support for our daughter and myself through thick and thin. After the shock of having a disease wears off, it suddenly becomes obvious that we as a family are better off than many around us. Just one more reason to be thankful.

During the 11 years since I was diagnosed with MS, my wife got a job at a local high school as an assistant librarian. This replaces our need for health insurance that had always been through my employers in the past. Fortunately, my wife recognized my work limitations which turned to unemployment, and took action to get a job that she could manage for our needs. Our daughter successfully completed high school and is about to complete college by focusing mainly on schooling and not on her Dad's shortcomings. Fortunately, I am able to maintain independence by driving and staying busy, albeit busy in different regards than before.

Maintaining stable physical and mental health is very important when dealing with disabilities. You'll note that I stress 'maintaining' because accomplishments take on new measures. Searching out medical professionals that address all my physical needs was no easy task. No one sent me a letter outlining the 5 Easy Steps to Achieving Good Health with MS now that things are different. Understanding that I was not going to get better like when I took antibiotics for 10 days requires much work to retrain our way of thinking about physical health. Exchanging ideas with others dealing with similar challenges through support groups is a start. Attending help seminars sponsored by pharmaceutical companies is another great way to make new contacts and hear from others dealing with similar disabilities.

Most important to me is having a realistic outlook for the future. Maintaining faith in God and knowing that he has a plan for the world of mankind eases many fears. It's no coincidence that my life has progressed to what it is today. I'm in a location where extensive medical help is readily available. Family and church friends are willing to help with my temporal needs as well as help me gain more in-depth understanding of God's love for the entire world of mankind. This time in medical history is rich with the most advanced options for dealing with my disability. Despite having MS, my life delivers much joy in many regards. I keep looking forward and hope and pray that others can overcome their infirmities as I have. I leave you with two very important words, "Stay Positive".

Natasha Marie

I was born Tasha Lynn. I do not believe that my parents were married. One of the things I remember from my very early years was riding in the car with my dad. I am in the passenger seat. I am not wearing a seat belt and I have no car seat. I'm sitting in the seat with my knees up to my chest. For some reason, my dad is very angry at me. We are driving over a bridge. He slows the car down and stops. He says to me, "go jump off that bridge". I remember feeling very rebellious, and said, "no". He starts the car up and we drive home. I was probably about 2 years old.

I remember a lot of yelling in my house. I was placed in foster care when my day care called the authorities because I had bruises on me that couldn't be explained by normal childhood activity. After I was placed in foster care, my parents didn't live together anymore. I remember going from foster care back to my dad's and his new partner's house, back into foster care, then from foster care to my mom's and new step-father, and back to foster care. I remember an incident from this time period. It is night time out and I am at day care. I'm playing with some toy–I think a doll house. My step mother comes to pick me up. She calls my name several times. I do not respond and she gets angry. At home she tells my dad, "she wouldn't come for me". My dad looks at me and says, "Tasha?" I remember feeling really scared. He grabs me and drags me to the bathroom.

Another time I am lying in my bed at night. I am calling out "mommy, mom" because I have to go to the bathroom. I remember hearing my mom mumble something to my dad. And he comes instead. In my mind, I'm thinking, "oh no".

I remember and still carry the scar on my elbow of being thrown against a wall by my dad. After I came to day care with bruises on my body which couldn't be explained by typical kid accidents–falling down, etc., I

261

was permanently removed from both my parents' homes and their parental rights were terminated. I remember being in foster care out in the country. In the living room of this house, there were two mounted deer heads. For some reason, I was really. . . well, not scared exactly. I didn't "trust" them. I had to walk past them in order to reach my room. Whenever I had to pass them I would have my back to the wall, but I always kept my eyes on them. I sidled past, always keeping my eyes on those deer. One day, the grandfather said to me, "you don't have to be afraid. Those deer aren't going to hurt you". I shook my head. He picked me up and walked closer to the deer heads. I started panicking and squirming, wanting to get away. He took my hand and made me 'pet' the deer saying, "See, they aren't going to hurt you."

Our oldest foster sister had wet her bed. She was six. We had company over. Our foster mother chased her around the upstairs balcony in front of company with a diaper. She was finally caught and the diaper put on her. We were told to go to our toy chests and find anything baby-related like bottles, pacifiers, etc., and bring them to her. Quite an impression to leave on a little kid.

For the simple reason that we had annoyed them, at one point our foster parents tied all three of us up to a huge box and just left us there in the long driveway. It was hot out and we were out in the country on a small farm. I finally said, "I'm bored, how about you guys?" I somehow got myself untied. They said "yeah". I untied them and we went off to play. Great way to start life.

I was adopted when I was four-years-old by a single lady who changed my name to Natasha Marie. I have been diagnosed with Fetal Alcohol Spectrum Disorder (obviously from alcohol consumed during my birth mother's pregnancy with me), Attention Deficit Disorder, Asperger Syndrome, and Post Traumatic Stress Disorder (PTSD). These diagnoses cause me to have a hard time not speaking before I think. I just blurt things out.

I remember an incident where I was in my new mom's small bathroom. I don't remember if I had all of my clothes on or not. I was in the process of raiding my new mom's band-aid stash. I remember I put band-aids randomly all over my body. I even put some on my 'privates' and over my 'boobs'. My new mom opened the door on me while I was doing this. She said, "There you are. . ." She saw what I was doing. She said, "Oh honey". Somehow I trusted her.

Kindergarten and elementary school went fine for me. My new mom was very attentive. I was in public school at this time.

Middle school was hell for me. I say that and people today say, "oh well yeah, middle school is hell for everyone". Well fine, but nobody knows what I went through. When I was in middle school, I was sexually assaulted. There was a boy in my class who was constantly picking on me who I didn't like for obvious reasons. Then all of a sudden this boy started being nice to me. After school one day he was talking very nice to me and asked me to come with him. I followed him into the locker room where he touched my breasts. I didn't like it and was trying to figure out how to get out of there when he pulled out his penis and told me to suck it. Now I really wanted to get out of there! I spit on it and he said he wasn't feeling anything. Fortunately, right then the principal was walking by calling his name. I was able to get out. I told my mom when she came to pick me up. I had to repeat the story not only that day to the principal, but also the next day to the police. Of course, everything was denied, both by this boy and by his mother. Only when there was going to be a trial, did this boy admit what he had done to me and then it came out that he had also sexually assaulted other girls at school. This was very traumatic. But it was on top of something else. I had always known that something had happened in my earlier life. I had flashbacks of incidents and acted some things out. (See band-aid story above). My mom never hid these facts and details from me. Nor did she hide that I was adopted. Not only had I been sexually assaulted by this boy, but also by my dad. Those were the flashbacks that I was having.

In middle school I was made fun of and bullied as well. The assault incident happened in public school. Because of all of this, my mom refinanced her house so she could send me to a small, private middle school. Because of the assault and my inability to concentrate, when I moved to the new middle school, I had to redo a year. I did well in the small school and continued counseling for all of my issues, especially the sexual assault. I would have gone to a fairly large high school only about 6 blocks from home, but I was scared. There had been reports of girls being assaulted in the stairwells. So, after middle school, my mom again refinanced the house so she could send me to a parochial high school in town. That is love.

After middle school, I would have some pretty gruesome dreams at night. Like other children dealing with trauma in their life, I liked movies with super heroes. Mine was 'Xena'. In my dreams, I used Xena's chakram, a sharp, round blade weapon like a boomerang, and I would walk up to my perpetrators. In my dreams I slit their throats after reminding them of what they did to me.

I was shy and self-conscious in high school but other than that, school went fine for me. I did have some special education support in high school, but graduated on time with my class at age 18.

I have been able to do many things in life, although some have been harder than others and as a result, I am on SSDI. I graduated from high school; tried a semester away from home at college but I was too homesick to continue. I was successful at working a couple of part time jobs over the years including the clinic job I just got. I have taken classes for several life skills things as well as belly dancing and throwing clay/pottery; I found a companion (who also has Asperger Syndrome); we had a commitment ceremony; bought a condo; I've gotten a job at a vet clinic I love; we adopted a kitten; and have traveled a lot.

Counseling has helped, however, I still think about the assaults a lot, and you could say that it is still a big part of my life. When my dog got very sick and had to be put to sleep, I don't know why, but this seemed to trigger a giant bout of PTSD. I had trouble coping. I was crabby. I felt anxious. I love the job I have at a veterinary clinic. They like me. They gave me extra hours; however I suddenly had trouble going to work. I would skip work and not call in, I would leave early (although I had the work done, I was leaving before my shift ended). This caused problems for my job. Suddenly my job developer/job coach was being summoned to straighten this out and get me back to work. I am mostly back on track at work, although I really don't understand why I can't leave early, if my work is done.

I have trouble tending to the obligations that I have such as actually getting myself out of the house. I get very anxious, make myself miserable thinking about actually leaving the house. This happens even if it is an activity I am interested in. My disabilities (maybe the PTSD) have caused me to sabotage my successes in life. I quit a job because I had trouble getting to know my co-workers since I only worked there one day a week. I felt self-conscious about doing the job and missing work, plus the duties I was assigned exacerbated my back problems which caused me to miss more work. I tend to perseverate on things. It could be an incident or my just needing to leave the house, so I make myself (and everybody else crazy).

One of our challenges is cleaning the condo. Both Eric and I have issues with hoarding, cleaning and generally keeping the condo picked up. We've even had the assistance of multiple life coaches as well as both my mom and Eric's parents trying to help us and get us to clean up. Somehow getting it cleaned up and then maintaining it just seems too hard.

I love reading books. I especially like mysteries and like to escape into the story so I don't have to deal with reality. I also like playing with my cat, and watching movies. In the summer, I enjoy going to the condo association pool. I have been able to gain some socialization skills by participating in LOV Dane activities such as outings, cooking group, book group, bowling, and pottery classes. I have taken belly dancing on my own.

I enjoy the fact that we have been able to purchase our condo and get out of an apartment. My mom is the oldest of 5 kids so I was adopted into a big extended family and have lots of cousins. Having a relationship with Eric has expanded my family as well as I am now part of his family. Now I have even more aunts, uncles, cousins, and friends. We go on vacation with his parents in their motor home and have been to Hawaii twice, a place I thought I would never get to. I feel loved and supported by the whole extended family which is nice. All in all, I feel that life is pretty good.

BIBLIOGRAPHY

Because of the dynamic nature of the Internet, any web addresses contained in this book may have changed since publication and may no longer be valid. The author has made an effort to ensure they were valid at the time of publication.

Introduction

"Chronic Illness or Disability." All About Counseling. https://www.allaboutcounseling.com/chronic.htm.

"Education & Research." British Film Institute. https://www.bfi.org.uk/education-research.

Maslow, Abraham H., "A Theory of Human Motivation," *Psychological Review* Vol. 50, No. 4 (1943), 370-396. http://psychclassics.yorku.ca/Maslow/motivation.htm.

The History of Attitudes to Disabled People. https://attitudes2disability.wordpress.com.

The Kim Foundation. https://www.thekimfoundation.org.

Chapter 1—What Is A Disability?

"Chronic Illness or Disability." All About Counseling. https://www.allaboutcounseling.com/chronic.htm.

"Disability." https://www.encyclopedia.com/social-sciences-and-law/sociology-and-social-reform/sociology-general-terms-and-concepts/disabilities.

Webster's Third New International Dictionary (Springfield, Massachusetts, Merriam-Webster, Inc., 1986).

Chapter 2—Disabilities–Born or Acquired

Clayton, Jane, and Jennifer Fitzgerald. *The History of Disability: A History of "Otherness."* Renaissance Universal. http://www.ru.org/index.php/human-rights/315-the-history-of-disability-a-history-of-otherness.

"Disability Statistics: Information, Charts, Graphs and Tables." Disability World. https://www.disabled-world.com/disability/statistics.

Pennington, Tess. "The Dangers of The Normalcy Bias." *The Daily Sheeple*, February 18, 2014; http://www.thedailysheeple.com/the-dangers-of-the-normalcy-bias.

U.S. Department of Health and Human Services, National Institutes of Health, National Institute of Mental Health, *Post-Traumatic Stress Disorder*, https://www.nimh.nih.gov/health/publications/post-traumatic-stress-disorder-ptsd/20-mh-8124-ptsd_38054.pdf.

Weir, Jennifer. *CODI: Cornucopia of Disability Information.* http://codi.tamucc.edu/index.html.

Wikipedia contributors. "Normalcy Bias. *Wikipedia, The Free Encyclopedia.* https://en.wikipedia.org/w/index.php?title=Normalcy_bias&oldid=974580789.

Chapter 3—Co-Morbid

National Institute on Drug Abuse. "Common Comorbidities with Substance Use Disorders Research Report." April 2020. https://www.drugabuse.gov/download/1155/common-comorbidities-substance-use-disorders-research-report.pdf?v=6344cb285ff0a098afa0909927de4512.

"The Other Dual Diagnosis." https://cow.waisman.wisc.edu/wp-content/uploads/sites/148/2017/06/the-other-dual-diagnosis.pdf.

Wikipedia contributors. "Comorbidity." *Wikipedia, The Free Encyclopedia.* https://en.wikipedia.org/w/index.php?title=Comorbidity&oldid=973458671.

Chapter 4—Some Statistics

"2020 Poverty Guidelines." U.S. Department of Health and Human Services, Office of the Assistant Secretary for Planning and Evaluation. https://aspe.hhs.gov/2020-poverty-guidelines.

"Chances of Disability—Common Causes." Council for Disability Awareness. https://disabilitycanhappen.org/common-causes/.

"Chances of Disability—Disability Statistics." Council for Disability Awareness. https://disabilitycanhappen.org/disability-statistic/.

"Disability Statistics." Cornell University. https://disabilitystatistics.org/reports/acs.cfm?statistic7.

"Disability Statistics: Information, Charts, Graphs and Tables." Disability World. https://www.disabled-world.com/disability/statistics.

"The World Bank in Social Protection." The World Bank. https://www.worldbank.org/en/topic/socialprotection.

Weir, Jennifer. *CODI: Cornucopia of Disability Information*. http://codi.tamucc.edu/index.html.

Chapter 5—Disabilities—No Respecter of Persons

"Famous People with Disabilities." Disabled World. https://www.disabled-world.com/disability/awareness/famous/.

Chapter 6—Movies Portraying People with Disabilities

Wikipedia contributors. "Category: Films about Disability." *Wikipedia, The Free Encyclopedia*. https://en.wikipedia.org/wiki/Category:Films_about_disability.

Wikipedia contributors. "List of Mental Disorders in Film." *Wikipedia, The Free Encyclopedia*. https://en.wikipedia.org/w/index.php?title=List_of_mental_disorders_in_film&oldid=974208577.

Chapter 7—Disabilities in History

Allen G. Breed. "Eugenics in N.C.: Victim, Son Fight for Justice." *The Seattle Times*, August 16, 2011. https://www.seattletimes.com/nation-world/eugenics-in-nc-victim-son-fight-for-justice/.

Associated Press. "Shocking History of Medical Experiments on People." *ABC News*, February 27, 2011.

Clayton, Jane, and Jennifer Fitzgerald. "The History of Disability: A History of 'Otherness.'" Renaissance Universal, http://www.ru.org/index.php/human-rights/315-the-history-of-disability-a-history-of-otherness.

"Disability Rights in Aotearoa New Zealand 2012." Disabled Persons Assembly, New Zealand. http://www.dpa.org.nz/resources/

sector-resources/the-convention-disability-rights-in-aotearoa-new-zealand/2012-monitoring-reports.

"Education & Research." British Film Institute. https://www.bfi.org.uk/education-research.

Frances, Allen J. "U.S. Mental Health Care Goes from the Worst to Even Worse." *Huffington Post*, June 2, 2017. https://www.huffpost.com/entry/us-mental-health-care-goes-from-the-worst-to-even-worse_b_10215720.

Frances, Allen J. "World's Best and Worst Places to be Mentally Ill." *Psychology Today*, December 28, 2015. https://www.psychologytoday.com/us/blog/saving-normal/201512/worlds-best-and-worst-places-be-mentally-ill.

Kamis-Gould, Edna, Fredrick Snyder, Trevor R. Hadley, and Timothy Casey. "The Impact of Closing a State Psychiatric Hospital on the County Mental Health System and Its Clients." *Psychiatric Services*, Vol. 50, No. 10 (October 1999), 1297-1302. https://ps.psychiatryonline.org/doi/pdfplus/10.1176/ps.50.10.1297.

Mike Adams. "Dr. Jonas Salk, Inventor of Polio Vaccine, Exposed as Criminal-Minded Scientist Who Conducted Illicit Medical Experiments on Mental Patients." https://www.naturalnews.com/031564_Jonas_Salk_medical_experiments.html.

Mike Stobbe. "Ugly Past of U.S. Human Experiments Uncovered." *NBC News*, February 27, 2011. http://www.nbcnews.com/id/41811750/ns/health-health_care/t/ugly-past-us-human-experiments-uncovered/#.Xzrpv-hKjIU.

National Center for Bioethics in Research and Healthcare (website), Tuskegee University, https://www.tuskegee.edu/about-us/centers-of-excellence/bioethics-center.

"Opioid Overdose." Centers for Disease Control and Prevention. http://www.cdc.gov/drugoverdose.

"U.S. Public Health Service Syphilis Study at Tuskegee." Centers for Disease Control and Prevention. https://www.cdc.gov/tuskegee/index.html

Wikipedia contributors. "Deinstitutionalisation." *Wikipedia, The Free Encyclopedia*. https://en.wikipedia.org/w/index.php?title=Deinstitutionalisation&oldid=974250687.

Wikipedia contributors. "Deinstitutionalization in the United States." *Wikipedia, The Free Encyclopedia*. https://en.wikipedia.org/w/index.php?title=Deinstitutionalization_in_the_United_States&oldid=973184928.

Wikipedia contributors. "Eugenics Board of North Carolina." *Wikipedia, The Free Encyclopedia.* https://en.wikipedia.org/w/index. php?title=Eugenics_Board_of_North_Carolina&oldid=966771956.

Wikipedia contributors. "Rosenhan Experiment." *Wikipedia, The Free Encyclopedia.* https://en.wikipedia.org/w/index.php?title=Rosenhan_ experiment&oldid=967445673.

Wikipedia contributors. "Tuskegee Syphilis Study." *Wikipedia, The Free Encyclopedia.* https://en.wikipedia.org/w/index.php?title=Tuskegee_ Syphilis_Study&oldid=974180004

Wikipedia contributors. "Ugly Law." *Wikipedia, The Free Encyclopedia.* https:// en.wikipedia.org/w/index.php?title=Ugly_law&oldid=962321015.

Chapter 8—Changes in the Disability Treatment Landscape

Allen J. Frances. "U.S. Mental Health Care Goes from the Worst to Even Worse." *Huffington Post*, June 2, 2017. https://www.huffpost.com/ entry/us-mental-health-care-goes-from-the-worst-to-even-worse_ b_10215720.

Anxiety and Depression Association of America (website). https://adaa.org.

Carter, Jimmy. "Mental Health Systems Act" (remarks on signing S. 1177 into law on October 7, 1980). The Presidency Project. https://www.presidency.ucsb.edu/ documents/mental-health-systems-act-remarks-signing-s-1177-into-law.

"Disability and Health." World Health Organization. https://www.who. int/news-room/fact-sheets/detail/disability-and-health.

"Education & Research." British Film Institute. https://www.bfi.org.uk/ education-research.

Kamis-Gould, Edna, Fredrick Snyder, Trevor R. Hadley, and Timothy Casey. "The Impact of Closing a State Psychiatric Hospital on the County Mental Health System and Its Clients." *Psychiatric Services*, Vol. 50, No. 10 (October 1999), 1297-1302. https://ps.psychiatryonline. org/doi/pdfplus/10.1176/ps.50.10.1297.

Thomas, Alexander R. "Ronald Reagan and the Commitment of the Mentally Ill: Capital, Interest Groups, and the Eclipse of Social Policy." *Electronic Journal of Sociology*, 1998. https://www.sociology.org/ejs-archives/ vol003.004/thomas.html.

Wikipedia contributors. "Community Mental Health Act." *Wikipedia, The Free Encyclopedia.* https://en.wikipedia.org/w/index.php?title=Community_ Mental_Health_Act&oldid=962765032.

Chapter 10—The Brain and the Role It Plays in Disabilities

Allen, John. "Head-on Collision." *On Wisconsin*. University of Wisconsin, Winter 2010, 22-27.

Cooley, Donald G., editor. "The Human Brain" in *Family Medical Guide*. New York: Better Homes and Gardens Books, 1973, 248-249.

"Executive Function." Encyclopedia of Mental Disorders. http://www.minddisorders.com/Del-Fi/Executive-function.html.

Malcolm Ritter. "Teen Brains Are Low on Control." *Wisconsin State Journal* (Madison, WI), December 3, 2007.

"Neurocognitive Disorder." National Institutes of Health, U.S. National Library of Medicine. https://medlineplus.gov/ency/article/001401.htm

Ron Seely. "Getting Inside the Brain." *Wisconsin State Journal* (Madison, WI), May 19, 2013.

"Severe Head Injury," National Health Service. https://www.nhs.uk/conditions/severe-head-injury.

Wikipedia contributors., "Organic Brain Syndrome." *Wikipedia, The Free Encyclopedia*. https://en.wikipedia.org/w/index.php?title=Organic_brain_syndrome&oldid=969877182.

Chapter 11—Diagnosing Children

"'Charlotte's Web' Marijuana Supposed Cure for Kids' Seizures But Doctors Skeptical." *CBS News*, February 18, 2014.

John Ingold. "Non-psychoative CBD Oil Made from Marijuana Plants Poised to Be Game-Changer." *The Denver Post*, March 30, 2014. http://www.denverpost.com/marijuana/ci_25450052/cbd-marijuana-oil-changing-game.

Saundra Young. "Marijuana Stops Child's Severe Seizures." CNN, August 7, 2013. https://www.cnn.com/2013/08/07/health/charlotte-child-medical-marijuana.

Chapter 12—Diagnosing Disabilties

American Psychiatric Association. *Diagnostic and Statistical Manual of Mental Disorders* (5th ed., 2013). https://doi.org/10.1176/appi.books.9780890425596.

"Living with Unseen Disabilities." https://livingwithunseendisabilities. wordpress.com/.

Shaw, Megan E. "Invisible Disabilities: Stigma and Belonging" (A Research Paper presented to The Faculty of the Adler Graduate School, in partial fulfillment of the requirement for the Degree of Master of Arts in Adlerian Counseling and Psychotherapy, September 2012). https:// alfredadler.edu/library/masters/2012/megan-e-shaw.

Chapter 13—Medication vs. No Medication and/or Self-Medication

Office of National Drug Control Policy, "Teen 'Self-Medication' for Depression Leads to More Serious Mental Illness, New Report Reveals." *Science Daily*, May 10, 2008. http://www.sciencedaily.com/ releases/2008/05/080509105348.htm.

Stratyner, Harris B. "The Truth About Self-Medicating Behavior." *Psychology Today*, March 30, 2009. https://www.psychologytoday.com/us/blog/ recovery-life/200903/the-truth-about-self-medicating-behavior.

Wikipedia contributors. "Self-medication." *Wikipedia, The Free Encyclopedia.* https://en.wikipedia.org/w/index.php?title=Self-medication& oldid=974242929.

Chapter 14—Acceptance of the Disability

Kessler, David. "The Five Stages of Grief." http://grief.com/ the-five-stages-of-grief.

Kingsley, Emily Perl. "Welcome to Holland" (poem). https://www.dsasc. ca/uploads/8/5/3/9/8539131/welcome_to_holland.pdf.

Kübler-Ross, Elisabeth. *On Death And Dying.* New York: Collier Books/ Macmillan, 1969.

Wikipedia contributors. "Five Stages of Grief." *Wikipedia, The Free Encyclopedia.* https://en.wikipedia.org/w/index.php?title=Five_stages_ of_grief&oldid=974249633.

Chapter 16—Shortages of Mental Health Providers, Community Services, and Funding

Associated Press. "Across Much of the United States There is Serious Shortage of Psychiatrists." *News-Review* (Petosky, MI), September 15, 2015. https://www.petoskeynews.com/featured-pnr/across-much-of-the-united-states-there-is-serious-shortage-of-psychiatrists/article_59c96bbe-4e37-5d51-aa4b-c34747d97a22.html.

Joe Smydo. "Psychiatrists in Short Supply Nationwide." *Pittsburg Post-Gazette*, March 16, 2014. https://www.post-gazette.com/news/health/2014/03/16/Psychiatrists-in-short-supply-nationwide-Pittsburgh/stories/201403160076?cid=search.

Samantha Raphelson. "Severe Shortage of Psychiatrists Exacerbated by Lack of Federal Funding." *NPR Wisconsin Public Radio*, March 9, 2018. https://www.npr.org/2018/03/09/592333771/severe-shortage-of-psychiatrists-exacerbated-by-lack-of-federal-funding.

Chapter 17—Non-Medical Therapies

Animal Therapy

Hall, Deborah. "Considering a Therapy or Service Assistance Dog for Your Special Needs Child? Pros and Cons." https://www.childrensdisabilities.info/therapy-service-animals/therapy-assistance-dogs.html.

Hubley, Linda. "Horse Therapy for Children with Special Needs." https://www.childrensdisabilities.info/therapy-service-animals/horse-therapeutic-therapy.html.

Art Therapy

American Art Therapy Association (website). https://arttherapy.org/

"Art Therapy" (blog). http://www.arttherapyblog.com/.

Wikipedia contributors. "Art Therapy." *Wikipedia, The Free Encyclopedia.* https://en.wikipedia.org/w/index.php?title=Art_therapy&oldid=972345983.

Music Therapy

American Music Therapy Association (website). https://www.musictherapy.org.

Dileo, Cheryl, Editor. *Envisioning the Future of Music Therapy*. Temple University, 2016. https://www.temple.edu/boyer/academicprograms/music-therapy/documents/ENVISIONING_THE_FUTURE.pdf.

"Music Therapy at Temple University—Frequently Asked Questions." https://sites.temple.edu/musictherapy/faq/.

Wheeler, B. L. et al. "Effects of Number of Sessions and Group or Individual Music Therapy on the Mood and Behavior of People Who Have Had Strokes or Traumatic Brain Injuries." *Nordic Journal of Music Therapy*, Vol. 12, No. 2 (2003), 139-151.

Wikipedia contributors. "Music Therapy." *Wikipedia, The Free Encyclopedia*. https://en.wikipedia.org/w/index.php?title=Music_therapy&oldid=970533561.

Mindfulness Meditation

Baer, Ruth A. "Mindfulness Training as a Clinical Intervention: A Conceptual and Empirical Review." *Clinical Psychology: Science and Practice*, Vol. 10, No. 2 (Summer 2003), 126-143. http://www.wisebrain.org/papers/MindfulnessPsyTx.pdf.

"Mindfulness Exercises." Mayo Clinic. https://www.mayoclinic.org/healthy-lifestyle/consumer-health/in-depth/mindfulness-exercises/art-20046356.

Pinter, Robbie. "Where Love Is." *Guideposts*, January 2015, 42-47. https://www.guideposts.org/friends-and-family/parenting/special-needs-children/where-love-is.

Shapiro, Shauna L., Gary E. Roberts, and Ginny Bonner. "Effects of Mindfulness-Based Stress Reduction on Medical and Premedical Students." *Journal of Behavioral Medicine*, December 1998, Vol. 21, No. 6, pp. 581-599. https://link.springer.com/article/10.1023/A:1018700829825.

Wegela, Karen Kissel. "How to Practice Mindfulness Meditation." *Psychology Today* (blog), January 19, 2010. https://www.psychologytoday.com/blog/the-courage-be-present/201001/how-practice-mindfulness-meditation.

Wikipedia contributors. "Mindfulness." *Wikipedia, The Free Encyclopedia.* https://en.wikipedia.org/w/index.php?title=Mindfulness&oldid= 974665479.

<u>Yoga</u>

A. L. Komaroff. "Yoga Can Help Ease Chronic Pain." *Wisconsin State Journal* (Madison, WI), August 20, 2015.

Chapter 18—Players, Procedures, and Protocols That Will Drive You Crazy

"Cutting" (for teens). https://kidshealth.org/en/teens/cutting.html.
"Cutting" (for parents). https://kidshealth.org/en/parents/cutting.html.
"Cutting and Self-Harm," HelpGuide International. https://www. helpguide.org/articles/anxiety/cutting-and-self-harm.htm.

Chapter 19—Advocacy

Curtis, Jill. "For Families of Children with Special Needs." https://www. childrensdisabilities.info/parenting/snparenting.html.
Edelson, Miriam. "Advocating for Your Child with Disabilities." https://www. childrensdisabilities.info/advocacy/advocacy-child-disabilities.html.
Hickman, Lori. "Someone I Love" https://www.childrensdisabilities.info/ advocacy/advocacy-someonelove.html.
Melnick, Karen. "How to Talk So Health Professionals Will Listen." https://www.childrensdisabilities.info/advocacy/advocacy- healthprofessionals.html.
Murray, Carolyn. "Acceptance." https://www.childrensdisabilities.info/ parenting/acceptance.html.

Chapter 20—The Realities of Every Day Life

Namkung, Eun Ha, *et al.* "The Relative Risk of Divorce in Parents of Children with Developmental Disabilities: Impacts of Lifelong Parenting." *American Journal on Intellectual and Development Disabilities,* Vol. 120, No. 6, 514-526. https://www.ncbi.nlm.nih.gov/pmc/ articles/PMC4624231/.

Chapter 22—Taking Care of the Caregiver

"Caring for a Sibling with a Disability: Easter Seals Siblings Study." Springfield, MA: MassMutual Financial Group, 2013. https://www.massmutual.com/mmfg/pdf/Sibling%20Study%20Key%20Findings_SC8200.pdf.

Chris Rickert. "Caring for Disabled Is Hard But Can Be a Gift." *Wisconsin State Journal* (Madison, WI), November 11, 2012.

Diament, Michelle. "Sibling Caregivers Find Responsibilities a Struggle." December 5, 2012. https://www.disabilityscoop.com/2012/12/05/sibling-caregivers-struggle/16899/.

Laura Henning. "Commitments: Taking Charge: Not Everyone Is Up to Caring for a Disabled Sibling. But Some Can't Imagine Life Any Other Way." *Los Angeles Times*, October 23, 1995. https://www.latimes.com/archives/la-xpm-1995-10-23-ls-60293-story.html.

"Mindfulness Exercises." Mayo Clinic. https://www.mayoclinic.org/healthy-lifestyle/consumer-health/in-depth/mindfulness-exercises/art-20046356.

Williams, Geoff. "Caring for a Sibling with Special Needs." *U.S. News and World Report*, May 14, 2013. https://money.usnews.com/money/personal-finance/articles/2013/05/14/caring-for-a-sibling-with-special-needs.

Chapter 23—Disabilities in the Educational Realm

"About IDEA." U.S. Department of Education. https://sites.ed.gov/idea/about-idea/.

Beth J. Harpaz. "For Some, All-Year School Didn't Live Up to Hype." *Wisconsin State Journal* (Madison, WI), July 13, 2012.

Bill Sizemore. "Virginia Joins Crackdown on Student Control Antics." *Wisconsin State Journal* (Madison, WI), February 16, 2015.

"Free Appropriate Public Education for Students with Disabilities: Requirements Under Section 504 of The Rehabilitation Act of 1973." U.S. Department of Education, August, 2010. https://www2.ed.gov/about/offices/list/ocr/docs/edlite-FAPE504.html.

Joanne Juhnke, Katie Austin Schierl, and Heidi Wilson. "Why We Must Stop Special Needs Vouchers." *The Cap Times* (Madison, WI), February 13, 2013.

Kimberly Hefling. "Government Weighs in on Discipline in Schools." *Wisconsin State Journal* (Madison, WI), January 9, 2014.

"Protecting Students with Disabilities." U.S. Department of Education. https://www2.ed.gov/about/offices/list/ocr/504faq.html.

Shawn Doherty. "Educating Donovan." *The Cap Times* (Madison, WI), March 10, 2010.

Wikipedia contributors. "Free Appropriate Public Education." *Wikipedia, The Free Encyclopedia.* https://en.wikipedia.org/w/index.php?title=Free_Appropriate_Public_Education&oldid=970537358.

Wikipedia contributors. "Individuals with Disabilities Education Act." *Wikipedia, The Free Encyclopedia.* https://en.wikipedia.org/w/index.php?title=Individuals_with_Disabilities_Education_Act&oldid=973169498

Chapter 25—Employment of Other-Abled

Anna Gouker. "Hiring People with Disabilities Makes Good Business Sense." *The Cap Times* (Madison, WI), January 8, 2020.

Stuart, S. C. "At This VFX Studio, Artists with Autism Make Magic for Marvel." *PC Magazine*, August 23, 2017. https://www.pcmag.com/news/at-this-vfx-studio-artists-with-autism-make-magic-for-marvel.

Weir, Jennifer. *CODI: Cornucopia of Disability Information.* http://codi.tamucc.edu/index.html.

Chapter 26—Housing

Dillman, Beth. "Disabled Renters' Housing Rights." https://www.nolo.com/legal-encyclopedia/disabled-renters-housing-rights-30121.html.

"Housing Choice Vouchers Fact Sheet." U.S. Department of Housing and Urban Development. https://www.hud.gov/program_offices/public_indian_housing/programs/hcv/about/fact_sheet.

"Housing Solutions for People and Families with Disabilities." Movin' Out. https://www.movin-out.org/.

Janet Portman, "Law Protects Rights of Disabled Tenant Seeking to End Lease," *Chicago Tribune*, June 26, 2009. https://www.chicagotribune.com/news/ct-xpm-2009-06-26-0906240580-story.html.

"Reasonable Accommodations and Modifications." U.S. Department of Housing and Urban Development. https://www.hud.gov/program_

offices/fair_housing_equal_opp/reasonable_accommodations_and_modifications.

"Rental Housing Rights for Disabled Tenants." FindLaw, July 25, 2017. https://civilrights.findlaw.com/discrimination/rental-housing-rights-for-disabled-tenants.html.

Ron Leshnower. "Know Your Rights if You Have a Disability: Be Aware of What a Landlord Must and Mustn't Do." *The Spruce*, April 29, 2020. https://www.thespruce.com/fair-housing-and-disability-rights-155902.

"Section 811 Supportive Housing for Persons with Disabilities Program." U.S. Department of Housing and Urban Development. https://www.hud.gov/program_offices/housing/mfh/grants/section811ptl.

Smith, Lisa. "Housing Cooperatives: A Unique Type of Home Ownership." Investopedia, February 28, 2020. https://www.investopedia.com/articles/pf/08/housingco-op.asp.

Chapter 27—Transportation

"Equity in Transportation for People with Disabilities." American Association of People with Disabilities. https://www.aapd.com/wp-content/uploads/2016/03/transportation-disabilities.pdf.

Rosenbloom, Sandra. "Transportation Patterns and Problems of People with Disabilities." In *The Future of Disability in America*, edited by Marilyn J. Field and Alan M. Jette, 519-560. Washington, D.C.: The National Academies, 2007. https://www.ncbi.nlm.nih.gov/books/NBK11434/pdf/Bookshelf_NBK11434.pdf.

"Transportation." The Arc. https://thearc.org/position-statements/transportation/.

Chapter 29—SSI/SSDI

"Difference Between SSI and SSDI." https://www.differencebetween.com/difference-between-ssi-and-ssdi/.

Froemming, Roy. *One Step Ahead: Resource Planning for People with Disabilities Who Rely on Supplemental Security Income and Medicaid*. Madison, WI: Wisconsin Board for People with Developmental Disabilities, 2009.

Robert, Teri. "Choosing SSDI or SSI for Your Disability." https://www.verywellhealth.com/ssdi-vs-ssi-which-is-best-for-your-disability-1719475.

Chapter 30—Grassroots Groups and Support Organizations

Assistive Technology Solutions (website). http://abilityhub.org/.

Children's Disabilities Information (website). https://www. childrensdisabilities.info/.

"Disability Organizations." http://abilityhub.com/links/organization.htm.

"Living Our Visions, Inclusively." https://lovdane.org/.

Wikipedia contributors. "Disability Rights Movement." *Wikipedia, The Free Encyclopedia.* https://en.wikipedia.org/w/index.php?title=Disability_rights_movement&oldid=969447349.

Chapter 31—Special Needs Trusts

Elias, Stephen. "Special Needs Trusts—The Basics." https://www.nolo.com/legal-encyclopedia/special-needs-trusts-30315.html.

Froemming, Roy. *One Step Ahead: Resource Planning for People with Disabilities Who Rely on Supplemental Security Income and Medicaid.* Madison, WI: Wisconsin Board for People with Developmental Disabilities, 2009.

Froemming, Roy. *Provisions: Sample Language for Supplemental Needs Trusts.* Madison, WI: Wisconsin Council on Developmental Disabilities, 1998.

Wikipedia contributors. "Special Needs Trust." *Wikipedia, The Free Encyclopedia.* https://en.wikipedia.org/w/index.php?title=Special_needs_trust&oldid=914638314.

Chapter 32—Jails and Prisons as Institutions for the Disabled

Alexander, Michelle. *The New Jim Crow: Mass Incarceration in the Age of Colorblindness.* New York: The New Press, 2012.

Aviva Stahl. "Children Locked Up for Life: 10 Shockers About America's Prison System." AlterNet, November 7, 2013. https://www.alternet.org/2013/11/children-locked-life-10-shockers-about-americas-prison-system/.

Barbara Herman. "Kalief Browder Suicide: Did Solitary Confinement Kill Him? Advocates On The 'Torture' Of Juvenile Detainees At Rikers Island." *International Business Times*, June 10, 2015. https://www.ibtimes.com/kalief-browder-suicide-did-solitary-confinement-kill-him-advocates-torture-juvenile-1960575.

Brad Plummer. "Throwing Children in Prison Turns Out to Be a Really Bad Idea." *The Washington Post*, June 15, 2013. http://njjn.org/uploads/digital-library/Throwing-children-in-prison-turns-out-to-be-bad-idea_Washington-Post_June-15-2013.pdf.

Brendan Farrington. "Florida Reduces Freddie Lee Hall's Death Sentence." *The Gainesville Sun*, September 8, 2016. https://www.gainesville.com/news/20160908/florida-reduces-freddie-lee-halls-death-sentence.

Chammah, Maurice. "How Germany Does Prison," The Marshall Project, June 16, 2015. https://www.themarshallproject.org/2015/06/16/how-germany-does-prison.

"Children in Adult Prison." Equal Justice Initiative. https://eji.org/issues/children-in-prison/.

Cohen, Andrew. "The Court's Emphatic Ban on Executing the Intellectually Disabled." *The Atlantic*, May 27, 2014. https://www.theatlantic.com/politics/archive/2014/05/hall-v-florida/371662.

Elizabeth Chuck. "For Mentally Ill Inmates, Health Care Behind Bars Is Often Out of Reach." *MSNBC*, February 12, 2012. https://www.ethicalpsychology.com/2012/02/for-mentally-ill-inmates-health-care.html.

"Facts About Developmental Disabilities." Centers for Disease Control and Prevention. https://www.cdc.gov/ncbddd/developmentaldisabilities/facts.html.

Haney, Craig. "The Psychological Impact of Incarceration: Implications for Post-Prison Adjustment." U.S. Department of Health and Human Services, The Urban Institute, National Policy Conference, January 30-31, 2002. https://aspe.hhs.gov/system/files/pdf/75001/Haney.pdf.

Joseph Erbentraut. "Germany's Prisons Could Not Be More Different from America's." *Huffington Post*, September 29, 2015. https://www.huffpost.com/entry/germany-prison-policy-prison-reform_n_5609b658e4b0dd850308ce1c.

Kamis-Gould, Edna, Fredrick Snyder, Trevor R. Hadley, and Timothy Casey. "The Impact of Closing a State Psychiatric Hospital on the County Mental Health System and Its Clients." *Psychiatric Services*, Vol. 50, No. 10 (October 1999), 1297-1302. https://ps.psychiatryonline.org/doi/pdfplus/10.1176/ps.50.10.1297.

Marc Benjamin and Barbara Anderson. "Without Proper Medication, Fresno Inmates Locked in Terror." *The Fresno Bee*, August 11, 2013. https://www.mcclatchydc.com/latest-news/article24751948.html.

Mariner, Joanne. "Prisons as Mental Institutions: The Mass Incarceration of the Mentally Ill." FindLaw, October 27, 2003. https://supreme. findlaw.com/legal-commentary/prisons-as-mental-institutions.html.

Noelle Phillips and John Ingold. "Aurora Theater Gunman Says He Hoped FBI Would Stop Him, Lock Him Up." The Denver Post, May 29, 2015. https://www.denverpost.com/2015/05/29/aurora-theater-gunman-says-he-hoped-fbi-would-stop-him-lock-him-up/.

Okasha, Ahmed. "Mental Patients in Prisons: Punishment versus Treatment?" *World Psychiatry*, Vol. 3, No. 1 (February 2004), p. 1. https://www.ncbi.nlm.nih.gov/pmc/articles/PMC1414650/.

Paul Elias. "High Court OKs Early Release Plan for California Inmates." *KPBS*, San Diego State University, August 3, 2013. https://www.kpbs.org/news/2013/aug/03/s-court-oks-early-release-plan-for-calif-inmates/.

Peter Holley, "Kalief Browder Hanged Himself After Jail Destroyed Him. Then 'a Broken Heart' Killed His Mother." *The Washington Post*, October 18, 2016. https://www.washingtonpost.com/news/post-nation/wp/2016/10/18/kalief-browder-hanged-himself-after-jail-destroyed-him-then-a-broken-heart-killed-his-mother/.

Renee Montagne. "Inside the Nation's Largest Mental Institution." *NPR Wisconsin Public Radio*, August 14, 2008. https://www.npr.org/templates/story/story.php?storyID=93581736.

Robert Barnes. "Supreme Court: Life Sentences on Juveniles Open for Later Reviews." *The Washington Post*, January 25, 2016. https://www.washingtonpost.com/politics/courts_law/supreme-court-juveniles-sentenced-to-life-have-option-for-new-reviews/2016/01/25/06e3dfc2-c378-11e5-8965-0607e0e265ce_story.html.

Smith, Phil. "'There Is No Treatment Here.' Disability and Health Needs in a State Prison System." *Disability Studies Quarterly*, Vol. 25. No. 3, Summer 2005. https://dsq-sds.org/article/view/571/748.

Steven Elbow. "Advocates Say Justice System Fails Inmates with Fetal Alcohol Disorders." *The Cap Times* (Madison, WI), May 14, 2008. https://madison.com/ct/news/local/crime_and_courts/advocates-say-justice-system-fails-inmates-with-fetal-alcohol-disorders/article_b1085688-c57b-11de-9059-001cc4c03286.html.

Stewart, Jean, and Marta Russell. "Disablement, Prison, and Historical Segregation." *Monthly Review*, Vol. 53, No. 3 (July-August 2001). http://monthlyreview.org/2001/07/01/disablement-prison-and-historical-segregation.

Susan Haigh. "States Revisit Mandatory Sentences for Juveniles." *The Morning Call* (Allentown, PA), August 18, 2013. https://www.mcall.com/sdut-states-revisit-mandatory-sentences-for-juveniles-2013aug18-story.html.

Torrey, E. Fuller, Aaron Kennard, Don Eslinger, Richard Lamb, and James Payle. *More Mentally Ill Persons Are in Jails and Prisons Than Hospitals: A Survey of the States.* Arlington, Virginia: Treatment Advocacy Center (May 2010), pp. 1–22. https://www.treatmentadvocacycenter.org/storage/documents/final_jails_v_hospitals_study.pdf.

Travis Waldron. "Rick Perry's Execution Record Includes the Deaths of Juveniles and the Mentally Disabled." *Think Progress*, September 2, 2011. https://archive.thinkprogress.org/rick-perrys-execution-record-includes-the-deaths-of-juveniles-and-the-mentally-disabled-67d0adf2b1e/.

Wikipedia contributors. "Deinstitutionalisation." *Wikipedia, The Free Encyclopedia.* https://en.wikipedia.org/w/index.php?title=Deinstitutionalisation&oldid=974250687.

Wikipedia contributors. "Deinstitutionalization in the United States." *Wikipedia, The Free Encyclopedia.* https://en.wikipedia.org/w/index.php?title=Deinstitutionalization_in_the_United_States&oldid=973184928.

Wikipedia contributors. "Hall v. Florida." *Wikipedia, The Free Encyclopedia.* https://en.wikipedia.org/w/index.php?title=Hall_v._Florida&oldid=958010392.

Wikipedia contributors. "Incarceration in the United States." *Wikipedia, The Free Encyclopedia.* https://en.wikipedia.org/w/index.php?title=Incarceration_in_the_United_States&oldid=974430858.

Wikipedia contributors. "Lunatic Asylum." *Wikipedia, The Free Encyclopedia.* https://en.wikipedia.org/w/index.php?title=Lunatic_asylum&oldid=972340761.

Wikipedia contributors. "Mentally Ill People in United States Jails and Prisons. *Wikipedia, The Free Encyclopedia.* https://en.wikipedia.org/w/index.php?title=Mentally_ill_people_in_United_States_jails_and_prisons&oldid=969882610.

Winstrom, Todd. "Rights of Persons with Disabilities in Correctional Settings." https://www.disabilityrightswi.org/wp-content/uploads/2017/08/correctional-settings.pdf.

Chapter 33—Death and Dying

"Back to School: Preventing Suicide." Mental Health America. https://www.mhanational.org/back-school-preventing-suicide.

Davis, Kelly. "Youth Suicide Jumped 56 Percent in Ten Years—I Was Almost One of Them." Mental Health America. https://www.mhanational.org/blog/youth-suicide-jumped-56-percent-ten-years-i-was-almost-one-them.

Gionfriddo, Paul. "How Can We Break the Back of the Growing Suicide Crisis." Mental Health America. https://www.mhanational.org/blog/how-we-can-break-back-growing-suicide-crisis.

"Suicide." Mental Health America. https://www.mhanational.org/conditions/suicide.

"Preventing Suicide." U.S. Department of Health and Human Services, Substance Abuse and Mental Health Services Administration. https://www.samhsa.gov/suicide.

"Preventing Suicide in Older Adults." Mental Health America. https://www.mhanational.org/preventing-suicide-older-adults.

"Risk of Suicide." National Alliance on Mental Illness. https://www.nami.org/About-Mental-Illness/Common-with-Mental-Illness/Risk-of-Suicide.

"Suicide Facts at a Glance." Centers for Disease Control and Prevention. https://stacks.cdc.gov/view/cdc/34181.

"Suicide Prevention." U.S. Department of Health and Human Services, Substance Abuse and Mental Health Services Administration. https://www.samhsa.gov/find-help/suicide-prevention.

Suicide Prevention Resource Center (website). http://www.sprc.org/.

"What the Data Says About Gun Deaths in the U.S." Pew Research Center. https://www.pewresearch.org/fact-tank/2019/08/16/what-the-data-says-about-gun-deaths-in-the-u-s/.